Constructing US Foreign Policy

This book seeks to address the roots of the hostility that has characterized the United States' relationship with Cuba and has persisted for decades, long after the Cold War. It answers the question of why America's Cold War era policy toward Cuba has not substantially changed, despite a radically changed international environment, going beyond the common explanation that American electoral politics and the Cuban lobby drive US policy toward Cuba.

Bernell argues that US foreign policy towards Cuba cannot be viewed as an objective response to a set of challenges to US interests and principles, and is better understood as a policy that is rooted in and informed by historical understandings of American and Cuban identities, which are themselves historically contingent. Examining a wide range of sources including government documentation and official speeches, this work explores the origins and perpetuation of a policy perspective that emphasizes Cuban difference, illegitimacy, and inferiority juxtaposed against American virtue, legitimacy, and superiority.

This work will be of great interest to all scholars of US foreign policy, International Relations, and Latin American politics.

David Bernell is Assistant Professor of Political Science at Oregon State University, where he teaches and conducts research in international relations, United States foreign policy, and international political economy. He is the author of *Readings in American Foreign Policy: Historical and Contemporary Problems* (2008), and also consults for the renewable energy firm, Think Energy, Inc.

Routledge Studies in US Foreign Policy
Edited by
Inderjeet Parmar,
University of Manchester
and John Dumbrell,
University of Durham

This new series sets out to publish high quality works by leading and emerging scholars critically engaging with United States Foreign Policy. The series welcomes a variety of approaches to the subject and draws on scholarship from international relations, security studies, international political economy, foreign policy analysis and contemporary international history.

Subjects covered include the role of administrations and institutions, the media, think tanks, ideologues and intellectuals, elites, transnational corporations, public opinion, and pressure groups in shaping foreign policy, US relations with individual nations, with global regions and global institutions and America's evolving strategic and military policies.

The series aims to provide a range of books – from individual research monographs and edited collections to textbooks and supplemental reading for scholars, researchers, policy analysts, and students.

United States Foreign Policy and National Identity in the 21st Century
Edited by Kenneth Christie

New Directions in US Foreign Policy
Edited by Inderjeet Parmar, Linda B. Miller and Mark Ledwidge

America's 'Special Relationships'
Foreign and domestic aspects of the politics of alliance
Edited by John Dumbrell and Axel R Schäfer

US Foreign Policy in Context
National ideology from the founders to the Bush Doctrine
Adam Quinn

The United States and NATO since 9/11
The transatlantic alliance renewed
Ellen Hallams

Soft Power and US Foreign Policy
Theoretical, historical and contemporary perspectives
Edited by Inderjeet Parmar and Michael Cox

The US Public and American Foreign Policy
Edited by Andrew Johnstone and Helen Laville

American Foreign Policy and Postwar Reconstruction
Comparing Japan and Iraq
Jeff Bridoux

Neoconservatism and American Foreign Policy
A critical analysis
Danny Cooper

US Policy Towards Cuba
Since the Cold War
Jessica F. Gibbs

Constructing US Foreign Policy
The curious case of Cuba
David Bernell

Constructing US Foreign Policy

The curious case of Cuba

David Bernell

R Routledge

Taylor & Francis Group

LONDON AND NEW YORK

First published 2011
by Routledge
2 Park Square, Milton Park, Abingdon, Oxon OX14 4RN

Simultaneously published in the USA and Canada
by Routledge
711 Third Avenue, New York, NY 10017

Routledge is an imprint of the Taylor & Francis Group, an informa business.

First issued in paperback 2012

British Library Cataloguing in Publication Data
A catalogue record for this book is available from the British Library

Library of Congress Cataloging in Publication Data
Bernell, David.
Constructing US foreign policy: the curious case of Cuba / David Bernell.
    p. cm. – (Routledge studies in US foreign policy)
    Includes bibliographical references and index.
    1. United States–Foreign relations–Cuba. 2. Cuba–Foreign relations–United States. I. Title.
    E183.8.C9B46 2011
    327.7307291–dc22   2010037876

ISBN: 978-0-415-78067-4 (hbk)
ISBN: 978-0-415-78067-4 (pbk)
ISBN: 978-0-203-82926-4 (ebk)

Typeset in Sabon
by RefineCatch Limited, Bungay, Suffolk

Contents

Preface

Pizza, all I wanted. That was always the first thought that came to my mind when I got to skip school and go to work for the day with my grandpa. Going to work with him was extra special because it meant taking a trip, a trip to some wonderful, far off place (about an hour or two by car) where we would complete the day in the best of all possible ways: by going for pizza.

Grandpa sold TV tubes, these days just one more ancient relic in the long line of obsolete technologies our society has used up and thrown away, but in the olden days (for me, at least), the 1970s, TV tubes were still good business. So my sister and I would get to play hooky and go spend the day with gramps on the road from Albuquerque, the place we called home, to Santa Fe, Los Alamos, or our favorite, Grants. Strangely enough, it was not Santa Fe, the exciting, popular "city different", or Los Alamos, the mysterious, hidden city, high in the mountains where Robert Oppenheimer, Richard Feynman and other scientific legends gathered decades ago to build the atomic bomb, but Grants, a small, dying mining town in western New Mexico, that rewarded us with our strongest memories of being with our grandfather. Perhaps it was precisely because the city was such a nondescript place, so devoid of glamour and history, that we were all better able to revel in the company. Perhaps, but to try to explain why those trips were so much fun is to tamper with the magic.

As we rode along the dusty highway (sometimes he let us drive even though we were far too young to do this legally) we could see for distances that seemed to stretch forever. The terrain was so flat, as if someone had taken a straightedge and run it along the ground. Only Mt. Taylor, jutting up in the distance, interrupted the perfection of the flattened horizon. Yet my sister and I really weren't aware of the significance of the land, of the ancient Indian ruins that we drove past, of the magnificent treeless landscape, the miles and miles of beautiful emptiness. The two of us had something better: we had grandpa. It was a special occasion indeed.

Mom and dad would always let us go. School seemed a distant second to them too, considering the competition. They knew how much fun we all had together, but more significantly, they knew it was important that we know this man well. My grandfather was not a famous man, he wasn't rich, and he wasn't educated either, but he was oh, so wise. And everybody knew it too, not least of all my parents. Gramps not only mesmerized his grandchildren, he had the same effect on everybody he met. Friends and family always came to him for help in difficult times, for advice about whatever subject. He may not have been an expert on the subject, but the details didn't matter so much. The genius he possessed was in helping people to go about conducting their lives as best they could. He always knew what the right answers were, or at least how and where to find them. He was the one we all turned to. And even though he was the center of attention, he always made you feel like you were the one in that privileged position. No parents were going to turn down this man's request to spend the day with his grandkids.

He would pass the time with us telling us stories about how he came to this country from Russia when he was a kid. He had lived in the Ukraine under the last Czar, in the chaos of World War I, and under the Bolsheviks when his family finally decided it was time to go someplace else. He told us about how his family moved from one European country to another for a few years, finding refuge wherever they could, for as long as they could. He told us about coming to America, dropping out of school (and warning us not to do the same) hustling a living during the Depression, being rich, being poor (rich is better, he advised us). And he always let us know how great a blessing it was that he was able to come to this country to live. He was not a zealot, uncritically defensive of his adopted home. He just knew. He had been there, at a time and place where just living one's life was often a difficult enterprise, and this was the good life. You could see it written on his face when he talked about the problems of being Jewish in Russia, of living in fear of war and then revolution, of the Depression and wondering each day if he might be fortunate enough to get a meal. There was a lot more in his stories than just the spoken words. He was endlessly fascinating.

Since his death several years ago there has been a conspicuous absence, diminishing the lives of all those he left behind. But we always remember him. One way we do this in the Jewish faith is to recite a prayer, the Kaddish, on the anniversary of someone's death. It is an unusual prayer. It is not recited in Hebrew, but Aramaic, the common language of the ancient Jews. This way everybody was able to understand it. Yet even more unusual than the fact that this Hebrew prayer for the dead is not recited in Hebrew, is the fact that it makes no reference whatsoever to death or dying. Not once. It is a prayer about the greatness of G-d. In the midst of sadness the Kaddish is recited to reaffirm our belief in a just and true G-d and the meaningfulness of life. It is a prayer that is used in other contexts, not only that of mourning, but when said in remembrance of someone it is always being used for dual purposes, to tell multiple stories, even though no direct reference is made to one of them.

That is one of the fascinating things about stories: their ability to tell us something by means of leaving something out. Usually the part we pay attention to is the part that is told to us. How many of us have not uttered the words "tell me that story again" to someone who has been able, at some time, to capture our attention, our imagination, with their rendition of some event from the past? We love a good narrative. But stories do more than entertain us. We use them to tell about who we are, what we value, how and why we are motivated to act. And a single narrative, like the Kaddish, can tell more than one story at a time. It depends on how you want to hear it, or read it. Furthermore, by the inclusion of one story at the expense of another, we can say something significant. We reveal a great deal when we choose to highlight something, to pick it out as important, and ignore something else that could have been told in its place.

It is no accident that my grandfather told of certain events in his life and not others. He had a particular view of his life that was captured best through certain stories which, through his telling, had a certain meaning. It doesn't mean he lied through omission, or misled us, just that there were some things that seemed important to him and a whole lot that didn't seem worth mentioning.

We hear stories every day, fiction and nonfiction alike. We know that fictionalized accounts are made up. On the other hand, we generally assume the others to be true. But even works of nonfiction have to be written, constructed, and manufactured. Is it really possible that a "fact" can be put through these processes, a "fact" chosen at the expense of others, and still end up unblemished by bias and interpretation? And can some "fact" even have meaning without these things? My answer to both of those questions is no. This being the case, the implication is clear: the meaning of a lot of stories is up for grabs, stories put out by journalists, government officials, business people. Their stories about the slice of the world that they happen to look at may be good ones, but they are not necessarily the only ones. It's possible that I can look at the same things and see them differently, and I often do.

So now it's my turn to tell a story. It's about my home, my country, the United States of America, and its long conflict with one of its neighbors, Cuba. My aim is to look at the stories that we in this country have told about ourselves to find out and to produce who and what we are, and who and what the Cubans are. The story of this longstanding fight has been told by the two governments along particular lines; they have each given the confrontation a certain meaning. I am going to tell another story about the confrontation, propose another possible understanding of it, and in the process suggest that the meanings we give to things may not be the absolute truth, but only one of many interpretations.

I only hope that in my storytelling abilities I can do justice to the legacy of the wise, respected, loved, and loving man I called grandpa.

David Bernell
Corvallis, OR
June, 2010

Acknowledgements

One of the things I have been looking forward to in completing this project, aside from the obvious goal of publishing the book, is the opportunity to thank the people who have made my work and my experience all the richer.

I have been lucky to work with some of the finest colleagues and intellectual mentors that anyone could ask for. William Connolly for years been a teacher, friend, mentor, and intellectual hero. His enthusiasm for the work he does and that of his colleagues cannot help but be contagious. Wayne Smith introduced me to the study of Cuba, with the insight and perspective that few will ever have. I would never have explored such an interesting topic as US policy toward Cuba had it not been for him. Steven David and David Campbell played an integral role in the development of this project. Carol Pech and Mo Healy are both great friends, excellent reviewers of my work, and savvy advisors with respect to getting published. Several friends and colleagues, including Kelly Erickson, Jason Philips, Tony Lang, and Doug Dow, offered their time and interest, discussing and debating the ideas addressed in the book. David Rosenblum and Alex Abeyta had a hand in this work too, by providing endless examples of how to put analytical thinking to practical use. And Phil Speros and Char Miller deserve a special thanks. They have been intellectual companions, wry observers, and most of all, true friends. Everyone should be so lucky as to have friends like Phil and Char.

Finally, and most importantly, there is my family. My mom and dad, Sue and Gordon, and my sister Julie, have given love and support, and no small measure of editorial commentary (usually directed at the author and not his work). Eli and Miles, my boys, whose sheer joy and enthusiasm for, well, everything provides me every day with the finest gift I could ever ask for. Saving the best for last, I thank my wonderful wife, Stephanie, for whom plain acknowledgement is woefully inadequate – she is simply the best. Knowing that I have finished this work (and not just because I will come unglued from my computer), she will be elated to see these words in print.

1 Introduction

> Cuba can gravitate only toward the North American Union, which cannot cast her off from its bosom.
>
> John Quincy Adams[1]

The bitter rivalry between the United States and Cuba has occupied a position as one of the principal political disputes in the Western hemisphere for the past several decades. Since the rise of Fidel Castro, the governments of these two countries have placed themselves on opposite sides of almost every major regional and global issue. They have long held vastly different ideas about what constitutes a good and just government, about what kind of international behavior is legitimate, and about the ends that foreign policy should serve. Moreover, they have not only harbored political differences, but maintained a very intense dislike of one another. The US has attempted to sustain a picture of Cuba as an international outlaw, the source of much turmoil, crisis and mischief in the world. Adding a personal dimension to the attacks, officials in Washington also have sought to demonize Castro, creating and continually advancing an image of him as the embodiment of evil. Although personal assaults are not often a predominant feature of Cuban accusations, due to the succession of American presidents, the image of the US depicted in Cuba is one of an imperialist giant, abusing its power, creating injustice, inequality and misery throughout the world. In sum, the relationship has been one of mutual hostility and contempt, fueled by the combination of differences in ideology, interests, culture and power, in tandem with their close proximity and contact.

Since the end of the Cold War, the antagonism directed toward Cuba and Castro from the United States government has in some ways intensified, resulting in further attempts to tighten the US embargo and isolate the island diplomatically. Such a heightened degree of hostility is not uncommon. The US-Cuban relationship has not been static throughout the decades. Rather, there have been periods of greater and lesser tensions. What is unusual is that an escalation in anti-Cuban sentiment and policy intensified with the end of the Cold War. The Cuban-Soviet connection, from its inception, was always identified in the US as the primary concern of American policymakers, the most important factor influencing Washington's stance toward the Cuban government. The close relationship between the two communist countries was regarded as a serious threat to American security, as it gave the Soviets a base of operations in the Western Hemisphere where they could advance their political and military objectives. Moreover, as a loyal ally of the USSR, Cuba used Soviet aid to advance the export of revolution, train and arm leftist guerrillas, deploy its own troops to prop up friendly regimes, and provide non-military aid in the form of doctors, technicians, construction workers, teachers and athletic trainers to a host of countries. While there were sometimes disagreements in the US over the extent of Soviet involvement in Castro's exploits, it was nonetheless widely agreed that the moral, material and human support by Cuba of guerrilla forces and established radical governments around the world was a threat to American global interests. (The disagreements existed generally in academics and journalism. The official US interpretation found in presidential speeches, congressional testimony, and State Department publications, emphasizing close cooperation between the two countries in the export of revolution, remained consistent over the years, with little attention devoted to ideological and policy differences that periodically marked Soviet-Cuban relations.) Even if Castro's efforts were not always conceived in the Soviet Union, and even if the Soviets only seemed to tolerate them at times, the two countries remained strong allies, sharing broad common goals and interests.

The problem

In consideration of all vast changes in the international system over the past 20 years – the collapse of communism in Eastern Europe and the former Soviet Union, and their disastrous effects upon Cuba, as well as the establishment of democratically elected governments throughout Latin America and the Caribbean, many of whom are increasingly critical of Cuba, the United States seems to be in the highly unusual position of having obtained exactly what it has long said it wanted. The Cuban revolution, by contrast, was significantly weakened since the collapse of the Soviet Union, and has remained so since this time, even though it has managed to avoid the same fate as befell the communist governments of Eastern Europe. The Cuban government suffers from economic hardship, the loss of its allies and trading partners, the end of its global projection of power in support of revolutionary movements, and the possibility – with the retirement of Fidel Castro and the uncertainty it brings for the future – that socialism at it has been practiced may not survive much longer on the island.

Yet American policy toward Cuba continues to follow the same path it has for decades, as if there had been no significant changes in the region or in the world. The arrival of Barack Obama in the White House has led to expectations (and concerns) that US policy could soon change. In April of

2009, soon after his inauguration, President Obama stated at a Summit of the Americas meeting that the United States sought a new beginning with Cuba, and that he was willing to have his administration engage the Cuban government on a wide array of issues. The President did initiate a change, lifting restrictions on family visits and remittances sent to the island. He also permitted investments there by US telecommunications companies, and resumed talks on migration that the Bush administration halted in 2003. He has, however, held off on more far reaching measures, insisting that Cuba first take steps to improve its human rights record and move toward democracy.

These conditions have long been central to US policy, and have been its stated goals. With great consistency to date, the United States has pursued a policy of isolating Havana internationally, increasing political and especially economic pressure, and encouraging the collapse of the government. Before President Obama relaxed some of the restrictions applied to US companies and Cuban Americans, the trend since the end of the Cold War had been toward greater pressure. President George W. Bush implemented a variety of changes over the last several years dealing with limited travel and cash transfers, and broadcasting into Cuba. These had followed The Cuban Liberty and Democratic Solidarity (Libertad) Act of 1996, (more commonly known as Helms-Burton, after its congressional sponsors), which itself followed *The Cuban Democracy Act of 1992*, all of which have attempted to impose costs on Cuba but have ultimately failed to achieve the desired results. Each effort has represented an attempt to strengthen the US embargo against Cuba in an effort to "squeeze" or "strangle" Castro and bring about his hastened demise. The 1992 act sought to forbid subsidiaries of American companies in third countries from doing business in Cuba. However, Havana has for years been eagerly seeking foreign investment, which has been forthcoming to a great degree. Helms-Burton enacted a secondary boycott, seeking to force US policy onto other countries by making foreign companies choose between either the American market or the Cuban market. Revisions to US policy by the George W. Bush administration were also characterized as applying pressure to Cuba, even though their targeted audience seemed often to be only a domestic one. The ultimate goal and hope has been to drive business out of Cuba, increasing the pressure on the regime and on the population who, according to the plan, would remove Castro from power. In spite of such goals, American policy has usually only managed to placate anti-Castro voters and anger US allies.

Two criticisms are made regarding the logic of this conduct. The first is that American policies are counterproductive. The argument is that if the goals of the US with respect to Cuba are a peaceful transition to democracy and the institution of free market capitalism (the oft-stated aims of the Bush, Clinton, Bush and Obama administrations) then the last action to take would be what the US continues to do. Should American policy be successful, and bring about the "strangulation" of Castro, what are the possible results? More likely than not it would be social upheaval, something which both

Raul and Fidel Castro, who have long advocated the use of violence to make and protect the revolution, and who have demonstrated little respect for human rights, might very well respond to with force, as opposed to quietly stepping down. The American government should be reminded that one of the cardinal rules of diplomacy is to allow one's enemies a face-saving way to avoid confrontation, that sometimes more can be accomplished with an outstretched hand than a clenched fist. The Sandinistas held free and fair elections only after negotiations with the US produced a deal. During the *contra* war, this did not happen. Spain after World War II provides another example, according to Wayne Smith, of how engagement worked better than ostracism. "Spain's major advances toward democracy came after the United States had normalized relations with it, signed an economic-military agreement with [it] in 1953, and allowed its admission into the United Nations in 1955."[2] Moreover, as the US maintains a policy whose success quite possibly leads to social violence and whose failure perpetuates economic difficulty, it fuels another undesirable outcome. In both cases, the embargo increases the potential for a large number of refugees to leave Cuba for South Florida, something that the Mariél episode and the refugee crisis of 1994 demonstrated is not in American interests, if it were not already apparent before. Nor, it is argued, do US actions advance the cause of human rights; they instead make it easier for Castro to crack down at home and justify repression. John Paul Sartre said that if the United States did not exist, Castro would have to invent it. However, such fabrication is not necessary because the US has helped provide Castro with sufficient cover to jail dissidents and squelch political opposition. Additionally, America's efforts to tighten the embargo, which include (unenforced) punitive measures against foreign companies that do not comply with US law, have only provoked quarrels with America's allies and major trading partners, rather than forcing the economic "strangulation" of Cuba. These outcomes, it is posited, are not what the US should want to encourage.

The second criticism directed at the logic of American policy is that the old threat to American security has vanished. If ever there was a need to guard against Cuba, that day is no longer. The Soviets, who represented the primary danger, are gone; Cold War is now an historical term. As the success of Castro's internationally-oriented foreign policy depended upon financial, political and military backing from the Soviet Union, Cuba's importance as a threat was only secondary. Cuba was rarely engaged by the US as an independent actor, but rather as a client or puppet state. Considering that Cuba is now poorer and weaker than it was when it had a patron, there is no reason for its significance to be elevated. Even if Castro posed a challenge to the US of his own accord, all of his global initiatives which the United States opposed have ended. Cuba is not a danger to the US. Thus any new expenditure by the US aimed at isolating or weakening the regime is a waste of time, money and effort, even if it might conceivably result in the downfall of the revolution.

Still, in spite of their debatable logic in the current setting, the policies begun during the Cold War remain. The question this book seeks to address is why this is so. What is it about the United States' relationship with Cuba that provides for the continuation, and even intensification of a Cold War policy into the post-Cold War era?

The first answer given to this question in the wake of the Cold War is almost invariably: domestic politics. Cuban voters and interest groups in the United States are said to have taken over American policy toward Cuba in order to advance their own personal interests at the expense of a genuine national interest. This view posits that successful lobbying efforts by organizations such as the Cuban American National Foundation have resulted in the continuation of the embargo and attempts to economically and diplomatically isolate Cuba. The lack of a security threat from Cuba makes the "capture" of US policy by a domestic ethnic constituency all the more possible.

This assessment stands in marked contrast to many others that have been offered as explanations over the years. There are, first of all, traditional theories of international relations, which consider general structures and systems around the globe that delimit the parameters of international politics. Specifically, there are three approaches that eclipse most others. There is the Realist argument which posits that in the anarchic international realm, states act rationally on the basis of interest in order to a) safeguard their security and acquire and hold power, and b) balance against rival powers or threats.[3] A Realist interpretation of US behavior toward Cuba would suggest that the United States would recognize the diminution of the danger, and without recourse to moral, ethical, legal or emotional considerations, devote little attention and fewer resources toward confrontation with Cuba. (These are, no doubt, oversimplifications. Realism does not represent a single, unified approach to analyzing international relations. Still, the differences within the group are not so great that they fundamentally question the general understandings of the exercise of power.) Looking strictly to the international setting of the Cuban problem, and not to domestic political concerns (elections, fundraising), the US would find no need for the continual attempts to isolate, contain, change and undermine Castro's regime, and such efforts should cease. The US might not be expected to embrace Castro, but at least not to actively seek to undermine the regime. Yet this clearly has not been the case.

There is the liberal internationalist perspective, which argues that states tend to evolve toward greater liberalism and democracy – and consequently to become more peaceful toward one another – when they become more economically developed, when they engage in global trade, when they open up to foreign investment, and when they are tied to international institutions that bind countries together through dense networks of associations, rules, laws, norms and practices.[4] Such logic suggests that greater economic development, along with participation in global economic institutions, would encourage greater rule of law in Cuba, as well as greater government accountability to both the Cuban population and to other countries. This view, informed by these assumptions, would argue that the United States should be willing to engage Cuba, conduct trade relations with it, and encourage US companies to invest and own property in Cuba. The US might also be expected to welcome Cuba back into the Organization of American States, or to take the logic even further, support its membership in the World Trade Organization and maybe even North American Free Trade Agreement NAFTA, along with a host of other global organizations devoted to economic development. Maintaining a policy similar to the one that the US has toward China would not be unreasonable according to this perspective. Yet none of these developments has yet occurred.

There are also a variety of economistic arguments that concern themselves with the logic of capital accumulation, investment, the acquisition of wealth, and the strength of the world capitalist system. Like the diversity in Realism, so too does this body of literature exhibit a multitude of variation.[5] One could argue that attempts to bring down Castro through embargoes and diplomatic isolation, no matter how futile they may seem (as evidenced by The Cuban Liberty and Democratic Solidarity [Libertad] Act of 1996, which tried to force a secondary embargo against Cuba due to the fact that no other nation will join the US in its embargo) represent an attempt by the US to hold out for the possible reassertion of overwhelming hegemony in Cuba. A situation whereby the economic strangulation of Cuba led to the collapse of the regime would certainly encourage political instability. This could indeed create an ideal situation for the US to intervene (not necessarily militarily) and reestablish its dominance over the island, dominance that would be even more advantageous than limited investment under the watchful and weary eye of the Cuban government. However, according to this reading, those who would be in a position to gain from holding out for the ultimate reestablishment of hegemony over Cuba are not those who are calling for continued embargo and Castro's removal. Rather, this capitalist class is calling for an opening to Cuba and opportunities to invest there, things denied by the US government, but paradoxically, welcomed by the Cuban government. (In addition to the agricultural sector, many US companies have been eager to do business in Cuba, including General Motors, Sears, ITT, Sheraton, Avis, Hyatt, and Gillette.)

In all three of these understandings, American policy toward Cuba represents an anomaly, running counter to what these approaches to the problem might expect. After all, not only has the Cuban threat to American security ceased, while most other countries besides the United States maintain diplomatic and economic ties to Cuba and welcome the country's participation in a variety of international institutions, but it is also the case that the reintroduction of foreign investment capital to the island is proceeding apace without US participation.

In addition to the theoretical considerations, there is an extensive body of literature which directly addresses the longstanding confrontation between the US and Cuba. The arguments in this literature offer several major explanations as to the sources of American policy. The first has to do with the nature and prevalence of US imperialism in Latin America, claiming that the "colossus of the North" has historically flexed its muscles in the region in order to achieve its ends, with the Cuban case as only another example of such behavior. The second concerns the understanding of Castro and the Cuban revolution as illegitimate and threatening, and is usually accompanied by criticism of American policy for not being sufficiently vigilant in the pursuit of Castro's ouster. The third addresses the array of historical issues and disputes regarding both countries which have been obstacles to normal relations. The fourth, already mentioned, consists of those who argue that American domestic politics are the primary impediment to a thaw in relations with Cuba.

The arguments that domestic American politics are the key to understanding its Cuba policy are notable at this time for their widespread acceptance. While there is undoubtedly a great deal of truth to this view, it only addresses the problem in part. It fails to explain why the US government, which has had a vigorous Cuban policy since the early 1800's, which has sought to annex, control and/or influence Cuba since the same period, and which has never treated the fate of Cuba as an inconsequential issue, seems to have simply turned over its Cuba policy to less than one percent of the American voters. In other words, until the late 1980s votes and campaign contributions were not recognized as the major determinants of US policy toward Cuba. Did so much change over the course of a few years that there remains nothing more upon which the US can base its Cuba policy? To argue this is to marginalize not only the history of US relations with all of Latin America, and Cuba in particular, but also the continuities in the global dimensions of American foreign policy.

However, even if one were to answer in the affirmative and say that the US government has essentially turned over its Cuba policy to a well-financed and well-organized special interest group, one would still need to explain why such a development occurred. Political success for an interest group is not the result of money and organization alone. These things must be accompanied by a goal, a program, an idea, a promise, a principle. With respect to Cuba, these things are readily available in grand, incontestable terms, encompassing an ideology as big as the promise of America itself – democracy, freedom, liberty, anti-communism, the rights of the individual. Characterizing their efforts as a struggle for the realization of these ideals in Cuba, advocates of current US policy have linked their cause with the most exemplary attributes of American identity. At the same time, they have been equally successful in characterizing their opponents as apologists of Castro and communism, or obstacles to the policy of bringing democracy to Cuba. The framing of the Cuban debate in these terms has spelled great success for those who advocate a "get-tough" Cuba policy. Having made the fight against Castro into a fight for these American ideals, they have not only emerged victorious, but have also highlighted the critical importance of appropriating and articulating those attributes of identity considered central to a polity.

The argument in brief

It is these concerns that inform this book, which addresses the question of America's Cuba policy differently from those mentioned earlier. What I submit involves two major arguments, one theoretical, one historical. The first is informed by the theoretical approach of people such as William Connolly, Michael Shapiro, Tzvetan Todorov, Roland Barthes, David Campbell, Cynthia Weber and Eldon Kenworthy, among others.[6] Drawing on their work regarding the power of discourse, strategies of representational practices, and the contingency of identity, I argue that historical under- standings of the United States and Cuba have been informed by particular representations of American and Cuban identities and differences which are prevalent in the discourse of US foreign policy.

I argue the significance of identity because it is not enough to say that US policy is motivated by interest or by principle, for one's interests and principles depend upon who one is, and who one is involves the establishment and maintenance of an identity, or several identities, which stand in marked contrast to the differences exhibited by one's enemy or adversary. Addi- tionally, these identities and differences are not given exogenously, outside of any context. They do not maintain a prior existence to political practice, or to debate and discussion over them. They are rather, constructions, products of words and deeds. This is not to say that Cuban identity, as seen from the US, is simply cut from whole cloth, conjured up out of the fertile imaginations of politicians, journalists, novelists or film producers. At the same time, the argument offered here does suggest that there is no unitary, fixed meaning to the idea of what Cuba is. The images, the attitudes, and the understandings evoked by the usage of the term are contingent, continually subject to reinterpretation. It has only been through recurrent interaction with Cuba that Americans have come to know this particular place. There is no essential nature that is grasped when the name Cuba is used, only spe- cific interpretations based upon a rather limited number of occurrences that have taken place within the greater context of inter-American relations. It is the dynamic of interaction and subsequent interpretation that allows for meanings to be constructed by language, imagery and deeds, be they the foreign policies of various countries, the arguments used to support or attack them, newspaper articles, political cartoons, films or a host of other practices. The identifying characteristics of these two entities – the US and Cuba – have been defined, established, defended and perpetuated through a more or less overt process of political and ideological construction that has taken place over a great period of time. As such, they are contingencies of history. They may foster self-sustaining tendencies and withstand attack, but nonetheless remain contingent, products of historical circumstance.

Moreover, the words, the names, the images and the interpretations do not necessarily tell about what Cuba really *is*. They describe things only in relational terms. Americans over the years may have said that Cubans are unfit for self-government or poor, yet these terms are inherently relational, as descriptive terms must be. Cuba cannot be understood in any of these terms without a (often unspoken) reference being made to something or someone else, that something else in American politics being the US itself. In other words, asserting an identity cannot be done without asserting a difference. It may be done only implicitly, or even be imperceptible, but it is inescapable. The two constitute one another. Thus if American political leaders over the years have described a place called Cuba, its form has been coupled with how they have imagined the US. This practice has been an essential component of American foreign policy, for a communist or underdeveloped Cuba cannot be understood as such without a democratic or developed counterpart to measure it against.

In consideration of this constructivist theoretical approach and its im- plications for the representation of identity, I make the historical argument that very little of what shapes American policy toward Cuba has changed since the end of the Cold War. By looking at different periods in the history of US-Cuban relations, from the Monroe Doctrine to the present, I examine the historical construction of identities which have been said to define the United States and Cuba with respect to each other, how they have come to be understood as such by American policymakers, how that has established the context in which American foreign policy toward Cuba takes place, and how American foreign policy results from these understandings. What I find is that particular American and Cuban identities have been constructed in the US, and that in accord with these representations, American policy toward Cuba is rendered sensible, justifiable and correct.

US policy toward Cuba is confusing only if it is viewed through Cold War/post-Cold War lenses. Viewed from a longer perspective that predates the Cold War, American actions reflect a great consistency. The consistency is that US foreign policy has been, and continues to be informed by those characteristics which are thought to constitute and distinguish Americans and Cubans. One set of characteristics involves the history of inter-American relations, whereby there exists in the US a presumption of American superiority. Throughout two centuries of interaction, there has been a continual representation in the United States of a Latin America that is inferior to the United States. This has been expressed in terms of American exceptionalism, racial hierarchy and Latin American underdevelopment. US superiority has also been understood by means of highlighting not only these differences, but similarities as well. This involves a focus on the idea that the Western Hemisphere is a unique territory, that all occupants of this hemisphere are Americans who share similar ideals, and that these considerations promote the idea of an "American family of nations." In spite of the use of representational practices that suggest unity, there is also an implicit understanding whereby the United States remains the first among ostensible equals.

Another set of characteristics concerns the role of Cuba as a communist state, both during the Cold War and after. In this era, officials of the United States government have consistently understood the Cuban revolution to be threatening and illegitimate, as well as unfree and undemocratic. Washington has consistently advocated the establishment of a democratic regime in Cuba, and has repeatedly pointed out the differences between the US and Cuba that inhibit the normalization of relations, with responsibility for the conflict belonging to Cuba.

The combination of these two sets of characteristics, the presumption of US regional hegemony and anti-communism, led to a rare occurrence. The US found itself faced with both a Soviet client state and ally, and an independent and troublesome neighbor. Cuba is the only country that has ever successfully managed to violate the limits of what had historically been permissible for a small, poor, Latin American country (by eliminating US influence and economic dominance), and then at the same time adopt communism as well. Castro's success in challenging US hegemony in Cuba while turning to communism and the Soviets provided the United States with a single location where the attributes that secured American superiority in the region meshed with those that were central to the struggle against communism. Cuba was simultaneously inferior, underdeveloped, unfree, dangerous and illegitimate.

With respect to both of these domains, I conclude that the historical understandings of these characteristics have not been substantially altered by the end of the Cold War and subsequent events in global politics. United States foreign policy has never managed to move beyond this double affront and accommodate itself to the Castro brothers and the Cuban Revolution. The rhetoric and practice of US policy continues to support the same representations that prevailed during the Cold War. The internal logic is upheld. In juxtaposing US and Cuban characteristics both before and after Castro's ascent, the US has consistently emerged superior in American representations of the relationship. US/Cuba, capitalist/communist, democracy/dictatorship, wealthy/poor, liberal/radical, free/enslaved, peaceful/threatening, developed/underdeveloped, advanced/backward, legitimate/illegitimate and superior/inferior – all of these pairings embrace the same hierarchy, which is reflected in US policies and the language that abets them. As the US is understood as democratic, free and legitimate, while Cuba is spoken of in terms of communism, non-democracy and illegitimacy, and as a threat to its own citizens, there is little reason to expect that a changed global setting should automatically prompt a reappraisal or fundamental change in US policy toward Cuba. By virtue of Washington's longtime understandings of the conflict, there is little, if anything, to suggest a change.

The course that this book follows from here is to explore in detail the dynamics involved in the exchange between historical representation, identity construction and the hierarchy of power, and the resultant effects on American foreign policy. The construction of Cuban and American identities is by no means a benign exercise. The language that sustains views of identity and difference serves the acquisition, preservation and exercise of power. Spoken and written words are to be understood not only as reflections of attitudes, beliefs and assumptions involved in the formation of policy, but as a set of political practices that nourish certain power relations.

It is important to state that the aim is not to point out whether or not the representations discussed (backwardness, threat and illegitimacy) are erroneous. Neither is the project to specify the "real" causes of US-Cuban antagonism, or to locate the ultimate sources of American policy by revealing heretofore unearthed sources of information. Rather, focusing mostly, but not wholly, upon official documents, letters, articles and speeches which are already part of the public record and are exemplary of their respective eras, I address the political consequences of specific modes of representation, to analyze the two-way relationship between the discourse of American foreign policy and the practice of it. Actions and reactions that may seem natural outcomes of a given situation are not natural. They must be produced as such – through the use of language and the meanings constructed via the usage and repetition of certain interpretations, understandings, words and phrases.

If Cuban action is or is not inherently hostile, dangerous, threatening or benign, then what is important is how and why such actions come to acquire or become inscripted in the US with such meanings. The aim here then, is to examine the historical construction of Cuba in the US with regard to hemispheric politics and the politics of anti-communism, to discuss the evolution of how, through the formative power of language and images, the US has come to order its world in such a way that Cubans, or Latin Americans, or communists must occupy certain roles and are prohibited from assuming others. American policy toward Cuba is to be understood not as a response to a series of objective facts, but as a series of undertakings which themselves are reflections of particular representations – practices that represent, interpret and produce what lies both within and beyond the water's edge.

A note on sources

As this analysis is concerned with US foreign policy, the focus is largely upon sources with a connection to the official organs of the US government. Not all of the documents examined should necessarily be considered official, but the vast majority comes from institutional sources or people who served as representatives or servants of the United States government and were in a position to say something that might have influenced American policy. For this reason various US presidents occupy a large part in this analysis. They are the major formulators and practitioners of American foreign policy; they give the clearest and loudest voice to both its origins and its practice. Still, they do not represent the sole object of analysis. In addition to presidential addresses, interviews and letters, the words of cabinet officials, Senators and Congressmen, soldiers, State and Defense Department documents, a few memoirs, and the occasional magazine article make up the bulk of the content under scrutiny, as they too are contributors to the dynamics that have served American policy and power.

Additionally, all of the passages quoted here are part of the public record, and several may be recognized by the reader. The point of tapping into an established and accepted record, whose contents are largely accepted as representative of their respective times, is deliberate. In spite of the fact the politicians may say one thing while they act for a different set of reasons, I would argue that the distinction often made between public rhetoric and the truth hidden behind the words is false. "All language is in fact rhetorical, whether it is intended to express the truth, accurately to reflect reality, or to persuade and manipulate." What public language does is to carry within it "implicit understandings of the world, of the objects which populate that world (such as the United States with its unique character and mission, the 'free world,' 'dominoes,' and the like) and of reasonable and acceptable forms of reasoning ... Examining even exaggerated 'rhetoric' provides a good indication of what makes sense in a particular environment at a particular time."[7] This is true of the assumptions, attitudes and prejudices that have informed historical and contemporary conceptions of "American-ness" and "Cuban-ness," offered up in the public record, whose open character serves to illustrate the extent to which that language is a reflection of its time and place. Informed by such an understanding, the book is organized as follows.

Organization of the book

Chapters 2 and 3 provide an examination of historical representations of Americans and Cubans over the past two centuries, looking at Cuba in the context of its place in the Western Hemisphere. Looking first at themes regarding conceptions of difference, I discuss American perspectives on exceptionalism, race and underdevelopment to explore how Latin America has historically been conceived of in terms of its inferiority to the United States. Special emphasis is placed upon the Spanish-American War as an example of how many of these themes played out at the time when the relationship between the United States and Cuba began to crystallize into the form it would take until the Cuban revolution. I then discuss a concurrent circumstance in which Latin Americans have also been regarded as part of a collective identity that encompasses the entire Western Hemisphere, a place where all are Americans. The focus is upon the language of geographic proximity, shared ideals of democracy and liberty, and the metaphor of "the American family of nations," whereby each of these serves an understanding based upon commonalities, but also serves to reproduce the superiority of the United States in inter-American relations.

Chapter 4 explores the historical representation of Cuba in the context of the Cold War and anti-communism. The focus here is on the early Reagan years to discuss the understanding of a Cuba whose ties to the Soviet Union and participation in revolutionary struggles around the world prompted an understanding in which Cuba was viewed as both an illegitimate government and a threat to the United States. In this context, since communist ideology was seen as an import from the Soviets, there could be no similarities to the ideals of the US, or to characteristics common to all the Americas, only differences. The chapter concludes with a discussion concerning Cuba's distinction as the only Latin American country that has ever successfully managed to eliminate US influence while adopting communism at the same time.

Chapter 5 address the post-Cold War environment and the continued recognition of Cuba as an enemy, in spite of both America's self-declared victory in the Cold War and Cuba's economic difficulties. It argues that with respect to both a regional hierarchy and anti-communism, the end of the Cold War did not substantially alter American representations of either the United States or Cuba. In light of enduring understandings that the US is democratic, free and legitimate, while Cuba is spoken of in terms of communism, non-democracy, illegitimacy, and human rights violations, the changed global setting has not automatically prompted a reappraisal or fundamental change in US policy toward Cuba. In fact, the revolution's durability represents, in and of itself, a challenge to an American under-standing of its proper place in hemispheric and global politics with respect to Cuba. By virtue of Washington's current understandings of the conflict, in which the Cuban revolution is not only an illegitimate dictatorship, but also a dying, failed regime with few friends, there has been little, if anything, to prompt or suggest a change. Thus if Cuban communism is more of a rotting corpse than a danger, it is, according to its American critics, still possessive of the same body that was and is worthy of disdain and therefore, continuity in American policy.

The concluding chapter offers a final assessment of US policy toward Cuba. It considers the tug between continuity and change, looking at how American policy reflects not only "the presence of the past," but also a distinct possibility for change since the arrival of President Barack Obama in the White House. It examines President Obama's words and actions to date, assessing the current debates over Cuba and the prospects for normalization of relations by analyzing policies such as his end to the bans on family travel and remittances to Cuba. It suggests that in spite of great continuity over the past several decades, a significant shift in policy is possible. It further suggests that the United States will eventually make such a shift. With each passing year, it becomes increasingly clear that US policy will not succeed, and that the Cuban revolution will be able to outlast not only the rule of both Fidel and Raul Castro, but also America's efforts of more than 50 years to fatally weaken it.

2 Latin America – A different kind of place

Those people are no more fit for self-government than gunpowder is for hell.
US General William R. Shafter[1]

All Latins are volatile people.
US Senator Jesse Helms[2]

That old Mexican lament "So far from God, so close to the United States," could apply equally as well to Cuba. Cuba's proximity to the US has made it the object of envy and attention of American presidents, congressmen, newspapermen, elites of all kinds, since the early days of the republic. Viewing the island as something of a cure-all for the economic and security concerns of the young nation, Thomas Jefferson wrote that he had

> ever looked upon Cuba as the most interesting addition which could ever be made to our system of States. The control of which, with Florida Point, this island would give us over the Gulf of Mexico, and the countries and the Isthmus bordering on it, as well as all of those whose waters flow into it, would fill up the measure of our political well-being. [3]

John Quincy Adams commented that "Cuba, almost in sight of our shores, from a multitude of considerations has become an object of transcendent importance to the political and commercial interests of our Union." Its strategic location, excellent harbor and economic potential gave it "an importance in the sum of our national interests, with which that of no other foreign country can be compared ... It is scarcely possible to resist the conviction that the annexation of Cuba to our federal republic will be indispensable to the continuance and integrity of the Union itself."[4] Later James Buchanan believed that Cuba would free the US "from the apprehension which we can never cease to feel for our own safety and the security of our commerce whilst it shall remain in its present condition."[5]

In the twentieth century up to the present time, American policies from the Platt Amendment, which gave the US to the right intervene in Cuba, ostensibly to protect Cuban sovereignty, to the Bay of Pigs invasion and Missile Crisis, to the *Cuban Liberty and Democratic Solidarity Act* of 1996 and the current revisiting of American policy testify to the continual concern in the US with Cuba's destiny. From the time the US gained its independence, the desire to possess or control or influence Cuba has been a recurrent theme in American foreign policy.

This persistent concern with the fate of Cuba is rooted in a view of the island that identifies it as both a Latin and an American entity, whereby both of these elements are significant. Such a view, which includes with it a series of representations, meanings, understandings and images, has remained relatively consistent since the early part of the nineteenth century, marking the entire region as part of a distinct geographic domain within a legitimate sphere of US influence. This chapter focuses on these representations, looking at various attributes of Cuban-ness, or Latin American-ness, and American-ness, analyzing how Cubans and Americans have been (and continue to be) depicted in American political discourse, and arguing how these under-standings contribute to American ideas and practices that bolster hegemony, influence, power and a sense of superiority. The objective is not to reveal prejudices and stereotypes with the intent of demonstrating their lack of correspondence to the real Cuba or the real United States, but to look at Cuban and Latin American identities through the language used to describe, understand and conceptually situate them in opposition to the United States.

This involves examining how various understandings of difference and sameness have developed over time. The language of difference addresses not only distinction, but also backwardness and inferiority.[6] It is implicated in a language of superiority and inferiority, or the relative backwardness of Latin America as compared to the United States, encouraging what I call "the myth of American superiority." In particular, the subjects of race and development have informed American notions of superiority/inferiority over the years. More than others, they have lent themselves to a understanding in which the United States of America retains a preeminent status in hemispheric politics.

However, as difference has meaning only in contrast to a reference point, Cuban backwardness has been historically represented as such by comparing it to an advanced US, the elements of which serve to secure the idea of American superiority and hegemony. These views of the US over time by its inhabitants has involved placing the terms America and American in a singular category, where Providence, the land, the frontier and American institutions have produced a unique nation, a nation defined by its exceptionalism. In tandem with positing difference based upon race and development, the idea of American exceptionalism renders a sharp distinction between the US and its neighbors. It provides for an interpretation of American behavior that is unlike that of other nations, and is ennobled by its origins in an exceptional place and its people. Thus it has been decisive in conceptualizing the United States as regionally superior.

The myth of American superiority

In discussing the idea of American superiority as a myth, I look to Roland Barthes, who describes the construction of myth through discourse.[7] In this view, myth does not mean falsehood. Instead, it is a language, or a "story that constructs meaning by mobilizing associations already extant in the culture and redeploying them toward new objects that then acquire the authority of those older meanings."[8] Hence, myth is not the same as a concept or an idea. It is instead "a mode of signification," in which "the fundamental character of the mythical concept is to be appropriated" in order to serve a particular end. Moreover, this understanding of myth reflects a sense that the "naturalness with which newspapers, art and common sense [and political personalities] constantly dress up a reality ... is undoubtedly determined by history." It maintains an awareness that what is construed to be true (in this thesis the characteristic attributes of identity) is contingent upon interaction, not upon objective truths that have been made evident as a result of that interaction. However, the perpetuation of such myths over time serves to render them as timeless.[9]

This understanding of myth as a process that tames language and meaning, and renders immutability out of historical contingency, is helpful in appreciating the US relationship with its fellow 'Americans.' (The tendency, or the need, to use the word American in two ways here may be some cause for confusion. In order to try to be as clear to the reader as possible, I will use the single quotes when I am referring to people of the entire Western Hemisphere, inhabitants of the Americas. Otherwise, the word will have its more common, parochial definition, being used to refer only to people of the United States.) This dynamic has contributed to a situation analogous to what Edward Said discusses in *Orientalism*: a relationship in which Western (or American) subjects, who understand another region in terms of its difference, backwardness and inferiority, effect their own hegemonic power over that region and its people. It is a situation in which the United States maintains its positional superiority, whereby the language and practice of American policymakers, like the practice of Orientalism, "puts the Westerner [United States] in a whole series of possible relationships with the Orient [Latin America] without ever losing the relative upper hand." This ascendancy, which spawns supporting institutions, vocabulary, scholarship, imagery, doctrines, even bureaucracies and styles, maintains as its principal component "the idea of [American] identity as a superior one in comparison with all non-[American] peoples and cultures."[10]

In a mythological understanding of a Latin America that has continually reproduced this superiority over successive generations, American leaders have regarded Cuba in a hemispheric context, where the island falls within an American domain, an almost natural sphere of influence, a place where the US has both a right and a duty to intervene in, control or influence political life. Such an outlook is best exemplified by the Monroe Doctrine.

This view of Cuba, as an entity within the US orbit, serves as an exemplar of how Americans have viewed their relationship to the rest of Latin America, especially Central America and the Caribbean. A presumption that the entire region lies within an American sphere of influence has long predominated in American thinking on the matter. In addition, this presumption has been coupled with another: that the US is more "advanced" than Latin America, a condition which has been blamed either on the Latin people themselves or on great social problems which happen to claim Latin Americans as victims. No matter the source, this understanding has led to a situation where, without really questioning its right to act in Latin America, the US has instead focused on the question of what to do with Latin America.

Usually one of two reasons have served as the rationale for the exercise of American power, often both: either there existed a potential threat to American national interests, security or else economic, or only US intervention could save the countries and/or peoples of Latin America from themselves. These aims were usually expressed in terms of promoting democracy or restoring order and stability. Yet both of these rationales rested upon the prior assumption among American leaders that the US was acting in its own "backyard" and thus could legitimately intervene in the region. Theodore Roosevelt stated it the most clearly when he claimed that,

> All this country desires is to see neighboring countries stable, orderly and prosperous. Any country whose people conduct themselves well can count upon our hearty friendship ... it need fear no interference from the United States. Chronic wrongdoing, or an impotence which results in a general loosening of the ties of civilized society, may ... ultimately require intervention by some civilized nation, and in the Western Hemisphere the adherence of the United States to the Monroe Doctrine may force the United States, however reluctantly, in flagrant cases of such wrongdoing or impotence, to the exercise of an international police power.[11]

The results of an outlook such as this – in which neighboring countries are targeted, in which instability, labeled here as "chronic wrongdoing" or "impotence," is to be eradicated, in which the US is identified as a civilized nation in contrast to neighboring countries, in which the US, in accordance with the Monroe Doctrine, can rightfully take the role of "international police power" – have considerable implications for reproducing the mythology of US superiority and Latin American inferiority. First of all, it reminds the reader (or listener) of those characteristics which are known to be good for nations and those which are known to be bad. Roosevelt himself does proclaim them, but he has no need to invent them. The qualities he chooses to talk about can be said to have withstood the test of time and can be readily agreed upon as either good or bad by both the wrongdoer and the policing power. (This is not as obvious as it seems, as in a later era, when communism was labeled as an evil, it would require its opponents to further define what was evil about it, a process that was continually challenged.)

Second, this outlook clearly establishes the US as a nation that possesses the favorable qualities Roosevelt describes, and none of the undesirable ones. Explicit recognition of this is not made, nor is it necessary, as it is already implicitly present. In fact, its absence makes an even stronger statement, as it is understood and assumed that the US is "stable, orderly and prosperous." Third, it is established that neighboring countries are potentially or actually disorderly, unstable or impotent, and thus uncivilized, in pointed contrast to the US. Fourth, this set of conditions presupposes the objectivity and legitimacy of the American order as well as the justice of any actions the US would take to uphold that order.[12] Violations of that order are, by definition, illegitimate and subversive.

Finally, all of these elements lead to the conclusion that the US maintains a degree of superiority over its neighbors. Possessive of certain qualities, seen as deficiencies, they may be forced to accept US intervention in order to eradicate them. By such a formulation, American leaders may reserve for themselves the right to act as the "community of judgment" regarding the proper course of Latin American affairs.[13] This situation not only makes Washington the judge and the executor, but also clearly precludes any consideration of the US as a possible candidate to be acted upon in the same manner. The right of intervention is both a duty and a privilege derived from a conception of American superiority.

The idea of US superiority is essential to the freedom to exercise power and to define the terms of reference in international dealings. Reinforced in a multitude of ways, the hierarchy of superiority/inferiority solicits a variety of images regarding Cubans and their Latin brethren. They have been imagined, at different times, as children, female, weak, poor, savage and unfortunate, but also deserving, ambitious to achieve, and desirous of democracy and/or free markets. A multitude of representations, or metaphors, are available. As Louis Perez argues in *Cuba in the American Imagination*, metaphorical representation has been one of the principal modes by which the United States has understood Cuba. Such modes of representation helped Americans in the past persuade themselves that Cuba, in some sense, belonged to them, and have continued to serve the goals of power and domination.[14] Yet what is notable about all of these representations throughout the decades is that they preclude an understanding of a Latin America that can enjoy a relationship with the US as equals. Even the love or practice of democracy can be made into a lesser quality than it is in the US, when it is characterized as merely aspirational or potential, or simply new to a particular place and therefore a) a copy of the legitimate original, and b) not as secure as its US counterpart. President George H.W. Bush's words provide an example of this when he stated that "freedom has made great gains ... right here in the Americas," and that he was "ready to play a constructive role at this critical time to make ours the first fully free hemisphere in all of history."[15] His words, unlike those of Teddy Roosevelt, are encouraging and promising, yet by speaking about recent "gains" and his willingness to be "constructive," he reflected (perhaps unavoidably, considering how much in his speech he actually did try to put the countries of Latin America on a comparable plane with the US) the presupposition of superiority. Like Roosevelt, Bush's representations have nurtured the idea that Latin America can be identified by its backwardness.

The idea of backwardness has been especially important in America's relations with its neighbors. The geopolitical underpinnings of American foreign policy toward Latin America have been significant, but they have not been exclusive. Again, the US relationship with Cuba serves as an exemplar of a greater appraisal. Cuba is/was not merely viewed from the US as a piece of territory, devoid of any characteristics other than location and capabilities. The character of its inhabitants, their institutions, culture, language, ideals, political and economic development, and of course, color, have all influenced American attitudes, beliefs and prejudices about Cuba and Cubans. As neighbors, fellow revolutionaries and Americans, the people of Cuba have been seen as sharing a common home and common ideals with the US as members of "the American family." However, in spite of the geographic closeness and the sometimes-invoked shared idealism, a stronger current has influenced American images and ideas even more, encouraging an understanding in which the US is divided from its neighbors by a huge gulf. While Cuba and Cubans are members of "the American family," they are also, at the same time, part of a place called Latin America, a term that defines not only a territory, but also a people, whose political, cultural and racial characteristics arose out of Spanish and Portuguese conquest, an altogether different foundation than the Anglo-Saxon tradition from which the US was cast. As the product of this conquest, Cubans and other Latin Americans are heirs to a different 'American' experience from the US, a different cultural and historical heritage.

What these divergent heritages represent, however, is not entirely agreed upon by Cubans and Americans. As I have discussed earlier, there is no single, stable meaning attached to the idea of Latin America, not among all 'Americans' or even in the United States. A Latin America that can represent a variety of different things is one which provides a myriad of possibilities for representing objects and objectives in American foreign policy. Imagined in terms of both similarity and difference, often simultaneously, and where the border between the two is not always clear, Latin Americans are depicted as family and savages, brothers and children, democrats and papists, benign and dangerous, free and unfree, friend and foe.[16]

In their dealings with Cuba over two centuries, a succession of American leaders have deployed all of these images to construct, understand, explain, encourage and/or justify their policies, not merely to gain support for policies whose real reasons could not be stated, but to construct their own understandings of Cuba and its people. Conjuring up a subject in terms of difference has involved, in varying degrees over time, looking at the qualities of an exceptional American specimen – one who is civilized, cultured, advanced, strong, manly, at the top of a racial hierarchy, rich, prosperous, developed and a guardian of democracy. This image is juxtaposed to an opposite Latin character – one who is uncivilized, backward, a mongrel, racially and culturally inferior, weak, effeminate, poor, underdeveloped and incapable of self-government. By contrast, conceptualizing Latin Americans who embody characteristics similar to the ones that Americans have often ascribed to themselves has involved the usage of language and rhetoric centered on geography (we are all inhabitants of the Western Hemisphere), idealism (the shared commitment that all 'Americans' do or should hold regarding liberty, freedom and democracy), and family (this place is home to the 'American family'), all of which comprise what has been called "The Idea of the Western Hemisphere."[17]

In spite of the multitude of ways in which Latin America can be portrayed, it is also the case that all these images, metaphors and understandings share a common feature: they contribute to a hierarchical conceptualization in which the United States enjoys a superior position to Latin America, Cuba in particular, and thus can more easily exercise its power in the region. Moreover, these representations have been continual features of US foreign policy, especially with respect to the subjects of exceptionalism, race and underdevelopment.

Exceptionally good

From the time that the Puritan minister Peter Bulkeley told his congregation, "the Lord looks for more from thee, then [sic] from other people ... Thou shouldst be a special people, a onely people, none like thee in all the earth," through the contemporary age when the first President Bush stated that "this nation, this idea called America, was and always will be a new world," there has been a continual self-reference in the US to the exceptional qualities that define the country and the people.[18]

Alexis de Tocqueville was the first to use the term with regard to the United States, stating that,

> The position of the Americans is therefore quite exceptional, and it may be believed that no democratic people will ever be placed in a similar one. Their strictly Puritanical origin, their exclusively commercial habits, even the country they inhabit, which seems to divert their minds from the pursuit of science, literature, and the arts ... a thousand special causes, of which I have only been able to point out the most important, have singularly concurred to fix the mind of the American upon purely practical objects.[19]

The myth of exceptionalism has been credited over the years for the rise of a peculiarly American ideology. This ideology is about "the free individual who was to attain his fulfillment by being an independent, rational actor in a free market unfettered by any oppressive collectivities, be they the state or social classes, organized religion or the army."[20] Seymour Martin Lipset identifies this idea – Americanism – in terms of an American Creed that consists of liberty, egalitarianism, individualism, populism and laissez-faire.[21] This itself is an outgrowth of Frederick Jackson Turner's thesis, which was described in "The Significance of the Frontier in American History." In Turner's interpretation the American was someone who originally had to "strip off the garments of civilization" before he could transform the wilderness and emerge as a "new product." The unique opportunities provided by the wide open spaces and extensive resources of the continent allowed for the emergence of the "self-made man" along the frontier, a person whose habits, mentalities and institutions produced a society, a history and an identity that were dramatically different from those brought from the Old World. This distinctly American dynamic gave rise to a society that was more open, more democratic and more equal than European society. It was more attuned to the aspirations of ordinary people who were less encumbered by institutional and governmental restriction.[22]

If the French, Italians, Chinese and others have been able to assert an identity in terms of culture, tradition or history, the US and the thirteen colonies before it have constructed identities in terms of one's relationships to society's political institutions: to be American is to enjoy freedom from the weight of state power with regard to speech, association, religion, etc. American-ness, what it means for many to be an American, is more about things social and political, not cultural. Or perhaps, to put it another way, the political has become the cultural. "Americanism," according to Lipset, "is to the American not a tradition or a territory, not what France is to a Frenchman or England to and Englishman, but a doctrine, what socialism is to a socialist."[23] What this means for the myth of uniqueness is that, as Richard Hofstadter commented, "it has been our fate as a nation not to have ideologies but to be one."[24]

More importantly, however, exceptional has not merely meant different, but better as well. As Michael Shapiro notes, "given the usual esteem within which the self is constituted," those who are different are invariably constituted as a less-than-equal subject.[25] Even before Tocqueville used the term, there existed conceptions of American greatness which placed the New World's inhabitants at the apex of a long line of a great historical and racial progression. The (white) American people were conceived to be part of a greater Anglo-Saxon tradition of greatness.[26]

In this reading the advance of civilization along a westward course had reached an endpoint. America was part of a teleology, representing the culmination of the grand sweep of history. As the logic went, the ancient civilizations of China and India were eventually eclipsed by the Western Civilization of Europe, whose corruption and decadence would eventually make way for an ascendant America. "The march of culture has always followed the sun's course" wrote August Friedrich Pott.[27] This idea was imported to America and found particular resonance by virtue of the east-to-west settlement of the North American continent. Thomas Jefferson noted that he had "observed this march of civilization advancing from the seacoast ... insomuch that we are more advanced in civilization here than the seaports were when I was a boy. And where this progress will stop no one can say."[28]

This ethos of progress was later incorporated into the idea of Manifest Destiny. As it was expressed by Senator Thomas Hart Benton, one of the most fervent advocates of America's role in the westward advance of civilization, it was the "disposition which the children of Adam have shown to follow the sun" which accounted for America's great triumphs.[29] To Benton, manifest destiny was a further proof of this. "It would seem," he said, "that the White race alone received the divine command, to subdue and replenish the earth! For it is the only race that has obeyed it – the only one that hunts out new and distant lands."[30]

Benton's reference to Adam was indicative of the especially lofty status America was assumed to enjoy over others, for this reading of America as a special place was not merely racial, but Providential, rooted in the enduring Puritan mythology of America as the place of God's new chosen people, living in a "new Eden," an "American Jerusalem," or "G-d's American Israel." "Wee [sic] shall be," said John Winthrop, leader of the new Massachusetts Bay Colony in 1630, "as a Citty upon a Hill, the eies of all people are uppon us."[31] From this place was to begin the regeneration of the world, and from this time the language of America as the land from which G-d would send Americans to renew the world became an important part of American political thought.

These ideas of exceptionalism have found strength in a multitude of occurrences in US history. They have been well documented by others and so I will only briefly mention their significance here. The success of the American Revolution was interpreted as an especially powerful sign that Americans were indeed marked for greatness. It did more than reinforce the moralistic tone of American uniqueness, it provided for a fusion of the Providential and the political, a form of religious nationalism, encompassing the idea that G-d had made it possible for this people to establish "institutions that made possible the protection of man's natural rights and allowed him self-realization ... Providence was working through the American people and American nation to achieve a new life for mankind."[32]

The results of the Spanish-American War provided further inspiration to proponents of the exceptionalist idea. No one better captured the rhetoric or the sentiment of this idea as well as Senator Albert Beveridge, an ardent expansionist who, championing the annexation of America's newly acquired Spanish territories, declared in a floor speech that drew applause from his colleagues, that

> God has not been preparing the English-speaking and Teutonic peoples for a thousand years for nothing but vain and idle self-contemplation

and self-admiration. No! He has made us the master organizers of the world to establish system where chaos reigns. He has given us the spirit of progress to overwhelm the forces of reaction throughout the earth. He has made us adepts in government that we may administer government among savage and senile peoples. Were it not for such a force as this the world would relapse into barbarism and night. And of all our race He has marked the American people as His chosen nation to finally lead in the regeneration of the world. This is the divine mission of America, and it holds for us all the profit, all the glory, all the happiness possible to man. We are trustees of the world's progress, guardians of its righteous peace.[33]

In this setting, a dichotomy is posited. The United States is the chosen land of liberty, a nest from which to fill a continent with one nation, while those not of "our race" are, by contrast, savage and senile, whose societies are places where chaos reigns. (Of course, the ostensibly noble effort Beveridge calls for, while steeped in a language of a divine mission, the march of civilization, and a special people, has also been implicated in the political practices of slavery, conquest, war, imperialism and the removal of Native Americans from their lands.)

The claim to exceptionalism has been continually emulated. If the vision of national greatness was captured by a call in the nineteenth century to fulfill a manifest destiny, its twentieth century variant was the call to fashion an American Century. In *Life* magazine, Henry Luce played the John O'Sullivan[34] of his day, calling forth an

America as the dynamic center of ever-widening spheres of enterprise, America as the training center of the skillful servants of mankind, America as the Good Samaritan, really believing again that it is more blessed to give that to receive, and America as the powerhouse of the ideals of Freedom and Justice – out of these elements surely can be fashioned a vision of the 20th century.[35]

America's important role in the Allied victory and its subsequent superpower status provided as big a boost as the American Revolution did in strengthening the idea of the US as an exceptional nation. The sign of that greatness was in America's position as the leader of the free world and the world's strongest power. Yet America's uniqueness was not merely in its strength and its past successes, but in its newly acquired role defending freedom around the world from the Soviet Union, which was understood as holding ambitions for world domination. There continued to be purpose in the unfolding of American history.

From the time President Truman stated that "the Communists in the Kremlin are engaged in a monstrous conspiracy to stamp out freedom all over the world," and that "it must be the policy of the United States to support free peoples who are resisting attempted subjugation by armed minorities or outside pressures," until the end of the Cold War, American political thought maintained its internal consistency and strength without changing: democracy and freedom challenged dictatorship and communism.[36] John F. Kennedy, who along with Ronald Reagan proved to be a master at using the language freedom vs. danger, declared that the US had been "granted the role of defending freedom in its hour of maximum danger" and pledged to "pay any price, bear any burden, meet any hardship, support and friend, oppose any foe to assure the survival and the success of liberty."[37] President Johnson expanded the role, declaring that the United States would "conduct a worldwide attack on the problems of hunger and disease and ignorance," as "only a people advancing in expectation will build secure and peaceful lands."[38]

Ronald Reagan too was especially adept at using the language of exceptionalism. In advocating "a crusade for freedom" to help "those who strive and suffer" for it, he deployed a language that was stirring precisely because it touched on the myths and ideologies that give resonance to the idea of an American mission.[39] He continued in the steps of his predecessors, privileging American democracy above all, establishing its intrinsic goodness through the identification of difference and danger in the Soviet Union. Moreover, his words also tended to resemble an earlier time, in which the language of success he used included a place for Providence. Reagan often ended many of his speeches with the phrase "G-d bless America," a practice not uncommon to many national figures. He also spoke of his belief that "this land was set aside in an uncommon way, that a divine plan placed this great continent between the oceans to be found by a people from every corner of the Earth who had a special love of faith, freedom, and peace."[40] In one notable example of this, he made a direct reference to the colonial beginnings, recycling the language of the Puritans by speaking of America as a "shining city on a hill," adding that "democracy is just a political reading of the Bible."[41]

Notwithstanding the wisdom of making grand pledges to act globally, as American presidents routinely did during the Cold War, the statements by these presidents are notable for this argument in that they reflect a sense of self-assuredness in a nation, a people and a government that is almost beyond measure. All of these speeches were lined with passages about America being the greatest or strongest or wealthiest nation on earth, but these qualities did not have to be explicitly stated. America did not have to be characterized with a string of superlatives. This much was already assumed, understood. The language of these promises reflected an *a priori* belief by the presidents and the people they spoke to that their government had the capabilities to accomplish all these tasks. Otherwise there would not have even been an attempt to begin them.

Without belaboring the point, suffice it to say that the post-Cold War world that succeeded Reagan only intensified the tendency to claim an exceptional greatness. After victory in a heroic struggle could be claimed, the first President Bush envisioned an America which would forge a "new world order," while President Clinton offered the reminder that "it's no accident that our nation has steadily expanded the frontiers of democracy."[42] The current wars in Iraq and Afghanistan have been steeped in similar language, expressing continuity in US history, imbuing them with purpose and direction, and implying righteousness and greatness, rather than acknowledging their contingent nature.

A final comment regarding the myth of greatness and exceptionalism concerns one of the results of America's self-proclaimed unique standing in the world. Throughout the years there has been a continual effort to represent American policy as disinterested, in which the US has acted, with regard to some issue, on behalf of a force greater than mere individual or state interest. Whether the motivation has been religious purity, manifest destiny, regional hegemony, superpower status and/or the spread of democracy, the representation of America by its policymakers is one of a nation with great responsibilities, a nation that acts to carry out its duties and obligation, not to selfishly profit. In contrast to other countries, which only have interests, the US has been characterized as distinct, and by implication, better.

This distinction has not only made American greatness a goal, it has served also as a premise: exceptionalism was seen to confer upon the US certain rights and duties. It legitimized a global mission.[43] To the early settlers their calling was that the "Lord looks for more from thee." The advocates of imperialism at the turn of the century could include with this a sentiment that the American nation was the part of the superior white race that had answered its calling improve the world.[44] The emergence of US leadership during the Cold War was only a variation on this theme of disinterest. As it was stated in NSC-68, which outlined American Cold War policy, Soviet designs had "imposed upon us ... the responsibility of world leadership."[45] Americans did not claim to have asked for these obligations, rather these duties had been thrust upon them. "Whether we like it or not," President Truman said in 1945, "we must all recognize that the victory we have won has placed upon the American people the continued burden of responsibility for world leadership."[46] This language enjoyed prominence throughout the Cold War. Reagan used it many times to rally support around his policy of arming the Nicaraguan *contras*, who sought to overthrow what Reagan described as an outlaw regime. Urging his countrymen to "help us prevent a Communist takeover of Central America," he argued that "there is no evading responsibility – history will hold us accountable."[47] The rhetoric was a perfect analog to that spoken almost a century before by Senator Albert Beveridge. Advocating an imperialist foreign policy, he had asked of his fellow Americans, if they failed, "What shall history say of us? Shall it say that we renounced that holy trust, left the savage to his base condition, the wilderness to the reign of waste? ... Shall it say that ... we declined that great commission?"[48]

This type of representation, of the US as selflessly taking responsibility for leadership, has significant consequences. It suggests what kind of subject the US is understood to be, and that those whom the United States is responsible for are, as opposed to subjects capable of taking responsibility for themselves, objects on whose behalf the US acts, protects and defends. It provides not only a warrant for action, but an obligation. Moreover, it bolsters an assertion that the United States remains above the fray, acting altruistically, doing what is necessary for the betterment of others, rather than seeking its own gain. These possible understandings, available to a country which has a long and established tradition of espousing its own uniqueness and superiority, have the double effect of not only reinforcing and reproducing the story of American exceptionalism, but also of legitimizing the actions taken in the name of that exceptionalism.

With respect to an understanding of Cuba reflected in American political discussion, the effect of the language of exceptionalism justifies a sense of superiority over Cuba. The position of the US is always privileged over Cuba's. By this reading America must do something about Cuba when there is a problem on the island. Additionally, it has the right to determine what is or is not a problem, and what is best for all the parties involved. The US, by this logic, must be partly responsible for Cuba and the condition of its people. With its actions grounded in this understanding, US policy toward Cuba is, by definition, legitimate. Maintaining an embargo is thus characterized not an act of aggression against another country, but an "effort to promote a peaceful transition to democracy in Cuba" so that the United States can "welcome a free Cuba back into the community of democratic nations."[49] Fault for any suffering in Cuba is thus the result of Cuban intransigence and resistance to change, not American policy. Conversely, any response by Cuba to challenge the US is, by definition, illegitimate. It is labeled a "communist totalitarian dictatorship," a type of regime which is characterized as deriving no legitimacy or support from the people.[50] By the logic of such an understanding of Cuba's role in the world versus that of the United States, it is both right and necessary for the US to take responsibility for Cuba's future.

Race, or white makes right

The mythology of American exceptionalism served to characterize the immigrants who had conquered, settled and populated much of North America as the pinnacle of Western Civilization. It provided for Americans a connection to the European roots of the United States, but did not wholly associate them with European history. In such a manner was a unique people imagined. If the singularity of this people was not always defined in racial terms, then race at least often served to identify those who did not belong to the exceptional group. Racial difference, then, has been a second important identifying characteristic by which Americans set themselves apart from others in their midst, who often were seen as standing in the way of progress, as inferior, and who did not merit equal treatment.

With respect to Cuba, Americans' racial attitudes formed in the wake of the Spanish-American War. These views were themselves informed by the racialist attitudes and assumptions that already permeated the American republic since the colonial period. They arose primarily out of experiences with Native Americans and African Americans, and later Mexicans. Along the westward traveling frontier and in the South, there was a continual interaction with people of different colors and different cultures, whose racial inferiority was deemed to be reflected in their enslavement, extermination and/or military defeat. Conversely, the enormous success of white Americans in conquering land and people was seen to constitute proof of their own racial superiority.[51]

In the same way that the rhetoric of exceptionalism helped provide a basis for a mythological hierarchy, so too did the conversation regarding racial difference. It championed the superiority of whiteness (and along with it Anglo-Saxon, or at least European heritage) and the inferiority of blacks, who were routinely placed at the bottom. Mixed-blood mestizos were located somewhere in between, but their precise standing was usually dependent upon the status of Native Americans who could either be above or below them. This was usually decided by whether or not Indians were involved in the particular struggle that prompted a discussion of racial worthiness. Out of this racial classification emerged not only a set of attitudes about the quality and moral worth of different races, but an assortment of practices, based on experience, about the proper way to treat and to talk about those assumed to be one's inferiors.

One of the results of this interaction, of particular experiences that encouraged a language of superiority/inferiority, was what Barthes terms "mythical speech." Mythical speech is a mode and form of signification that is "made of material that has already been worked on so as to make it suitable for communication." It "presupposes a signifying consciousness" in which representations deployed in the present have long since crystallized around referents whose meanings have been established in the past.[52] By the time the war with Spain occurred, and American occupiers began to have close contact with the Cuban people, the mythical speech of race that had already been worked on so as to make it comprehensible, was redeployed in a new setting. The views and habits Americans had formed through their interaction with Native-Americans, African-Americans and Mexicans were easily and quickly applied to relations with Cubans.

Native Americans

The racism that predominated in the earlier days of the republic seemed to be of a gentler version than that which would come to dominate by the middle of the nineteenth century. By that time, the experiences that Americans had with Native Americans, black people and Mexicans converged with the leading scientific "discoveries," or more accurately, interpretations of the day. Reginald Horsman, in *Race and Manifest Destiny*, points out that in America, in the late eighteenth and early nineteenth centuries, views on race were informed by Enlightenment thought – views which posited that all mankind was of one species and that all mankind was capable of improvement. If one group of people had advanced further than others, it was because of differences in environment and the different histories and possibilities these environments produced, not innate, unchanging and unalterable racial differences. Still, no thinking or influential person doubted the hierarchy of race in which white people occupied the apex.[53]

Originally the native population of the Americas represented souls to be saved by the Spanish and then the English colonists, yet when it became clear to those colonists that the indigenous peoples had little desire to give up their land and way of life and become good Christians, "savage" became the primary label for them.[54] Later, the rapid westward movement of the frontier and the importation of Enlightenment ideas from Europe seemed to tame this view for many in the eastern United States. It became much easier to appreciate Indians from a distance, but any optimistic view of Native Americans proved to be rather short-lived.

Henry Knox, Secretary of War under President Washington, represented an excellent example of how conflicting ideas regarding the Indians existed simultaneously. He not only made war against them, telling them they would be destroyed if they did not submit, but in trying to bring about an end to one of the many frontier wars, he said to several tribal leaders that he sought ultimately to provide for the tribes, "all the blessings of civilized life, of teaching you to cultivate the earth, and raise corn; to raise oxen, sheep and other domestic animals; to build comfortable houses, and to educate your children, so as ever to dwell upon the land."[55] Further reflective of the possibilities still held out at the time for Indians, he went so far as to address the tribal leaders against whom he was currently making war as "brothers." Propaganda or not, the use of such terminology is important in that it represented, at the time, acceptable language for public rhetoric, whereas a few decades later this would neither be acceptable nor convincing language to a Secretary of War or an American public, much less Native Americans.

While those away from the frontier and actual fighting might have been magnanimous toward the Indians, those in closer contact with them, political and military men, were reinforcing the image of Indian as a savage. After a particularly bloody battle, William Henry Harrison, Governor of Indiana and future President, wrote in a letter communicated to Congress that "the Indians manifested a ferocity, uncommon even with them. To their savage fury, our troops opposed that cool and deliberate valor which is characteristic of the Christian soldier."[56] Recalling a meeting with his Secretary of State, President John Quincy Adams noted that he concurred with Henry Clay's view that, "it was impossible to civilize Indians; that there never was a full-blooded Indian who took to civilization. It was not in their nature. He believed they were destined to extinction, and, although he would never use or countenance inhumanity towards them, he did not think them, as a race, worth preserving." Adams himself agreed, albeit unenthusiastically, with these conclusions, saying that he "fear[ed] there is too much foundation" for them.[57]

Though defenders of Native Americans persisted throughout the century to make a case for a humane policy, political power was exercised primarily by people who believed Indians to be inferior and who expected them ultimately to be completely pushed aside by white Americans. Moreover, when Native Americans were removed from their lands, their resistance was used to further condemn them as savages, such that any aggression against them was hailed as manly, while Indian resistance was condemned as beastly. "They are demons, not men," said one congressman. "They have the human form, but nothing of the human heart ... If they cannot be emigrated, they should be exterminated."[58]

Because the policy of Indian removal that resulted in extermination proceeded so successfully, as the end of the century approached, vilification gave way to pity. The rise of industry, the spread of railroads and the dwindling frontier all pointed toward the demise of the Indians. Their fate was one of two: destruction or life on the reservation. In either case, they would emerge a defeated people, because they were seen as fundamentally anathema to white civilization and that civilization's progress, symbolized by the completion of the transcontinental railroad. General George Custer summed up the dilemma best. In spite of his efforts to eliminate Indian obstacles to American expansion, he wrote that nature intended the Indian to be in a savage state. "Every instinct, every impulse of his soul inclines him to it ... He cannot be himself and be civilized; he fades away and dies." In the technological society that the US was fast becoming, Custer believed that they had a grim future. Even if the Native American could be left to his way of life, "when the soil which he has claimed and hunted over so long a time is demanded by this to him insatiable monster, there is no appeal; he must yield or it will mercilessly roll over him."[59]

Custer believed that reservations were of little recourse as well. They would not give assistance to the Indians so that they could "develop a means of livelihood compatible with civilization," nor would they "snatch the remnants of the Indian race from destruction," as the advocates of the "peace policy" claimed. They would only mean degradation, making Indians "grovel in beggary, bereft of many of the qualities which in his wild state tended to render him noble." The only solution, according to Custer, was to allow the native tribes to hunt and roam, provided they did not obstruct the advance of civilization. "At best the history of our Indian tribes ... affords a melancholy picture of loss of life."[60]

Still, in spite of the fact that the last of the Indian wars prompted feelings of pity on the part of many Americans, it was the pity of a victorious people who had completely conquered a land and a people. It was a pity that could be aroused only by victory. And in that victory there were also rewards. As Indians were either destroyed or sent to reservations to remain under the tutelage of the US government, as Americans had expanded from a "city upon a hill" across a continent, as no opposition seemed to stand in the way of progress, it would not be unreasonable for white Americans to conclude that the defeat of the Indians had resulted from their racial superiority in physical and moral power.

African Americans

The possibility for African Americans to join white civilization was deemed to be even smaller than the Native American held. If the indigenous way of life was a counterpoint to civilization, the Native American himself as a living being occasionally held out hope to whites who had encountered them. Where African Americans were concerned, however, the obstacles were even greater, as blackness itself was viewed as the primary defect of the "Negro" race. Long before scientific reasons were advanced to assert the innate inferiority of black people, American colonists brought with them English prejudices associating things white with purity and goodness, and things dark with baseness and evil.[61] In America, the degradation of black people was a part of daily life. They were seen as lower not simply because they were slaves, but were slaves because of their inferior nature.[62] Still, the influence of Enlightenment views on race produced an ambivalence in America such that Thomas Jefferson, in his *Notes on the State of Virginia* wrote, "Whatever be their degree of talents, it is no measure of their rights," but also that, "I advance it therefore, as a suspicion only, that the blacks, whether originally a distinct race, or made distinct by time and circumstance, are inferior to the whites in the endowment both of body and mind."[63] Benjamin Franklin, who also believed in the possibility of correcting the deficiencies of blacks, nonetheless stated that,

> The number of purely white People in the World is proportionably very small ... I wish their numbers could be increased. And while we are, as I may call it, scouring our planet, by clearing America of woods, and so making this side of our globe reflect a brighter light to the eyes of the inhabitants in Mars or Venus, why should we ... darken its people? Why increase the sons of Africa, by planting them in America, where we have so fair an opportunity, by excluding all blacks and tawneys, of increasing the lovely white and red?[64]

Any view that held out possibilities for members of lower races to be raised was easily eclipsed by the prevailing belief that dark-skinned people were inherently inferior to white people and always would be. As the nineteenth century progressed, the inferiority of African Americans was increasingly attributed to their physiology, and no environmental or intellectual uplift could change this supposed fact. Moreover, the 'facts' came to be generated not merely out of the institution of slavery, nor out of prejudice or personal contact with people who were supposedly inferior, but from the cutting-edge scientific research of the day. When leading scientists of the nineteenth century began to discuss the hierarchy of the races in scientific terms, it lent further legitimacy to the prevailing standards, reinforcing the racial stereotypes and prejudices, strengthening the idea that inferior peoples were inferior precisely because of their given, unalterable race.[65] The methods were varied as to how to arrive at the hierarchy that was already believed to exist, but the hierarchy always held. Whether the method of investigation was craniometry, polygeny or recapitulation, engaged in by reputable, acclaimed scientists, various bodies of data were consistently provided to 'prove' the already determined conclusion that whites occupied the pinnacle of human development.[66] Even if a new theory or set of data contradicted a previous view, the old facts that did not fit were quietly forgotten. There was hardly a dearth of "scientific" voices joining the chorus to proclaim whites at the top of a natural hierarchical structure, while relegating others to varying degrees of inferiority. It was part of the scientific terrain of the day throughout most of the nineteenth and early twentieth centuries. Not at all removed from their own social contexts, but rather deeply reflective and productive of them, some of America's and the world's leading scientists, working with "a rich body of data that could support almost any racial assertion ... selected facts that would yield their favored conclusions according to theories currently in vogue." As Stephen Jay Gould argues, rather than pursuing "truth before all," scientists "tend to behave in a conservative way by providing 'objectivity' for what society at large wants to hear."[67] And Americans, in both southern and northern states, were a receptive audience. Not only might such scientific objectivity assuage the guilty consciences of people implicated in expansionism, extermination of the Indians and the mistreatment of black people, but so too would it be exactly what the people of a conquering nation were expecting to hear.

It is not that all agreed on the policies of slavery, discrimination and conquest, actions whose justifications were couched in the racism of the day, only that widespread racism went largely unquestioned. Such views were common regardless of one's politics, in stark contrast to today when racism is usually implicated in certain political leanings. For example, Louis Agassiz, the most well-known proponent of scientific theories of racial superiority/inferiority in the nineteenth century, was an opponent of slavery, as was Charles Darwin. Both firmly believed in the inherent inequality of race, yet their scientific and/or personal beliefs about the inherent inequality of races did not predetermine their political convictions. Abraham Lincoln said that "there is a physical difference between the white and black races which I believe will forever forbid the two races living together on terms of social and political equality ... there must be the position of superior and inferior." In a more candid (and less public) moment he wrote: "Negro equality! Fudge! How long, in the Government of a God great enough to make and rule the universe, shall there continue to be knaves to vend, and fools to quip, so low a piece of demagogism as this."[68] Yet this same racist also liberated American slaves.

The point here is not simply to identify racism and condemn it, while besmirching the names of people such as Agassiz, Darwin and Lincoln. To accuse people in these periods of being racist is akin to accusing Americans today of believing their country to be the strongest in the world. Racism was a product of the times, something that was widely believed. Whether one was a liberal who wanted to uplift, a conservative who wanted to maintain order, or any other variation, one could be a racist as the result of a sober, reflective consideration of differences in people. It was not necessarily the result of overt hatred. It was, rather, a part of the American political and social landscape.

Latin Americans

The bulk of the early American experience with different racial groups, and consequently racial investigations and attitudes, involved interaction with black people and Indians in the early part of the nineteenth century. Later, Mexicans, Cubans and other Latin Americans come to occupy a greater concern in the US, reflecting the concerns of a nation expanding into territories that were inhabited by a different kind of dark-skinned people. As the US began to covet, claim and take land from Mexico and Spain, the people of these regions were increasingly inscribed with innate backwardness and weakness. As justifications for US policy, it is not necessarily the case that these characterizations were only cynically deployed. Such sentiments were often genuine and/or "scientific." Their appearance as directed against a particular group seems only to reflect the timing of American encounters with them.

Latin Americans generally enjoyed the benefits of not being placed on the bottom of the racial hierarchy, but their relative worth was not always agreed upon. Sometimes, the so-called "mongrel" races of America's southern neighbors were viewed with greater disdain than even the Indians, who were occasionally seen as a pure breed. Senator John C. Calhoun, arguing against the incorporation Mexican territory at the end of the Mexican War, stated that to admit Mexicans into the Union would be admitting "impure races, not as good as the Cherokees or Choctaws."[69] When the territory was incorporated, it was commented that "the pueblos, or town Indians of New Mexico, are by far the better part of the population," and that "there are no people on the whole continent of America, whether civilized or uncivilized, with one or two exceptions, more miserable in condition or despicable morals that the mongrel race inhabiting New Mexico."[70]

The same metaphors and images associated with the innate inferiority of Native and African Americans were applied to the Latin American as well, who was often portrayed as an animal, a savage, a half-breed, a child, a being guided by passions, wants, and hungers. An American army officer stationed in New Mexico stated that the Mexicans "were content if they could satisfy their animal wants."[71] Stephen Austin, for whom the capital of Texas was named, said of them that "the majority of the whole nation as far as I have seen them want nothing but tails to be more brutes than Apes."[72] The *Illinois State Register*, even more forcefully stated in 1846 that Mexicans "are reptiles in the path of progressive democracy ... and they must either crawl or be crushed."[73]

By the end of the nineteenth century, an imperialist policy with respect to non-contiguous lands enjoyed great support among American leaders such as Theodore Roosevelt, Henry Cabot Lodge, Elihu Root, Henry Adams, Albert Beveridge and Alfred Mahan. Yet if the outright conquest of such lands had many influential backers, the problems facing an expanding America were different in 1900 than they had been 50 years before, and this was especially notable in the case of Cuba. With respect to earlier acquisitions such as the Louisiana Purchase and the conquest of Northern Mexico, the republic had little trouble annexing sparsely populated lands in an era of rapid territorial expansion and manifest destiny. However, the same conditions were not present in Cuba in 1900. First of all, as the US had already stretched across the continent and developed a large industrial sector, its fortunes had come to be tied more to economic, and not necessarily territorial, expansion. Second, Cuba had a relatively large population; it was not a vast, sparsely inhabited region that was readily available to new conquerors. Third, the strong Cuban movement for independence, which had prompted the US intervention to begin with, would not be easily pacified. Finally, the population consisted mostly of mestizos and black people, two groups that had generated a great deal of acrimony and fear in American politics, and who would ultimately make the America debate over annexation not about Cuba, but about Cubans.

The Cuban people ...

The last of these items, the nature of the Cuban people, proved to be of great importance in deciding the course of Cuba's future. Based upon observation of the American occupation forces, it was decided early on that Cuba's tropical climate was "admirably adapted to the white man" and that "the American race will not degenerate" there.[74] So American policymakers were not preoccupied with what Americans in Cuba could or could not do. However, they were not so certain about what the Cubans could or could not do. More specifically, the concern at the time was if the Cuban people were inherently precluded from self-government, either in the form of outright independence, or as a part of the United States. And that in turn depended upon the nature of the Cuban people.

Throughout the nineteenth century the image of Cubans in the United States was not terribly flattering, involving concerns about the capacity of Cubans to maintain self-government. This was not surprising as no administration in the 1800s cared for anything that might lead to Cuban independence. Just as Jefferson had hoped to eventually acquire Cuba, so too did his successors. John Quincy Adams, invoking a law of "political gravitation," said that Cuba, once "disjoined from its own unnatural connexion [sic] with Spain, and incapable of self-support, can gravitate only towards the North American Union, which, by the same law of nature, cannot cast her off its bosom."[75] In fact, as Louis Perez argues, proximity tended to conflate "location and distance into a usable premise for possession," which was inscribed with a meaning that was "commonly understood as a fulfillment of a divinely ordained destiny."[76] These views regarding political gravitation or providential imperative became accepted wisdom, and "over the course of seventy years ... an uncommon consensus ... developed around the fate that destiny had fixed for Cuba: at some indeterminate point in the future, Cuba would be a part of the American union." Whether one cited national security concerns, economic benefits, the need to civilize, manifest destiny, fear of a black-run republic as an example to African-Americans in the US, or any other reason, "in the end, Cuba was simply there, and so close."[77] The result was deemed inevitable.

This sense of inevitability converged squarely with the idea that Cubans could not maintain a government. Jefferson pointed out that history "furnishes no example of a priest-ridden people maintaining a free civil government." Henry Clay determined that "if Cuba were to declare itself independent, the amount and character of its population render it improbable that it could maintain its independence." John Adams, among the most pessimistic, considered the appearance of democracy in Latin America about as likely as its appearance in the animal kingdom.[78] During the Ten Years' War in Cuba (1868–78), the Grant administration refused to recognize the Cuban insurgents. His Secretary of State, Hamilton Fish, "made no effort to conceal his low esteem of the intellectual and moral quality of the Cubans, believing a population consisting of Indians, Africans, and Spaniards incapable of self-government."[79] And at the end of the century, William McKinley did not recognize the republic of *Cuba Libre* as part of American intervention.

In the year or two preceding the American declaration of war against Spain, the view that Cubans were incapable of self government experienced a temporary eclipse, replaced by a more favorable image. Rebellion in Cuba, which had erupted in 1895, was portrayed in romantic terms of liberty-loving Cubans versus cruel Spaniards, the forces of freedom against the forces of tyranny. The rebellious Cubans were described as analogous to America's founding fathers, and widely praised. Members of Congress were especially outspoken in the effort to romanticize the Cuban revolt, one declaring that "Cuba today is fighting for the same principles that we contended for at Bunker Hill."[80] Especially influential were the newspapers of William Randolph Hearst and Joseph Pulitzer, which ran stories to portray Cuban heroism and righteousness. Filled with generous embellishments or even outright lies, their journals inflamed public passions and eventually aroused a great deal of public support for war against Spain.

This favorable image was contrasted with an opposite image of Spain. From a very early time in US history, American opinions of that country were informed by the myth of the "black legend," a condemnation of the Spanish that embodied the idea that Spain's supremacy had been a blight and a curse. The legend highlighted the cruelty with which the Spanish dealt with the Native Americans they encountered, their religious intolerance and medieval-era institutions. The cruelty, violence, greed, brutality and authoritarianism with which Spain was seen to have treated its colonies made up the better part of the Spanish legacy to New World.[81] Steeped in this mythology, American leaders had an understanding upon which they could easily draw in their vilification of Spain. Furthermore, the yellow journalism of the time reinforced the image of the treacherous and cruel Spaniard. Despite the fact that information provided by the press was often greatly embellished or even untrue, "the constant bombardment of the public with stories of Spanish atrocities convinced most of their readers that Spanish rule in Cuba was inherently brutal, repressive, and illiberal."[82]

Once the US entered the war, however, the images changed. The Cubans, who had been portrayed as liberty-loving heroes, were described by the US soldiers who encountered them as "the dirtiest, most slovenly looking lot of men I had ever seen," and "a collection of real tropic savages" who would neither fight nor work. "They stood by, inefficient, inactive ... the Americans made the sacrifice." Cubans were described as "armed rabble," "barbarous cutthroats," "villainous," "vermin," and "utter failures," whose ability to "hold off many thousands of Spanish troops" was considered "strange." Moreover, the Americans noted that "a large proportion are of negro blood," or that they "were all negroes." This rather contemptible, "worthless" band, "made up very considerably of black people, only partially civilized," amounted to "the most ragged, hungry, and motley looking crowd [the American soldiers] had ever seen." Even the description of the Cuban's color was denigrating; not only was he "black" or "Negro," but he "ranges from chocolate yellow through all the shades to deepest black with kinky hair." As these views became increasingly widespread, it was soon no longer the case, as had been previously asserted, that this "wretched mongrel lot" was reminiscent of America's founding fathers.[83]

Meanwhile, the Spanish brutes were given a makeover as well. Once the fighting ended, the Spanish were conferred with a variety of newly discovered virtues. They were held by the victorious Americans to be honorable, courageous fighters, who were worthy opponents, only overcome by a superior army. Moreover, their physical appearance resembled that of the Americans more than it did the Cubans. The Spanish were whiter than the Cubans, the Americans found, providing even more common ground for the former adversaries. As the Spanish attributes were rewritten, the abuses of the military government and its leader, "Butcher" Weyler, were forgotten, while any favorable qualities were emphasized. In contrast to the Cuban "ragamuffins" who were the "worst specimens of humanity," the Spanish in the end were deemed worthy of American admiration.[84]

This recasting of characters in the Cuban drama represented a return to those understandings of racial worth which placed Americans and Europeans on a higher plateau than mestizos, and it had an effect upon the arguments about what to do with Cuba after the war. If Cubans were not the white, freedom-seeking upright men that America's founders were, then the Cuban independence that the US claimed to be fighting for demanded reconsideration. "Can the Cubans govern themselves?" came to be one of the most important questions to answer before Cuba's fate could be decided.[85]

The answer to that question, from every quarter, was a resounding no. General James Wilson of the US occupation force in Cuba suggested that before any decision was made regarding the fate of the island, the Cubans needed "to show that they are not tropical and revolutionary, not a mongrel and vicious race, not disqualified by religion or impaired social efficiency for carrying on a stable government, or becoming American citizens."[86] His was a relatively generous attitude in that he held out the possibility for the Cubans to prove themselves. Secretary of War Root expressed that Cubans were "wholly ignorant of the art of self-government.[87] American soldiers serving in Cuba agreed, saying that "those people are no more fit for self-government than gunpowder is for hell," and "they are no more capable of self-government than the savages of Africa."[88] The best that could be hoped for, according to Major George Barbour, sanitary commissioner in Santiago, was that one day "the people of Cuba may become a useful race to the world, but to attempt to set them afloat as a nation, during this generation, would be a great mistake."[89]

The idea was that Americans might be able to teach the Cubans how to behave properly given enough time. "We are going ahead as fast as we can," said Governor-General Wood, as if remaking the Cuban individual were like constructing a building.[90] All that seemed to be necessary was a checklist of all the values and behaviors to be inculcated – Cubans were characterized as lazy, ignorant, unenlightened, improvident, dishonest, stupid, impractical, weak-minded, and childlike. With enough time and proper American teaching, the Cubans could progress, being "regulated and tempered by people of American birth."[91]

Time was especially important in remaking the Cuban so that he could participate in self-government. "We must wait until the children of today are old enough to think for themselves, and absorb American ideas," said one observer. Another predicted an even longer wait: "The present generation will have to pass away before the Cubans can form a stable government." After all, it was surmised, "Spain did not allow them to think for themselves."[92] The Cuban people "had no experience in anything except Spanish customs and Spanish methods which have grown up for centuries under a system opposed to general education and self-government." They were, according to General Wood, "a race that has steadily been going down for a hundred years."[93] It would not be a quick task to uplift that race.

Such an argument was also consistent with the idea that Cubans (and other Latin Americans) were analogous to children, members of an underdeveloped race not mature enough to govern itself. Senator Orville Platt commented that, "in many respects they are like children. They are passionately devoted to the sentiment of liberty, freedom and independence, but as yet have little real idea of the responsibilities, duties and practical results of republican government."[94] This was also seen as a virtue, in that Cubans could be controlled like children. In this hierarchy the metaphors of training or disciplining a childish race reinforced a paternalistic mindset of superiority/ inferiority that fueled and sanctioned imperialism. As Perez argues, representing the colonized like children not only privileges the colonizer, it also provides "a coherent cognitive framework into which to inscribe the pursuit of self-interest as a matter of self-righteous purpose."[95] Moreover, the policy not only reflected American power and American interests, it was grounded in the scientific wisdom of the day. At the time of the American intervention in Cuba, the phrase "'they're like children' was no longer just a metaphor of bigotry. It was not merely an insult hurled by politicians, newspapermen and soldiers, but a description offered by respected scholars.[96]

All of these understandings of what Cubans were, how they looked, how they acted, and how they could not be counted on, diminished their moral worth in the eyes of the Americans who occupied the island, governed it, and decided upon its future. Yet regardless of how one imagined Cubans, as savages, mongrels or children, they could not, in the face of such attitudes, be left to their own devices. Thus, responsibility for their well-being had to be taken up by the US. In a sense, American leaders at the time gave themselves no choice. Everything they believed about their own worth and capabilities as compared to the Cubans necessitated that the US maintain control of the island. This made it easier for the conqueror to take control of the land and the people with a clear conscience.

... and their fate

If Cubans were roundly deemed inferior, incapable of self-government, this agreement did not translate into an agreement on what to do with Cuba. Both sides in the debate wanted to maintain some form of control over Cuba, but for an island inhabited by an inferior race, there was more than one possibility. Cuba could either be made part of an empire, out of fear of contamination by people who would otherwise become citizens, or it could be formally annexed by a country whose superiority would render insignificant any drag exerted by the Cubans.

These options, however, contradicted the Teller Amendment. Enacted before the war with Spain, it said that the US "disclaims any disposition or intention to exercise sovereignty, jurisdiction, or control over [Cuba] ... and asserts its determination ... to leave the government and control of the island to its people."[97]

For the annexationists, neither the Teller Amendment nor the asserted inferiority of the Cuban represented a real problem. An ardent imperialist like Senator Beveridge, who proclaimed the supremacy of America and spoke of its destiny to rule much of the world, found the backward and deplorable attributes of Cubans to be ultimately irrelevant. The task of civilizing and teaching and making good citizens of them was not beyond American capabilities. Saying that "history and contemporaneous fact do not justify the belief that this element, left to itself, increases the Cuban capacity for self-government," he argued that "[G-d] has marked us as His chosen people, henceforth to lead in the regeneration of the world." The argument in this case was about much more than the particulars of Cuba, but about "His great purposes, revealed in the progress of the flag, which surpasses the intentions of Congresses and Cabinets."[98] By such reasoning was the United States to gain control over Cuba and extend its dominion through the Pacific Ocean. By invoking this language and this purpose, Beveridge provided the (white) American with his greatest burden and his greatest opportunity: the self-sanctioned control of vast territories and millions of people for the good of all involved.

In more practical terms this argument asserted that the racial inferiority of the Cubans would not diminish the United States. In the event of Cuba's annexation, Americans would begin to pour into the island "and within three, four, or five years that island would be thoroughly Americanized." Therefore, it could be suggested that the "speedy and practicable way to Americanize Cuba is to take her into the union as soon as possible."[99] Others agreed with the strategy, but were divided over the tactics, saying that "the policy with regard to Texas was right – the policy by which we first recognized her independence – then filled her with Americans, and then took her in."[100] The problem for all in this arrangement was how to properly Americanize Cuba, which meant removing the political influence of the black and mestizo Cuban population by overwhelming them with greater numbers of white Americans. The most blatant example of this sentiment was provided by Senator Newlands in 1903, when he said, "I hear it often said that Cuba would be desirable if for half an hour she could be sunk into the sea and then emerge after all her inhabitants had perished." Yet rather than remark upon the cruelty of such a wish, he continued, noting that "today Cuba has been practically dipped into the sea" as a result of the civil war, which diminished the population by half."[101] In other words, it was not necessary to wish for the death of the Cubans so that the island would be in pristine condition for the US, because that wish had practically come true already. Thus was there all the more reason to annex the island immediately.

Opponents of annexation argued that if independence should not be granted to Cuba because the people were unfit for self-government, then admitting Cuba to the union would give the people self-government anyway. Worse, it would give an inferior people a voice in the affairs of the US, the same concern that had been voiced upon the annexation of the southwestern United States. At that time, it was argued that the US constitution was not "for people of every color, and language, and habit"[102] and that Mexicans were a "sad compound of Spanish, English, Indian, and negro bloods ... resulting, it is said, in the production of a slothful, indolent, ignorant race of beings."[103] The fear, as Senator John Clayton put it, was that, "Aztecs, Creoles, Half-breeds, Quadroons, Samboes, and I know not what else – 'ring-streaked and speckled' – all will come in, and, instead of our governing them, they by their votes, will govern us."[104]

The same fears motivated the anti-annexationists with regard to Cuba. Senator Platt thought that "the project of annexation may, and ought to be, dismissed ... The people of Cuba, by reason of race and characteristic, cannot be easily assimilated by us ... Their presence in the American union, as a state, would be most disturbing." Besides, "with the Negro problem in our Southern States pressing upon us for solution," argued John W. Foster, "do we desire to aggravate the situation by adding a million more of the despised race to our voting population?"[105]

The agree-upon option turned out to involve holding to the letter of the Teller Amendment, avoiding the thorny issue of race, and still maintain control over the island. In this way, the "United States could use the island for its own purposes, but Cubans could have the headaches of day-to-day governing."[106] This policy was accomplished in the Platt Amendment, a rider to a defense appropriations bill to which the Cubans had to submit before the American occupation force would leave. Included in the Cuban Constitution, it stated that a) Cuba could not enter into any treaty without the consent of the US, b) the US could acquire a naval base, c) Cuba could not assume a national debt, and d) the US maintained the right of inter-vention.[107] As the provisions were included in the Cuban constitution, forcibly acquiesced to by the Cubans themselves, they ostensibly represented an agreement between two countries, not an imperial dictate by the US. Formal appearances were kept up, just as American officials wanted it. As Secretary of War Elihu Root put it, "it is better to have the favors of a lady with her consent, after judicious courtship, than to ravish her."[108]

The arrangement seemed ideal. Summarizing the virtues of the agreement when the question of annexation arose again in 1903, Henry Cabot Lodge pointed out that Cuba "has embodied in her constitution the clauses of the Platt Amendment ... She has done all that we asked her to do" while the United States had "all the control in a military and political point of view that we can possibly desire in regard to that great island." The US could have all it wanted in Cuba without the "distasteful aspects of having the Cubans incorporated into the Union."[109] The argument carried the day, allowing the Platt Amendment to remain the cornerstone of US policy toward Cuba until 1934.

In that period the US exercised its right of military intervention four times. But the US did much more than send troops. If the US could not formally take over Cuba, it did informally, as the island became intertwined with the US. When the Cuban republic began in 1902, its government and its army were North American creations. Soon the same could be said for its economy, which became inexorably tied to the US market. Americans began to invest in land in Cuba, then expanded into mining, banking, utilities and transportation. The economic and political muscle of the US was tremendous. It was often noted that the most powerful person in Cuba was not the president, but the US ambassador. In addition to this, American customs and habits and styles all permeated Cuban society. "That Cubans came in such close contact with US society guaranteed that vast numbers of them would think like North Americans, act like North Americans, look like North Americans, and generally derive their cultural, social and ethical orientations from North American sources."[110] All of this had been established by the 1920s, and the result was twofold. First, Cuba had in effect become a part of the US. Second, it was a subordinate part, a *de facto* colony, whereby American actions in Cuba were not subject to any democratic processes. Moreover, the relationship quickly crystallized in this unequal form. Marked by American military interventions, political dominance and economic might, the dynamic between the two countries reproduced and reinforced the image that Cubans were inferior to Americans.

Cuba in the early part of the century represented perhaps the most acute example of such interaction. Yet the same type of relationship existed between the US and other countries of the region, especially in Central America. From the time of the war with Spain until the Good Neighbor Policy, the United States intervened militarily in Latin America and the Caribbean a total of thirty-one times.[111] The assumption of superiority was not merely confined to American interaction with Cuba, but characterized the entire region.

Franklin Roosevelt's Good Neighbor Policy and his efforts during World War II to secure support from all of Latin America began to change the nature of inter-American relations. The first change was truly a break from the past. Roosevelt said that "singlehanded intervention by us in the internal affairs of other nations must end," and as far a military intervention was concerned, it did (for a time), even though the US did continue to wield a strong hand diplomatically and economically.[112] The second change was a shift in the language of the deficiencies of Latin Americans, from the hierarchy of race to the hierarchy of development, which did nothing to alter the view that the US remained superior to its Latin American neighbors.

Underdevelopment

While the subject of race was commonly addressed to explain US superiority in the nineteenth and early twentieth centuries, it was eventually eclipsed in the post-World War II era by the language of underdevelopment. At this time countries became categorized as underdeveloped by the application of economic criteria such as per capita income, size of GNP, levels of industrialization, size of the middle class, educational achievement and political maturity, which was reflected in the presence, or absence, of democratic processes. Development at this time was something that seemed both inevitable and necessary, and the lack of it required explanation. For the modernization theorists, underdeveloped countries lacked certain integral components that would remove the shackles holding them back. The problem was internally rooted, but it was also temporary. Walt Rostow's *The Stages of Economic Growth* was the most well-known of the modernization critiques, identifying the lack of financial investment required for "takeoff" as the primary cause of underdevelopment. Others identified the lack of a civic culture and other values associated with Western democracy, and the void of political institutionalization in newly independent countries.[113] For the most part, this school of thought reaffirmed what had been, and continues to be, some of the major underpinnings of American foreign policy toward developing nations.

Challenges to this interpretation, the dependency and world-systems theories that gained adherents in the 1970s, argued that underdevelopment was not internally rooted, but was part of an exploitative global process, the result of years of colonialism and the world capitalist system. In this analysis, the social, political and economic were all intimately related, and in poor countries all were at the mercy of the world's rich nations, whose development created the underdevelopment of others.[114] At the same time, these theorists did not question the desirable qualities of development or the need for it throughout the poorer parts of the globe. Just like those they critiqued, they too reflected in their writings a belief in and a bias against backwardness.

In this way the language of underdevelopment resembles the language of racial difference and hierarchy. Even though the two topics are seemingly unrelated, there is an important similarity in that each refers to the same topic: the "backwardness" of people who happen to be both poor and dark-skinned. In spite of the fact that racism and developmentalism treat separate themes, both have worked in a similar manner to construct a Latin America that has been seen as inferior to the US. The term underdeveloped is less pejorative than is backward, but by identifying Latin Americans in terms of lesser and greater, based not upon race but upon development, the term serves to uphold a regional hierarchy while it informs and justifies a hegemonic US policy based upon superiority.

The postwar era marked the turning point in American understandings of backwardness in Latin America. In the 1930s Senators and Representatives could still proclaim in congressional debate that in South America, "wherever the mongrel prevails, wherever the mixed breed prevails ... there is a decay of civilization," and that "to the South of us, especially in the Caribbean area, where mixtures of whites, Negroes and Indians are most common, the disastrous consequences on the national life of those peoples are only too clear." Even Franklin Roosevelt during World War II said of the Argentines that "you have to treat them like children."[115] After the war, however, the language underwent a modification, reflective and productive of a changed understanding of the nature of Latin America's problems. In the US government a sense of Latin American underdevelopment was steeped in theories of economic modernization, which held that progress could be achieved in lesser developed areas with US help. Modernization could proceed in traditional societies through the diffusion of modern (American) values and institutions. Foreign aid and investment, trade, technical aid, development loans and educational exchange were all facilitators of progress, which would result in economic, as well as political and social advancement.

In Cuba this outlook had practical results (as opposed to much of the rest of Latin America) due to the close ties that bound the two countries together. While there was little direct aid provided to Cuba by the US (American largesse in the region as a whole largely followed the ascent of Castro), American capital increasingly dominated the economy, holding most of the telephone companies, electrical utilities, railways and oil refineries. Americans owned almost half of the sugar industry, the largest sector of the Cuban economy, and provided most of the professional experts to service the sugar sector. So too was the tourism industry dominated by Americans, both as owners and as tourists. On top of this, American subsidiaries had interests in every industry from retail to autos to manufacturing. All the while the resident community of Americans in Cuba grew, especially in the 1950s.[116]

This was welcomed by President Batista, whose developmentalist program for the country was well-served by the presence of American capital. As the US and Batista embraced each other, the view that modernization could happen and was happening in Cuba took hold. A Commerce Department report in 1956 stated that "the worker in Cuba is ... ambitious enough to respond to incentive, he has wider horizons than most Latin American workers and expects more out of life in material amenities than many European workers ... His goal is to reach a standard of living comparable with that of the American worker."[117] In these short statements was reflected an official view that continued to dominate American foreign policy toward Cuba even after the topics of annexation and intervention had lost their salience: the inferiority of Cubans as compared to Americans. Such inferiority was not merely about material wealth as measured at the moment, but about the ability of Cubans, through hard work, to achieve their desires, incentives and ambitions, things which supposedly defined an essential nature of Cuban people in general. Granted, they were equipped with a desire to be like

Americans, and had "wider horizons than most Latin American workers," but while the aim was elevation rather than denigration (recall the statement that Cubans were no more fit for self-government than gunpowder was for hell), the tactic (to use the inferiority of Cubans as a referent) and the result (the continued assumption of US superiority) were the same as when the argument was about self-government. Perhaps even more telling, Cuba was seen as the pinnacle of Latin American development.

If Cuba served as the example that American economic involvement was beneficial to underdeveloped countries, this view took on real urgency after Vice-President Nixon visited South America in 1958 and was greeted in several countries by stone-throwing, insult-hurling, angry crowds. At first the assessment was that "the demonstrations ... were Communist inspired and staged." President Eisenhower expressed the view that while there were economic causes to explain Nixon's reception, more important was that "there is a habit, as we know, of the Communists to try to exploit and take leadership in any unrest."[118] Thus were the people contrasted with the communists as two groups who had interests that were opposed. Further analysis, however, expressed another opinion. In a report to the president, Milton S. Eisenhower, who had been sent by his brother to the region to make a report and recommendations, advocated a new set of policies focusing on economic relations. Arguing for commodity price arrangements and a regional development bank to counter the growing sentiment that Americans enjoyed a high standard of living at the expense of Latin Americans, he said that the people "know that low standards of living are neither universal nor inevitable, and they are therefore impatiently insistent that remedial actions be taken."[119] It was the US which had to provide the necessary assistance.

After the rise of Castro made clear that discontent in the region could have consequences greater than angry crowds and demonstrations, President Kennedy embarked upon the greatest postwar development project in Latin America, the Alliance for Progress. A dual effort to develop the region quickly with a massive influx of US aid, it was also intended to create the conditions necessary to prevent the arrival of more Castros. Announcing the program, Kennedy characterized the region as one where "millions of men and women suffer the daily degradations of hunger and poverty. They lack decent shelter or protection from disease. Their children are deprived of education."[120] This represents one of the most overt expression of Latin Americans as backward without actually using the word. There was, of course, no hesitancy in Kennedy's speech to stress the suffering in people's lives, as the aim was to rally his listeners in a campaign against it. Yet in arousing noble sentiments in a noble cause, there was an effect that was similar to what the language of race did in an earlier era.

Imagine Kennedy's statement being made one hundred years before. There is not much in the structure of his argument that deviates from how people had denigrated black people, Indians and mestizos at the time. One needs only to make a simple change or two in order to make his comments resemble an earlier attitude now deemed illegitimate. First, a sentence at the end could be added, such as "I advance it therefore, as a suspicion only, that Latin Americans are inferior to the whites in the endowment of both of body and mind." This would have the effect of making poverty and degradation the consequence of a more fundamental problem, and would not differ greatly from statements made about Cubans and Mexicans in the last century. Another modification of Kennedy's words could be the replacement of language that describes what Latin Americans lack. Substitute mental faculties for education, or ignorance for hunger and poverty, and one is left with a statement that would not be out of place in an earlier era. Of course, any speech can be given a complete makeover with enough changes. But the changes required to get from what is considered to be a legitimate critique to an illegitimate one are not so extraordinary. The structure of the argumentation of Kennedy is strikingly similar to that of Jefferson, Teddy Roosevelt, Senator Platt and a host of others who openly expressed their belief in American superiority and Latin American inferiority. The same prejudice that was explicitly voiced in the nineteenth century is also betrayed in the twentieth century, only more subtly. It is obscured by the fact that the stated intention of American policy is worthy and honorable – to eradicate poverty, prevent suffering and help the poor.

The recognition of this prejudice has not lessened its effect, only its conspicuousness. Almost a decade after Kennedy and his promise of the Alliance had faded, Nelson Rockefeller stated, in the *Report on the Americas* he submitted to Nixon, that "our neighbors need to be reassured ... that we want to continue to work with them, regardless of the form of their government, to help them raise the level of their lives."[121] Yet Rockefeller was wise to the fact that,

> Other nations have deeply resented the way in which the United States has carried out its assistance programs. As part of the aid effort the United States has intervened, usually with the best of intentions, in almost every aspect of their economic policies and programs. It has too often tried to do things *for* them, because it felt it could do them better. This subconscious paternalism was less effective not only because it was resented, but also because it did not give the other nations an incentive to assume responsibility and initiative themselves.[122]

Even though it can be argued that the US learned from this critique and began to turn toward trade as opposed to aid in its development programs, the shift still did not completely eradicate the superiority/inferiority implied in US foreign policy. The first President Bush introduced the "Enterprise for the Americas" during his tenure, a proposal to increase trade and foreign investment in Latin America. He made a point of praising several governments in the region as the "bold pioneers of a new path to development," and called the proposal an effort to "create incentives to reinforce Latin America's growing recognition that free-market reform is the key to sustained growth and political stability."[123] Yet he could have been talking about NAFTA, the Caribbean Basin Initiative or the proposed Free Trade for the Americas Treaty. All of the development initiatives that have been tried over the years, whether or not one agrees with them, share a common feature: the conviction that Latin America lags behind the United States in material wealth. While this may not be a startling proposition, it betrays an official mindset in which American policy is guided by the fact that the US is in some way better than Latin America, and that it has a responsibility to offer leadership and guidance and assistance to its neighbors. The motivations may be admirable and noble, and the policies might even be helpful to their intended beneficiaries, but at the same time the impetus to promote development perpetuates a hierarchy, in which the US and Latin America cannot be equals, except perhaps at some point in the distant and unidentifiable future. President Kennedy's description of life in Latin America paints a clear enough picture of poverty as opposed to a country strong and powerful enough to "bear any burden, pay and cost, fight any foe." President Bush reveals the same bias. Though his initiative was a trade proposal and not an aid package, the assumption of an unequal relationship is obvious. "Bold pioneers on a new path to development" are people who have not achieved development, only those who have tried other paths and failed. Furthermore, a growing recognition in the power of free markets to promote political stability indicates that political stability is not something that characterizes the region.

The point is not to be critical of the aims and motivations of policies that promote development. After all, there is hardly an objection raised to a desire to eradicate poverty. Rather than critiquing the wisdom or efficacy of initiatives such as the Alliance for Progress, or gauging the degree of accuracy involved in characterizing the people of Latin America as poor or deprived, this reading of the US-Cuba relationship seeks only to consider the consequences of a particular mode of representation: one in which Latin America, as a distinct entity separate from the United States, is written and spoken of as underdeveloped and inferior.

In a subtler fashion than the language of racial differences, but in a similar manner nonetheless, the language of development works to preserve hierarchy and hegemony so that American superiority is assumed, unquestioned and reflexive. The repetition of such an understanding of Latin American identity thus involves what Edward Said termed a tradition of continuity, embodying a continual accumulation of material from which to construct an identity, a tradition in which succeeding generations are linked by a common language, a set of practices, and a set of received ideas which outlive any single era.[124] Such an accumulation has led to a certain stability of interpretations that fuel an understanding of American superiority over its neighbors.

3 Latin Americans as fellow travellers

Faith in freedom is the enduring essence of our hemispheric cooperation.

John F. Kennedy[1]

We are in a very true sense the guardian and big brother of these little republics.

Franklin D. Roosevelt[2]

The relegation of Latin America to an inferior status is not only effected by means of highlighting difference. It also has derived from a discourse which emphasizes shared identity. Cubans and their Latin American brethren have often been represented in the US as poor, weak and stupid "mongrels," children or even apes, yet they also have at times enjoyed a very different status: as members of an American family of nations, as fellow democrats, as brothers and sisters, as fellow 'Americans'. In spite of their seemingly favorable qualities, in these representations, like those which highlight difference, US hegemony is reinforced, providing for what Eldon Kenworthy calls a dynamic of "control-through-sameness," the exercise of power by the selective elimination of difference in order to enforce conformity and silence dissent.[3] Neither set of representational practices negates the other. Rather, as William Connolly argues in discussing the Spanish conquest of America, "these two modalities can support complementary strategies of domination, one supporting conquest of the other in the name of the universal superiority of the conqueror's own identity and the other neutralizing resistance to colonization by understanding the customs of the other well enough to launch a campaign of conversion."[4]

In this chapter, the focus is on an understanding of "control-through-sameness" as a complement to strategies of negating difference as they regard the sustenance of American superiority over Latin America. I draw upon the work of Kenworthy to discuss how the deployment of a discourse of shared identity, like that geared toward difference, also has provided a positional superiority in which the US has never lost the relative upper hand over Latin America.

It is important to note that the argument here is not one in which the aim is to demonstrate that all statements and representations regarding Cuba and Latin America reinforce US superiority in the Western Hemisphere. After all, it could be argued, if statements concerned with both sameness and difference serve a hierarchical relationship, then there is nothing that Americans can say about Latin America that does not justify and perpetuate control, dominance and hegemony by the US. However, the point to be made here is not that there is no way out of this dilemma for the US and Latin America alike, only that there are a variety of possibilities and strategies for representing superiority and inferiority, and that they can and do involve understandings of both differences and similarities regarding the peoples and countries of the hemisphere.

The assumptions and representations that comprise the project of control-through-sameness have their antecedents in the early days of the republic and have been continually reproduced up to and including the present. In these understandings, markers other than race and development are used to posit similarity and difference. These markers are grounded in an alternative understanding of what makes America different. Rather than locating a common identity in a heritage that predates independence, and which hearkens back to Europe and its peoples, the idea that there is a distinct American family of nations is grounded only in the Western Hemisphere, and does not usually predate the movements for independence in the region. According to this reading of political identity, the world is ordered in a very different way. The line between where 'we' and 'they' lie falls primarily in a place not where distinctions based on race, culture and nationality are highlighted, but rather upon geographical proximity and a sense of regional cohesion that Europeans and others cannot rupture. In this understanding, with a division made between hemispheric politics and other politics, Europeans, who had earlier been closer soulmates to Americans than were fellow residents of the Western Hemisphere, become the excluded outsider.

Imagining a Cuba and a Latin America that are seen in terms of similarity and a common identity with the US and its citizenry has involved the deployment of what has been called the Idea of the Western Hemisphere, the sentiment that this half of the globe is, can be, and should be seen as a distinct entity in the world. Kenworthy has called this idea as the America/Américas myth, which is based upon "old images and ideas that comprise a myth of US-hemispheric relations that has acquired paradigmatic status."[5] I will simply refer to the idea of unity, be it assumed or explicit, enforced or voluntary, which has served to characterize US-Latin American relations at various times in their history. In all of these cases the emphasis is on the notion that the Western Hemisphere is more than a geographical term identifying a stretch of territory. It is also to be regarded as a concept, a belief and/or a goal. Comprised of a language that centers around geography, idealism and family, this concept posits an assumption of 'American' unity that is continually referred to by American political leaders. Where 'Americans' are members of the same family, sharing a common home, revering the same ideals of democracy, freedom, liberty, anti-colonialism – those things that led to the establishment of independence among almost all the nations of the Western Hemisphere – the language used serves to render a single 'America' out of the entire region. The concept presupposes that all 'Americans' share this heritage, a common understanding that the founding of all our countries was based on ideas and ideals, not on monarchical claims to territory through hereditary wars or intermarriages. Thus 'Americans' are different from Europeans and other non-'Americans'. Born out of lofty ideals, nurtured in a pure environment known as the New World, 'Americans' were to be essentially different – democratic, free, and peaceful. Much in the same way that the idea of American exceptionalism has been a powerful force in US history, this exceptional quality of people and place has often been expanded to include the entire Western Hemisphere, a special area that is home to democratic ideals and the family of distinctly non-European peoples who espouse them.

Addressing first how the idea of unity is grounded in geography, I will discuss the Monroe Doctrine as the premier example of an understanding which posits the Americas as a singular place for all 'Americans', while it simultaneously reserves space for US hegemony and superiority over its neighbors. Next I will turn to a discussion of the ideals of democracy and liberty, as they have been defined and used by the US government, looking at how they have been constructed as 'American' values and how they serve as both a goal and a premise. Finally, I will consider how the metaphors of family and home are employed in American political language to describe the Western Hemisphere, and their service in promoting the cause of unity through shared identification. In discussing all of these examples, I highlight how they contribute to an understanding of American superiority over Latin America, and to the practices of US dominance and hegemony.

The Monroe Doctrine

The language of unity and the various metaphors spawned by it have their sources in the early years of the republic. They have been expanded upon and given new dimensions over the years, but the original formulations were derived early by the nation's founders. Though this sense of unity has been strongly represented in the Monroe Doctrine, Thomas Jefferson was one of the first to encourage the Idea of the Western Hemisphere. Arthur Whitaker argues that by the time it appeared in the Monroe Doctrine, it had already been fully developed by Jefferson. All the important elements are included in his letters to Presidents Madison, Monroe, and others.[6]

Even before the republics of Spanish and Portuguese America had won their independence and the Holy Alliance of the non-democratic powers of Europe had coalesced – two of the primary reasons behind Monroe's postulating that the Western Hemisphere was exceptional and in need of permanent separation from Europe – Jefferson began to formulate the idea of an 'American' system. Responding to Mexican and Cuban revolutionaries in 1808, he stated that "we consider their interests and ours to be the same, and the object of both must be to exclude all European influence from this hemisphere."[7] Ever distrustful and fearful of said influence, he observed that "the European nations constitute a separate division of the globe; their localities make them part of a distinct system; they have a set of interests of their own in which it is our business never to engage ourselves." Conversely, the Americas had "a different system of interests flowing from different climates, different soils, different productions, different modes of existence." Because "America has a hemisphere to itself," it must also "have a separate system of interest which must not be subordinated to those of Europe."[8]

President James Monroe, whose name is forever attached to this sentiment in the Monroe Doctrine, produced the statement that gave full force to this now long-established understanding. The British had originally proposed issuing a joint statement opposing the further acquisition of territories in the Americas, something that served both countries. However, Monroe rejected that appeal at the urging of his Secretary of State, John Quincy Adams, choosing instead to issue a statement unilaterally. While British cooperation in keeping the hemisphere Europe-free at that time was an attractive idea, (considering that the US could not enforce such a wish) it was also something of an oxymoron. If there was to be a unique, common, 'American' home, it would have to be made, articulated and defended (at least rhetorically) by 'Americans,' or in the more practical sense of what came to pass, by the United States. In so doing, Monroe could respond not only to a threatening Russia, which had interests in colonizing the Oregon territory, and Spain, which was refusing to recognize the newly-independent Latin American countries, but also Britain, which made claims on the US-coveted Oregon territory and maintained considerable influence in the Caribbean. Thus Monroe stated that,

> the American continents, by the free and independent condition which they have assumed and maintain, are henceforth not to be considered as subjects for future colonization by any European powers ... we should consider any attempt on [Europe's] part to extend their system to any portion of this hemisphere as dangerous to our peace and safety ... with the Governments who have declared their independence and maintained it, we could not view any interposition for the purpose of oppressing them, or controlling in any other manner their destiny, by any European power in any other light than as the manifestation of an unfriendly disposition toward the United States.[9]

Announcing this policy in 1823 to deal with his cabinet's fears about Russian, Spanish and British aims with regard to land that the US hoped to eventually acquire, Monroe elucidated a set of principles that not only specified a warning to Europeans to stay out of the Western Hemisphere, but that also placed the United States at the peak of a regional hierarchy. In this sense, there are, as Eldon Kenworthy notes, two Monroe Doctrines: the one that informed American foreign policy until the US officially repudiated it by the time of Franklin Roosevelt, and the one that appears as a myth in US domestic political discourse.[10] The first was enshrined by continual interventions, such as those initiated by McKinley, Teddy Roosevelt, whose corollary to the Monroe Doctrine provided the most well known rationale for the enactment of an interventionist foreign policy, and Woodrow Wilson. The second Monroe Doctrine, however, has long since been invoked as a means of lending authority to a variety of political positions, in spite of its official rejection and the claim that it has been eclipsed by the end of the Cold War. "Just as most citizens believe in a Constitution they cannot accurately describe, so the Monroe Doctrine conveys a vague, proprietary feeling of this being 'our' hemisphere without the speaker taking responsibility for the diplomatic consequences."[11] The claim has been that the United States has legitimate concerns in Latin America, and that it may act on them as it sees fit with a greater degree of autonomy than it may act elsewhere in the world. President Monroe, proclaiming the Americas for 'Americans', inspired what has become a foundational myth of American foreign policy. Its two greatest effects have been "the establishment of the concept of the Western Hemisphere Idea, and the creation of a paternalistic attitude in the United States toward the countries to the south; after all Washington had been the guarantor of Latin American independence."[12] Monroe made it clear that even though the US maintained elements of similarity to its neighbors (almost all had successful revolutions against European powers in the name of democracy and self-determination, and sought to protect them by preventing the reestablishment of European hegemony), it also intended to be superior to them.

Monroe's address contained within it one of the earliest official characterizations of how the US conceptualized its relationship with the newly independent Latin American states. Describing the outlines of a particular international structure, Monroe revealed how his administration defined America's relationships with the rest of the world. In the first instance he located the Americas in relation to Europe: the Western Hemisphere, the common home to a large number of newly-independent states, were now to be regarded as a special non-European zone, for 'Americans' only. At the same time, however, he postulated a particular order within 'America' itself, such that his words simultaneously invoked both the equality and the inequality of Latin America in relation to the US. His statements expressed the extent to which the US was in a superior position in the hemisphere. European interference was a problem only because it would antagonize and threaten the United States. In this respect, Latin America is considered unimportant in and of itself. It is only noted secondarily, to the extent it is noticed at all. Of course, it is entirely understandable that the young government in Washington would place more emphasis on its own safety in expressing concern about the reintroduction of European power into the hemisphere. This outlook is certainly accepted as legitimate for a government. Nonetheless, debates about legitimacy aside, Monroe's address is noteworthy in that it explicitly communicated how the US viewed the newly-independent Latin American states. They were places where US security could be threatened, and thus their defense, safety and well-being were considered to be the business and responsibility of the United States. By identifying Latin American independence with US security, and by appointing the US guarantor of that independence, Monroe asserted an American superiority that could justify aggressive and interventionist foreign policies.

The irony of the Monroe Doctrine is that it was formulated out of a sense that the Americas should be different from Europe. Yet in the rejection of a European system that involved a politics of spheres of influence, Monroe gave sanction to an interpretation of hemispheric politics that postulated, staked out and justified a US sphere of influence, where it could act, or potentially act, with relative autonomy, and thereby hold ascendancy in the region. Imperialism was not just for Europeans anymore.

The themes embodied in the Monroe Doctrine, the interest in preventing European encroachment in the Americas while ensuring US power and influence, have been consistently invoked since the founders expressed them, through the years when the physical presence of European armies and navies was real, and even after the United States became the premier military power in the region. Theodore Roosevelt, in his well-known corollary to the Monroe Doctrine, asserted an American right of intervention as the "international police power" of the region, but even that could be seen as an effort to eliminate any possible European influence. One concern at the time was that governments in the Caribbean that could not pay their debts might provoke European governments to impose controls upon them. Preempting such a possibility in the wake of the Dominican Republic's insolvency became part of the rationale that led to Roosevelt's proclamation of the right to intervene, which was soon followed by the US taking over collection of the country's customs revenues and eventual military occupation.

Not even superpower status diminished this concern, as during the Cold War, when the enemy's presence was not merely physical but ideological. For example, when the Eisenhower Administration undertook action to overthrow the government of Guatemala in 1954, the policy was a reproduction of the Monroe Doctrine, warning against non-American, i.e., Soviet threats in the hemisphere. Soviet influence in the region, which was seen in and of itself as a threat, might not result from an invasion, nor possibly even from a Soviet presence, but simply the infiltration of alien and hostile ideas. It could be invisible. Still, the source was obvious: by definition, communism in Latin America could not be indigenous, only the result of Soviet influence and conspiracy. The result was that at the inter-American conference of the OAS in 1954, Secretary of State Dulles engineered the passage of the

Declaration of Caracas, a resolution that conformed to the Monroe Doctrine in spirit, if not in letter. It stated that "the domination of the political institutions of any American State by the international communist movement, extending to this Hemisphere the political system of an extracontinental power, would constitute a threat to the sovereignty and political independence of the American States," adding that such a development would justify "appropriate action in accordance with existing treaties."[13]

Though this was clearly an attempt to justify intervention in Guatemala, Dulles insisted that the declaration was "designed to protect and not to impair the inalienable right of each American State freely to choose its own form of government and economic system and to live its own social and cultural life."[14] Intervention was what the Soviets had done through their infiltration. Any action taken by the US against the government of Guatemala, which was seen as communist infiltrated, would be, by such reasoning, a restorative action, designed only to return the country to its previously untainted state, back into the American family of nations. Thus could Dulles defend intervention as the means for preserving self-determination, espouse collective security to defend unilateral action, and project US superiority through instruments based upon juridical equality (the Rio Treaty and the OAS).

After the success in overthrowing the Guatemalan government, the same logic was used repeatedly to justify action against many states such as the Dominican Republic, Nicaragua, Grenada, and of course, Cuba. In Cuba the Monroe Doctrine was especially important during the Cold War in making the American case against Castro's legitimacy, as he was someone who had "betrayed the Cuban revolution," and turned the country into "an instrument of the foreign policies of ... extracontinental powers."[15] According to this construction of the Cuban problem, Cuba was not free and independent; it was a Soviet puppet, a "bridgehead of Soviet imperialism in the Western Hemisphere and a base for Communist aggression, intervention, agitation and subversion against the American Republics." Nor did Cuba experience a real revolution. Rather Castro and the Soviets had "subverted the wholesome Cuban social revolution to communism." There could be no greater violation of the Monroe Doctrine than the Cuban revolution. It was, according to Secretary of State Rusk "incompatible ... with the inter-American system," as it had turned an entire country over to a European power. Thus there could be no greater task with regard to Cuba than to bring it back into the "family of the hemisphere" by eliminating all outside influences.[16]

The continual reiteration this mythic Monroe Doctrine simultaneously strengthens and naturalizes it. The substantial power its invocation wields renders it as foundational to US foreign policy as is the Constitution to domestic policy.[17] This is why it has been such an attractive option for officials to use, both explicitly and implicitly, to generate support for specific conduct, such as intervention in Guatemala or isolation of Cuba. Ronald

Reagan did exactly this in the 1980s trying to make the case for funding the *contras* in Nicaragua. He stated that "our commitment to a Western Hemisphere safe from aggression did not occur by spontaneous generation on the day that we took office. It began with the Monroe Doctrine."[18] Similarly, the power of the Doctrine's hold on the American imagination is revealed in its invocation to dismiss certain policy alternatives. Then CIA Deputy Director Robert Gates, in advocating an assertive policy in Central America to remove what was seen as Soviet influence and power, made plain what opposition to that policy meant when he stated that, "if we have decided to totally abandon the Monroe Doctrine, then we ought to ... acknowledge our helplessness and stop wasting everybody's time."[19] In deploying this rhetoric, Gates framed the debate in terms that would be virtually unchallengable by others. To concede such ground to Gates (which the talk of "abandoning the Monroe Doctrine," apparently believed to be a rather heretical thought, was meant to do) would reduce the discussion to whether or not Cuban and Soviet ties to Nicaragua represented a threat to the US or Central America. On this terrain it is much easier to win an argument, as it concerns the wisdom of being cautious, vigilant and skeptical, while countering a potential problem that is only very small, versus the potential danger in ignoring a problem whose results cannot be foreseen and which could someday grow unmanageable. These options, of course, support the more actively interventionist policy in which the United States, as guarantor of the security, freedom and democracy of others in the region, is both permitted and obliged to act in their defense.

'American' ideals

In addition to the concerns of the Monroe Doctrine, which address the hemisphere-wide interest in keeping European (or other outside) influence out of the Americas, and protecting the region as a US sphere of influence, there is also a proactive element to the hemispheric idea. Introduced by Jefferson, this involved an understanding that the Americas were not merely to be a zone of exclusion, but one that would foster genuinely 'American' characteristics, among them democracy, liberty, freedom, anti-colonialism, independence and peaceful cooperation.[20] These would serve as both a goal and a foundation for all the Americas.

At the conclusion of the war of 1812, Jefferson wrote to President Madison that "we cannot too distinctly detach ourselves from the European system, which is essentially belligerent, nor too sedulously cultivate an American system, essentially pacific."[21] And only a few months before the Monroe Doctrine was enunciated, he wrote to Monroe that, "while [Europe] is laboring to become the domicile of despotism, our endeavor should surely be, to make our hemisphere that of freedom."[22] Steeped in a tradition that had characterized America as a "shining City on a Hill," where colonists had come in the name of freedom, Jefferson reproduced this understanding so that it not only applied to the new American Republic but to all the hemisphere itself.

The common interests that Jefferson identified were elaborated upon by Henry Clay, who expressed them as elements of a common political identity grounded in a set of shared ideals. Arguing in the House of Representatives for the US to recognize the newly-independent governments of South America still engaged in revolution against Spanish rule, he claimed that

> We behold there a spectacle ... interesting and sublime – the glorious spectacle of eighteen millions of people, struggling to burst their chains and to be free ... There can not be a doubt that Spanish America, once independent, whatever may be the form of the governments established in its several parts, these governments will be animated by an American feeling, and guided by an American policy. They will obey the laws of the system of the New World, of which they will be a part ... We are their great example. Of us they constantly speak as brothers, having a similar origin. They adopt our principles, copy our institutions, and in many instances, employ the very language and sentiments of our revolutionary papers.[23]

By such a reading, the inhabitants of the Western Hemisphere are a united community, and an enduring one. In 1962, when the OAS passed a resolution recognizing a "Communist Offensive in America," the body used language that could have been formulated by Jefferson or Clay. It pointed out that regional values include "the faith of the American peoples in human rights, liberty and national independence as a fundamental reason for their existence, as conceived by the founding fathers who destroyed colonialism and brought the American republics into being." They further comprise "the right of peoples to organize their way of life in the political, economic and cultural spheres, expressing their will through free elections, without foreign interference."[24] From the earliest days of independence through the present era, there has been a well-articulated conception that this part of the world is home to a politics that is fundamentally 'American', essentially different from Europe and other regions. Relying on a sense of global space, in which isolation was a virtue, and including the ideals of freedom, liberty, independence, democracy and peaceful cooperation, the language suggests a distinct 'American' identity that was to be juxtaposed with the difference of outsiders.

This articulation of sameness, however, did not preclude US superiority. In fact, it did just the opposite, allowing for the adoption of strategies that foster greater control by means of co-optation. By representing all 'Americans' as a single people and their history as a unified narrative, the idea of unity can be readily deployed in an effort to produce, define or defend American interests in the Western Hemisphere, whereby the referent is the same for both nation and hemisphere. Moreover, it is with great ease that this referent can be shifted from the United States to the entire hemisphere. It was prevalent in the words of Jefferson and Clay, and it remains in use. Witness Vice President Dan Quayle's statement that "the Americas, North and South, are destined to shape the future together ... [a] new era is here, bringing with it an irreversible attitude of 'we Americans,' North and South, 'we Americans,' building on our common values."[25]

The collective identity inherent in this type of imagining has provided the United States with occasion to continually speak of its foreign policy as something being done in the name of democracy. For example, in the year preceding America's declaration of war against Spain, the Cubans rebelling against the Spanish were portrayed as reminiscent of America's founding fathers. In Congress, the sentiment that "they are just like us" was reflected in statements comparing the American Revolution to the Cuban fight for independence. It was claimed that "the Cuban patriots are fighting for the same rights and independence and home government that our ancestors fought for and won," and that, "the fight for Cuban independence is similar to our own."[26] These views were muted first in the executive branch by President McKinley, then by those who later occupied Cuba. Yet once annexation was rejected, the idea of the democratic Cuban was resurrected. As the stated American aims in Cuba moved from liberation and pacification to ensuring "stability," even the much maligned Cuban could be involved in the democratic project. Teddy Roosevelt pointed out, after Cuban independence, that "the path to be trodden by those who exercise self-government is always hard, and we should have every charity and patience with the Cubans as they tread this difficult path."[27] Thus, proponents of democracy may be unpracticed, but this does not preclude their designation as democrats.

When Washington's relationship with the government of Cuba began to deteriorate in the first years of Castro's rule, it became increasingly attractive for American officials to speak well of the Cuban people. After 1959, American leaders such as Adlai Stevenson, US delegate to the United Nations, began to invoke the name of the Cuban people as an entity who "desire to seek independence and freedom" and "to bring democratic processes to Cuba."[28] This has been a consistent effort. John F. Kennedy spoke of a people who "look forward to the time when they will be truly free," while President George W. Bush stated that "the Cuban people continue to act with dignity and honor and courage. In Cuba, advocates of liberty ... honor political prisoners who have sacrificed for the cause of freedom."[29] If it was Castro and his comrades who "betrayed the revolution," then it could easily be said by Secretary of State Dean Rusk and his successors that the US had "no quarrel with the Cuban people – only with the regime which has fastened itself upon that country."[30] The Cuban people are represented like all other 'Americans', people who claim democracy and freedom as both their right and their desire. At the same time, the United States is represented as a country that professes to have always upheld these ideals. These views lend themselves to a presumption of unity in the Americas, whose people are inherently "tied to a project that must not be denied inasmuch as it is driven by forces nobler and more powerful than mere mortals."[31]

This conflation of identities among all "Americans" accomplishes two things. First of all, it serves a strategy of co-optation. Rather than seeking control through the language of difference, the invocation of shared identity projects a "universalism subjugat[ing] the particularity of the other to its own particular code with universalist pretensions."[32] This prejudice of equality identifies those attributes deemed to be worthy of attainment, and not only allows the relevant parties to climb aboard the bandwagon, but requires it in order for them to maintain legitimacy in US representations. Those who do not subscribe to an American ideal of democracy are cast outside the family of democratic nations, while those who do are welcomed by the US into the legitimate community of democratic nations. The idea of welcoming other countries into a place where the US has long been also serves the assumption of superiority by invoking a reminder that the United States arrived at the democratic ideal first, and has always known that this was the goal to be aspired to and attained. President George H.W. Bush said in 1990 that "we in the United States welcome our Central and South American neighbors into the ranks of democracy."[33] Just as the wording of the Monroe Doctrine revealed a paternalistic attitude toward those who would join the US in practicing democracy or any other mission, so too do references to how the US is pleased by recent developments in Latin America and how it welcomes them.

The second accomplishment of the conflation of identities is that it takes the idea of hemispheric unity and changes it from a goal into a premise for further cooperation. Most often, but not exclusively, this has been in the field of trade. In the same year that Bush welcomed the new democracies, he also offered a proposal of free trade for the entire hemisphere in the "Enterprise for the Americas Initiative." As a start on this offer, he negotiated the North American Free Trade Agreement with Canada and Mexico, saying that "NAFTA represents the first giant step toward fulfillment of a dream that has long inspired us all – the dream of a hemisphere united by economic cooperation."[34] His was by no means a new idea. Long before him in the 1880s, Secretary of State James Blaine sought to realize his vision of Pan-American unity through trade and finance. In a manner similar to the logic of the 1990s, whereby unity deriving from geography and democracy served as a premise for action, Blaine and his fellow Pan-Americanists based cooperation upon similar foundations. One congressman spoke in favor of calling a conference to promote trade, stating that "all the countries with which we seek to cultivate amicable and commercial relations, with the exception of one, are republics, and because of the similarity in forms of government, there is a bond of sympathy between them and us."[35]

When common ideals are portrayed as a premise to action, rather than a goal, one consequence is that the politics of determining and agreeing upon a common ground are not only silenced, they are precluded from ever occurring. This serves to strengthen the common identity, for "a politics of the common good is essential both to sustain a set of identities worthy of admiration and to enable the public to act self-consciously in support of justice and the public interest as they emerge in the common life."[36] The idea of the common good, which suggests an attractiveness based upon both universality and moral worth, further secures the hegemony of the collective identity through the delegitimation, denaturalization and marginalization of that which stands in opposition to it.

The American family

While the entailments of unity have included a grounding in geography and the fostering of particular ideals, they are also inclusive of another element, for not only is the Western Hemisphere portrayed as a special zone, for "Americans" only, where democracy, freedom and liberty shall flourish and be cherished, it is also home to "the American family." The metaphor of family adds further impetus to the idea of hemispheric unity as it emphasizes sameness, and with it similar perspective and collective action. Yet, like other elements of identity – geography and idealism – it has simultaneously undermined the shared identity it alleges by introducing and reinforcing an understanding of US superiority.

There is a long tradition in American foreign policy of peppering the rhetoric with metaphors of family. Especially prevalent since the end of World War II, references of this sort are to be found in numerous official speeches and documents. While references to family do less to undermine an implied equality than do metaphors of brothers and sisters (which is discussed later), they work to enforce an understanding where joint behavior is sought, deemed favorable, and rewarded by their connection to hemispheric idealism. President Kennedy provides an example of this in the quote at the beginning of the chapter. He stated that "faith in freedom is the enduring essence of our hemispheric cooperation," and that "our moral unity as a family of nations rests on the ultimate faith that only governments which guarantee human freedoms, respect human rights, and vindicate human liberties can advance human progress."[37]

This theme, the connection between a member of the family and shared ideals, equates filial ties with democracy, freedom, human rights, liberty and progress. In this formulation, the bonds of family are both cause and consequence of embracing these "American" ideals. Because all countries in the region are members of the same family, they all, by definition, subscribe to a set of values that are inherent to the hemisphere. At the same time, it is also the case that because a country embraces these values, it is family. Cuba serves as an example of this. President George H.W. Bush expressed the hope that, "someday soon [Cuba] will join the family of democratic nations."[38] This can only occur, according to US policy, when the people of Cuba are victorious in their struggle for democracy. The Cuban people are represented such that their membership in the family is assumed. They are true democrats and are eventually to be welcomed back. However, as their government is non-democratic, the country as a whole must be, albeit temporarily, understood as existing outside of the family.

The language of family also promotes and justifies a sense of responsibility over others. Even without the presumption of the US as the head of that family, the idea encourages that each member has an obligation to look out for all other members. President Eisenhower warned of the importance that "every member of the American family of nations should feel responsible for promoting the welfare of all."[39] By this logic the Declaration of Caracas, the isolation of Cuba, the funding of the *contras*, invasion of The Dominican Republic, and a host of other actions are entirely justified as they come to be seen a part of a hemispheric code of action, whose origins lie in family relations.

Concurrent with using the metaphor of the American family, there also has been an inclination to refer to the peoples and states of Latin America as brothers or sisters. Recalling the earlier quote by Henry Clay, what he saw when he looked south were 'Americans,' very much like Americans, whom he referred to as brothers. James Monroe too spoke of "our southern brethren" and echoed Clay in admiring their adherence to an 'American' system of politics.[40] Franklin Roosevelt used the metaphor of "guardian and big brother" to describe the United States' relationship to Latin America, while John F. Kennedy said that "all who fight for freedom – especially in this hemisphere – are our brothers."[41] More recently, a State Department publication released in 1994, extolling the virtues of 34 out of 35 countries in hemisphere which enjoy "political freedom ... respect for human rights ... and open economies," (Cuba was the outlier) called those 34 countries "sister republics."[42]

Perhaps a closer approximation to the role the US at one time envisioned and sought to play in the hemisphere has been that of a father, although using such language would be considered too offensive, especially to those who would be characterized (explicitly or not) as children.[43] In a similar vein, after George Orwell published *1984*, it would be difficult, if not impossible, for an American official to use the phrase big brother and guardian as Franklin Roosevelt did. For Orwell made clear what the stakes were in a relationship defined by guardians and big brothers. The role implies surveillance, the reporting of bad behavior and teaching by example, and it easily merges with the role of the father, where discipline, punishment, control, and teaching are central. The role of an alleged equal quickly and smoothly slips into a role defined by inequality. The language of (big) brotherhood is not quite the same as speaking of fathers and children, but a similar paternalistic spirit can be invoked.

The language of "sister republics" serves a similar dynamic, but there is an added element. If little brothers need to be taught responsibility, sisters are sometimes in need of protection. With regard to Cuba, especially in the nineteenth century, there was a tendency to feminize the country. In the 1850s Cuba was referred to as "Queen of the Antilles ... breathing her spicy, tropic breath, and pouting her rosy, sugared lips."[44] As Michael Hunt points out, historically, in contrast to the more usual brutish depiction of the Latino, under certain circumstances a more positive feminine depiction of Latin Americans was employed, that of "a fair-skinned and comely señorita." She was personified as a figure who Uncle Sam could sweep off her feet, and "save from some sinister intruder."[45] This representation figured prominently in the 1890s, especially in political cartoons before and after the Spanish-American war, which pictured Cuba as white maiden, without blemish, wearing a white dress. She might be seen in tattered clothing, carrying the torch of freedom like the Statue of Liberty, struggling for liberation against the brutish or fiendish, generally dark-skinned Spaniard, or she might be seen as passively awaiting salvation by the US.[46] In either case, these representations of the feminine Cuba gave impressions of purity and weakness, both of which warranted a strong, manly, superior United States to intervene, to save her, and maybe even to bring her into his home.[47] This point is emphasized by Louis Perez, who points out that feminine representations of Cuba gave Americans more than adequate reason to preempt the Cuban claim to self rule, and instead justify their own power and influence.[48]

Jutta Weldes makes a similar point regarding US behavior toward Cuba during the Cold War. She argues that,

> if the Latin American states were "sisters" in the "American family", then the "communist threat" amounted to their "seduction". The invocation of the particular metaphor brought with it the quasi-causal argument that, given the opportunity, "the Communists" will "seduce" these "sister republics" away from both their "American family" and from the path of virtue, that is, from the straight and narrow pursuit of the shared values of "American civilization". As the defender of these values, it was the familial obligation of the US to prevent the "seduction" of its "sisters" by the Soviet Union or the "international communist movement" ... This argument implied as well that the US and OAS actions taken against the Castro regime, such as the trade embargo ... were not violations of Cuban sovereignty. They were instead the fulfillment of a familial obligation.[49]

The metaphor of the American family provides for a further extension that is related to the importance of geographic proximity embodied in the Monroe Doctrine: the notion of the region as a neighborhood or common home. In this elaboration, the states of Latin America, particularly those in Central America and the Caribbean, are represented as America's neighbors, or alternatively, the backyard or doorstep of the United States. Franklin D.

Roosevelt provided probably the most well-known example of the neighbor metaphor in his Good Neighbor Policy, whereby the US refrained from direct military intervention in Latin America, in contrast to the previous three decades, when the US had intervened more than two dozen times. He proclaimed that he would "dedicate this nation to the policy of the good neighbor – the neighbor who resolutely respects himself, and because he does so, respects the rights of others."[50] His usage was by no means the first. Rather he borrowed from an already established tradition of referring to Latin Americans as neighbors. Teddy Roosevelt, in announcing a policy usually thought to be the opposite of the later Roosevelt, made his pronouncement to "neighboring countries" which were admonished to remain "stable, orderly and prosperous." And before him, Secretary of State James Blaine, deplored "the condition of trade between the United States and its American neighbors," advocating a Pan-American Congress to promote "the friendship of [the United States'] American neighbors."[51] To this day, the practice of speaking of neighbors survives. More recent examples involve the efforts to promote free trade in the Americas. Upon the signing of NAFTA, President George H. W. Bush spoke of the fact that "relations between the United States and its neighbors have never been better."[52] And upon proclaiming Pan American Day in 2010, President Obama said that as "More than 200 years of history ... have reinforced the strong bonds of friendship and common purpose among the nations and people of the Americas," the US would continue to "partner with friends and neighbors across the Americas."[53]

The practice of talking about neighbors, Teddy Roosevelt notwithstanding, has generally been used in situations where American leaders were interested in promoting a policy to strengthen unity and cooperation. This stands in contrast to the strategy of using the words backyard or doorstep, whose use is more often associated with describing and alerting the people of the US to a perceived threat. The metaphor has been used repeatedly with respect to Cuba, probably more so than with any other place. President McKinley justified US intervention in part because, "it is right at our door."[54] Decades later Kennedy spoke of Cuba as a "dangerous and malignant enemy on our very doorstep." Similarly, Douglas Dillon, recalling the Cuban missile crisis, noted that it "was something they started in our own backyard."[55] Expanding the reach of the yard that lay in the US domain, Ronald Reagan found great use for the metaphor in defending his policies in Central America. He asked the American people if they were willing to "permit the Soviet Union to put a second Cuba, a second Libya, right on the doorstep of the United States."[56]

Like early characterizations of America as an empty land, where the indigenous populations were ignored by white conquerors and settlers, the imagery of neighbors, yards and doorsteps implies that there is a house and a neighborhood that is in need of protection. By these formulations, Cuba and Central America have become merely pieces of territory upon which a struggle is to be played out. The states and peoples of the region are less understood as actors than the stage upon which important players act. This view is coupled with the presumption that the sanctity of the American home or neighborhood must be protected from outside and dangerous influences. Accordingly, the implication is that the property actually belongs to the United States, or at least that the US maintains responsibility for it.

The representation of Latin America as home to the American family, where brothers and sister republics live in the same neighborhood, inscribes a place with characteristics that locate the US in a hegemonic position and provide for certain possibilities regarding relations between the US and its neighbors. These characterizations serve to reinforce the image of unity based upon shared identity. They undergird a myth whereby an 'American' hemisphere can be articulated, its interests defined and defended, its characteristics written, its ideals espoused, its pacific system produced, its inhabitants imagined as family, its territory spoken of as a home with a yard. And of its understanding as a location characterized by unity, there shall be little doubt.

This language of identity encourages and warrants US hegemony, intervention and superiority, as the US has taken to speaking for and acting on behalf of others in the hemisphere. It serves to silence dissent while securing an identity. Perhaps Eldon Kenworthy describes the dynamic best when he points out how if,

> there is obvious silencing in dismissing another as inferior ... there also is silencing in speaking for others because you know them so well ... at the core of silencing through identification is projection: attributing to another one's own needs and goals ... Speaking for the other because we know them so well slides into acting for the other when we have the power to do so, and finally into overriding their expressed desires in the name of defending their best interests.[57]

The tug within

One final comment remains regarding the identification of Latin America with the United States as suggested by the historical representations presented in this and the previous chapter. There is and has been a tension in American foreign policy concerning what Latin America is and what it means to American policymakers – is the place fundamentally similar to or different from the United States? The official language already quoted indicates this ambivalence in that it protests too much, continually reiterating that we are all 'Americans' from north to south who are united and have common values. The tug was evident in 1826 when the United States approved a proposal to send two delegates to the first inter-American conference in Panama, but because of protracted Congressional debate over whether or not to even participate, sent them just in time to arrive after the Congress had ended. It was evident during the Spanish-American War when a rapid shift in representations of Cuban identity occurred, turning him from a freedom-fighter into a wretch in a matter of weeks. It occurred when Ronald Reagan exhorted his neighbors to defend democracy in the hemisphere by standing against communist tyranny and infiltration in Nicaragua, while at the same time acting unilaterally to protect "America's doorstep." And it continues to the present, as George W. Bush spoke of providing "a powerful rebuke to dictators and demagogues in our backyard."[58]

This ambivalence is well described by Tzvetan Todorov. While looking at a different subject, he explained how the appreciation and sympathy the conquistadors displayed toward the Indians led not only to an enhanced understanding of the Indians, but also to their denigration and destruction, inasmuch as the Spaniards spoke only *of* the Indians, they never spoke *to* them. He noted that "it is only by speaking to the other (not giving orders but engaging in a dialogue) that I can acknowledge him as a subject, comparable to what I am myself ... unless grasping is accompanied by a full acknowledgment of the other as subject, it risks being used for purposes of exploitation, of 'taking'; knowledge will be subordinated to power."[59]

This explains why there is a continual slippage between the language of common identity and of difference in US representations of Latin America, and also why both types of representations serve US power and superiority over the region. There has scarcely been a time in which the United States has engaged in a dialogue of equals with Latin Americans. Only since the first President Bush took office might one argue that there has been any semblance of an equal relationship in the language used. For example, Bush said that "as we in the United States welcome our Central and South American neighbors into the ranks of democracy, we must offer them our help and something more: we must offer them our respect, the respect due one free nation from another, and the outstretched hand of partnership."[60] Likewise in the Clinton Administration, Secretary of State Christopher stated that "the United States and the nations of Latin America can make real progress if we work in partnership."[61] Yet even these statements, in spite of the change from earlier formulation, do not eradicate a sense of US superiority. Help, respect, and partnership are things that the United States has to offer other countries, such that the US is granting rewards to those who have reached a condition sufficiently similar to that of the US. In effect, the US was offering congratulations and presents to those who have joined the American bandwagon. The invitation of partnership and help thus do not have to involve any concessions or changes on the part of the United States, only a sense that it has been in the proper place all along and only now are others coming to join it.

Like so many other formulations of shared identity, an 'American' partnership, where help is provided, also reaffirms a Latin America that is spoken to and is spoken for, thus perpetuating the tension inherent in US policy toward the region. And like formulations based upon difference, they reinforce an understanding that promotes the superiority of the United States.

If this ambivalence is indicative of a general framework that has both informed and been the product of American behavior, its more ambiguous aspects rapidly disappeared in the face of the Cuban revolution. When the rupture with the regime of Fidel Castro occurred, the concerns of the United States about the Cold War and communism prompted a rereading and rewriting of Cuba and Cubans, reserving for the government no attributes of identity and for the population no relevant attributes of difference. This phenomenon was especially striking during the Reagan Administration, whose reading of Cuba is addressed in the next chapter.

4   Cuba, the Cold War foe

Cuba is today the country that shows most clearly the failure of the communist system.

Jeanne Kirkpatrick, US Representative to the UN[1]

We will focus on the source of the problem.

Thomas Enders, Former US Assistant Secretary of State[2]

A photograph of Castro adorning the cover of a State Department publication from 1986 entitled "Human Rights in Castro's Cuba" presents the American viewer with a paradox.[3] It shows a rather unflattering picture of the man, portraying him as old, tired and fat (or at least overweight). Yet these are by no means his only, or even his primary characteristics. This Castro also appears to be quite evil and dangerous.

A black and white photo, it is taken from Castro's right side. He is bespectacled and graying, and wearing his usual army fatigues. Yet they are a bit tight, and thus cause his belly to paunch out over his belt. This usual sign of aging is compounded by the fact that Castro is not standing completely upright; he is slouching a bit, and so also appears to be tired. At the same time, however, it is clear that this is a picture of a strong and determined leader. Strong, because, in the blurred background is a faceless crowd, the unseen masses who have come (or have been forced) to come listen, cheer and show support for their leader. Determined, because even more ominously, while Castro seems to be waving to the crowd, or perhaps asking for quiet so he can speak, the angle of his outstretched arm and his hand look as if he is making a "heil Hitler" gesture. Like everything else in the photo regarding Castro's physical stature, it seems to be a weak, flimsy gesture – the arm is not completely straight, or at a very high angle – as if he is simply too old and too tired to do anything with great energy. However, the eminently recognizable salute, weak as it is, suggests the greatest of evils. Finally, to drive the point home even further, adjacent to the picture is a quote from Castro: "Within the revolution, everything; against the revolution, nothing."

The photograph is rather successful in conjuring up a good many of the sentiments that the Reagan administration held so deeply about Castro, Cuba, communism and the Soviet Union. It skillfully embodies what the US government said and wanted the world to believe about Castro's Cuba: that it is a force to be reckoned with, strong enough by virtue of its Soviet support, and evil enough by virtue of the same origins, to threaten the United States and the worldwide freedom it defends. More than that, however, the photo portrays a figure who is a repository of contradictions. The first and obvious impression is that Castro is portrayed like a Nazi, making the telltale salute of the Führer. Moreover, the blurred faces of the crowd in the background seem geared to remind the viewer of the unbelievable sway Hitler held over his subjects, who appear by the tens of thousands, if not more, wildly cheering their leader in the many newsreels of the era. We are admonished to remember that, ever so enthusiastically, a vulnerable people can easily be led down a dangerous path by an evil man spouting lies, hate, terror, violence – madness. Castro the communist is given a makeover as a fascist, but the labels themselves are not really important. Communist, fascist, both share enough threatening features to be understood as something to fear and to fight. As totalitarian challenges to the liberal democracy of the West and of the US, they are variations on a theme. Thus it may not seem so unusual that Castro emulates the Nazis with his salute. It is a rather easy leap to transfer the characteristics of one hated dictator to another. What is important however, are not the particulars of this or that person, this or that ideology, but the portrayal and recognition of danger. And this Castro is clearly dangerous.

Simultaneously, however, this Castro is portrayed with an inherent weakness, a sense of being tired and worn out. He has gray hair and glasses (no matter that he has worn them for decades). He is getting fat, and his wave to the crowd looks halfhearted. All signs of age, no doubt, but not merely Castro's. Adorned in his military garb, yet without the strength and dynamism that is usually associated with the military, Castro, in a lackluster stance, suggests that not only is this weakness personal, it is also inherent in what Castro represents: communist dictatorship, revolution, a challenge to the West, the US and capitalism. These things are old, tired, weak, aging, dying. They are on the decline. Communism, once considered progressive, dynamic, a model for the future and an ideal of the young, is shown here to now be conservative, static, passé, tried and failed, the dream of only the old. And if, in this photo, this waning ideology and its adherents are losing strength, they also lack color, literally. The photo is printed in black and white, and the tones are shades of gray, suggesting something dull, lifeless, unappealing and dying.

Still, diminished though he may be, the figure here does not appear to be pathetic, only overworked. Defeated he is not. The Castro in this picture may be someone who has worked long and hard, and needs a rest, but he will not take one because his task is not done. He may be getting older, but he is not enfeebled. Age appears here to be not only weakness, but experience, coupled with a certain resoluteness, a determination to persevere, a will to fight on. As with the pictures of Hitler, the imagery seems to say that the power of his convictions is more than enough to carry this body and its (evil) mind for a long time. Even in an aging, weak man, who represents an aging, stifling movement, Castro's Hitleresque gesture (and its implications), his commitment (or fanaticism), and his ideological motivations are not to be taken lightly. This Castro still has plenty of fight left in him. After all, as Fidel Castro himself said, "against the revolution, nothing."

The thousand words the picture is worth

The Reagan administration, which produced the document that displayed this photo, understood very well the power of pictures, be they on television, the movies or photographs. This group of politicians was especially adept at using images effectively to achieve numerous political successes. One type of image continually used involved a "spontaneous" video clip (in reality these were always orchestrated events) of Reagan riding a horse on his ranch, which served to depict the President as strong, capable, rugged and wholesome. Just as those images were supposed to inform an audience about the identity of the American president, so too does this picture of Castro on the cover of the State Department publication tell a story about Castro's identity. And just like the images of Reagan riding a horse, this picture is not simply some average photo that just happened to appear on the cover of an official document. There are a multitude of pictures of Castro available for such use, so this picture had to be deliberately selected. It had to be one which could evoke a variety of associations, understandings and memories that reinforce an image of Castro as evil and dangerous, in spite of his diminished strength. It is for specific reasons that this illustration was selected over others; the State Department and the administration had an agenda.

But this fact can easily be overlooked when viewing a picture – an object that is often thought of as neutral and objective, passively recording reality, revealing without prejudice information about the people and things in it. The photo of Castro is none of these things. In order for it to be successful in portraying an evil and determined, but still vulnerable enemy, such forgetting on the part of the viewer is crucial. Yet if one refuses to forget that it required a deliberate act to choose and disseminate this photograph, then this picture becomes a mirror. While the photo does tell a story about Castro, it tells a far richer and more interesting story about those who sponsored, wrote and distributed the document. The image presented here, then, is not necessarily that of Castro. It is instead *Reagan's* Castro, a man who existed more in Washington than in places such as Havana, Moscow, Mexico City or even London and Paris.

Reagan's Castro is a man who can be found in the story told by the photo. His qualities as portrayed in the picture depict a photographic representation of the Reagan administration's Manichaean view of global politics, in which the Cold War defined almost all global conflict from the arms race to social revolutions to Middle Eastern terrorism. A clear division between good and evil, us and them, democratic and dictatorship, freedom and communism, benign and dangerous, peaceful and warlike, upstanding and subversive, legitimate and illegitimate characterized this perspective. This last pair implies further divisions of strong and weak, stable and unstable, robust and frail, unbreakable and breakable. In an effort to generate support for its foreign policy, the Reagan administration continually used rhetoric marked by these divisions, trying to encourage and reinforce an understanding of global politics along these lines, whereby the United States embodied the former in each of these pairings, and Castro and communism embodied the latter.

It is this dynamic – involving the discourse and the policies regarding Cuba and communism in the Reagan years – that I shall address in the chapter. While the previous two chapters sought to show how the United States effected its power and superiority with regard to Cuba as part of Latin America, this chapter seeks to explore the relationship of the United States to Cuba in the latter's capacity as a communist country, to look at how Cuba was represented during the Cold War, not as backward or underdeveloped, but as dangerous and illegitimate. The argument does not address the degree of accuracy in this representation, nor is it concerned with gauging the credibility of the Cuban threat, a project already undertaken by many others. Additionally, it does not seek to locate the ultimate source of Reagan's policy, be it in ideology or geopolitics, for this is a question that concerns the truth or falsity of the Cuban threat. Both ideology and geopolitics can be described as the source of the same American foreign policy. Characterizing Reagan's foreign policy as ideologically or geopolitically driven has been as much a reflection of agreement or disagreement with the policy than anything else, such that the labels are simply two ways of characterizing a single mode of representation concerning danger and illegitimacy. It is this mode of representation, and its consequences, that I focus upon here, looking at how Castro and Cuba were constructed to fit into a Cold War framework marked by rigid identities and differences.

The reasons for choosing the Reagan era are twofold. The first is that while the obvious era to discuss might be the early years of the Cuban revolution and Castro's turn to communism, as evidenced by the large amount of books and articles written about those years, it has already been extensively studied. In focusing on the treatment of Cuba during the Reagan years, I not only avoid covering ground that has already been well-documented and analyzed, I can also examine a period in US-Cuban relations that has not come under as much scrutiny as is perhaps warranted. A second, and more important reason is that the Reagan administration's rhetoric and policies toward communism in general and Cuba in particular are exemplars of the greater Cold War period. As examples of some of the most forceful political attacks directed toward Castro's Cuba, they provide a very clear view of the formulation and practice of US anti-communist policy when it was stated quite unambiguously. If there is no superlative that can be attached to Reagan's policies and words regarding Cuba, they do nonetheless appropriately represent the official American reaction to the Cuban revolution, as well as Cuba's significance in American foreign policy. And lastly, there are a great number of official documents involving US policy toward Cuba that were generated during this period. The number of policy statements and special reports released by the State and Defense Departments was quite extensive, offering up a rich collection this is not only worthy of study, but one that reflects the concerns, policies and worldview of the Reagan Administration.

The importance of Cuba's role as Cold War foe to the United States is that it resulted in a situation where the United States was confronted with two major adversaries embodied in a single Cuban government. Castro was both a troublesome neighbor who flouted US hegemony, and a communist and Soviet ally. Once he aligned with the Soviet Union and declared Cuba a Marxist-Leninist state, he gave rise to the volatile combination of the Monroe Doctrine and the Cold War. His success at both staying in power and eliminating American influence on the island provided the United States with a single site where the attributes that secured American superiority in the region were combined with those that furnished it with a global mission against communism. Cuba was at once backward, underdeveloped, dangerous and illegitimate in American understandings. The combination of these characteristics, which had long been represented as defects, worked in tandem with the stated principles and interests of America's Cold War foreign policy to give rise to an unyielding hostility, whereby the tension between sameness and difference that had continually been manifested in American foreign policy toward Cuba disappeared. In its place came clarity, in which no attributes of common or shared identity existed between Castro's revolutionary government and the United States.

This clarity, marked by Cuba's total conversion to an unambiguous enemy, was achieved quite rapidly, the result of two phenomena. First of all, Castro quickly overstepped the bounds of what historically had been permissible. Cuban leaders had never been allowed to be as independent and radical as Castro. Once the Eisenhower administration become convinced that Castro could not be coaxed or coerced into changing, US policy too changed quickly from a "wait-and-see" approach to outright hostility.

In conjunction with this, but on another level, this rapid transformation of Cuba is explained by the circumstance that alternative modes of representation were readily available to US policymakers who had decided that Castro was a troublemaker. As "identity is established in relation to a series of differences that have become socially recognized," Castro could be placed in a category that included other Latin American leaders whom the US found distasteful for one reason or another, and he could be included among the ranks of communist revolutionaries.[4] The social and cultural roots of identity formation and interpretation not only assist in establishing the dichotomy of good/evil, US/Cuba, which could be quickly employed to effect opposition, negation and hostility, they also serve to ground the competing representations in an established historical and social setting. This is because returning to the words of Roland Barthes, the language of democracy versus communism is a form of "mythical speech," a mode and form of signification which is "made of material that has already been worked on so as to make it suitable for communication." This language already contained within it a "presupposed signifying consciousness" in which representations of communism had long since crystallized around referents commonly regarded as dangers.[5] Thus, while the characteristic features of Cuban identity were quickly converted into those of difference in the early 1960s, they were also just as quickly embedded in an already established understanding about the threat and illegitimacy of communism. The "mythical speech" of communism had long been "worked on" such that Cuba quickly and easily fit into its new place. Moreover, due to the tendency to "congeal established identities into fixed forms, thought and lived as if their structure expressed the true order of things," Cuba's placement in the enemy camp gave added sustenance to already established set of dichotomous representations whose objectivity was further naturalized.[6]

By casting Cuba in the unfavorable terms of communism, dictatorship, etc., the rhetoric deployed by members of the Reagan administration attempted to preserve and strengthen the long established understandings involving the essential goodness of the United States and the inherent evil of communism, which represented and pursued a range of differences. The characteristics associated with communism and its illegitimacy that were attributed to Cuba and its patron, the Soviet Union, served to clarify what the US response to them should be. These dangers, i.e., differences, had to be challenged, neutralized, and if possible, eradicated. Communists were not merely different in this dichotomy they were entirely negated, stripped of any morality, of any goodness, of any worth. As the counterpoint to communism, the US could thus presuppose its morality, goodness, and worth, and proclaim its own standard of conduct as the correct one. Furthermore, since such an understanding provided for the added assumption that this American standard was objective, not rooted in the particularities of American ideology and history, it endorsed the idea that there was an inherent justice in America's responses to the actions of communists around the world. Ultimate responsibility for conflict lay with the communists, those who broke the rules of civilized nations, not those who set the standard of conduct. The desired result was the strengthening of American self-certainty and further delegitimation of communism and its adherents.

In the case of posing a challenge to Cuba in the 1980s, this intensification and affirmation of anti-communism was reminiscent of the early 1960s, and not an isolated incident in Cold War history. It is instead characteristic of the heights reached in the rhetoric of anti-communism and the assertion of American identity. In the 1960s and 1980s these heights brought with them a reassertion of American power in a renewed effort to challenge the illegitimate alternative posed by the Soviet Union and its allies. In both of these eras too, there were calls by the American leadership for a change in attitude in which Americans were admonished for their complacency and/or doubt. Also in both periods, official representations of Cuba advanced a completely uncompromising understanding of the country as a Cold War threat whose defects and dangers were repeatedly and vehemently articulated. This is not to say, however, that Castro was not vilified during other periods. The Cuban government has consistently been characterized as a communist interloper in the region, while the people themselves have been represented as members of the American family who had been enslaved by a regime that was ultimately foreign in nature.

While these characterizations have been continuous features of American rhetoric about Cuba since 1960, by 1981, when Reagan entered office, the reintensification of the uncompromising stance toward Castro included some changes as well. The Cold War was by then 20 years older, and much had happened in the intervening years. The interpretation of those years by Reagan and his supporters was that the Soviets, with a great deal of help from the Cubans, had asserted themselves around the world at America's expense. (This was a prevalent theme, expressed by foreign policy analysts and practitioners such as Jeanne Kirkpatrick, Norman Podhoretz, Alexander Haig, Irving Kristol and Eugene Rostow, as well as organizations such as The Committee on the Present Danger and The Committee of Santa Fe – a conservative organization that took up the topic of US policy in Latin America). One could explain the problems afflicting the world and the United States by understanding that crucial fact, which identified the origins of these problems and their respective solutions.

As one of the world's leading communist adventurers and expansionists, Castro was an important part of this interpretation. He was the quintessential communist. He possessed all the negative characteristics mentioned earlier which marked the enemy. A focus upon those qualities, after Presidents Nixon, Ford and Carter had tried to reestablish more normal relations with the Soviet Union and Cuba, was an important part of articulating a worldview whose central feature was the ideological faultline between the US and the Soviet Union. This meant that Castro, Cuba and the Soviet Union had to mean something a bit different than they did during most of the 1970s, when deténte dominated and accommodation with Castro seemed possible. The most notable and emphasized features of their identities was once again their danger and illegitimacy, as this was a crucial aspect of a larger project involving the reinterpretation of a global politics which made ideological sense to the Reagan team. The first task in this project was to interpret the state of the world and tell how the US had arrived there.

Writing the right history

Part I: Self-doubt

The primary actors on the Reagan team came to power reflecting a growing current in American conservatism. The sense that the Soviet Union had made great gains in the 1970s, at the expense of the United States, had begun to take hold not only in the Republican Party, but also among many Democrats who were quite critical of President Carter (Jeanne Kirkpatrick, Daniel Moynihan, Henry Jackson, Norman Podhoretz, and Lane Kirkland, to name a few). Anxious to reverse this national decline, a problem which was both cause and consequence of the concomitant Soviet ascendancy, a growing number of people and organizations began to reformulate the nature of the debate regarding American power, American purpose and American action, bringing into existence variety of conservative or right-wing organizations. (In addition to the Committee on the Present Danger, there were others such as the Moral Majority, the Heritage Foundation and the Richard A. Viguerie Corporation).

Reconstructing the world within the frame of this viewpoint involved both a reconceptualization of international conflict and the reintroduction of a political language that sharply divided the world in two. The effort, aimed at encouraging a reimagining of the conceptual space of international conflict, sought to accomplish nothing less than redrawing the boundaries of the discursive territory upon which any debate took place. The result sought was the characterization of any conflict around the world, be it in Cuba or anywhere else, as part of the global confrontation with the Soviet Union. Thus if the United States was not involved in some regional or local conflict, it almost certainly should be, the implication being that American absence meant a net Soviet gain.

Yet if the perceived gains and superiority of the communists around the world (e.g. nuclear superiority, Nicaragua, Grenada, El Salvador, Afghanistan, Southeast Asia, Angola, Ethiopia) were understood as part of a worldview that feared communist adventurism and imperialism, that perspective also included another aspect: a lack of will on the part of the United States to confront the enemy. The Soviet Union and communism were seen to be on the move, dynamic. The US, in the face of such dynamism, was not meeting the challenge. It was "everywhere in retreat."[7] As the Committee on the Present Danger asserted, "the principal threat to our nation, to world peace, and to the cause of human freedom is the Soviet drive for dominance based upon an unparalleled military buildup." By contrast the United States was complacent. What was needed was "a conscious effort of political will ... to restore the strength and coherence of our foreign policy." The committee members called upon the United States and its allies which "still ha[d] time to protect their vital national interests ... but that time is growing short."[8] This crisis was not merely strategic, it was, as the Committee of Santa Fe put it, metaphysical.[9]

These critics and others such as Paul Nitze, Jeanne Kirkpatrick, Irving Kristol, Norman Podhoretz, Richard Pipes, Gene Rostow, Alexander Haig and Colin Gray (many of whom were members of the Committee on the Present Danger) faulted President Carter for carrying out a misdirected, weak foreign policy.[10] Their growing discontent with what they saw as American self-doubt – attributed to defeat in Vietnam, Watergate, oil crises, the disclosures of corruption and criminality in government, and a string of Soviet gains – reflected a belief that the United States was crippling itself, as its population and leaders subscribed to a theory of inevitable decline, with potentially disastrous consequences.

During the presidency of Jimmy Carter, this attempt to reconstitute an American sense of self around notions of strength and global action became increasingly widespread. The critics of Carter rejected the argument, ascendant in the 1970s, which asserted that the United States could no longer maintain the preeminent global position it had held since World War II. This interpretation of international relations held that a successful foreign policy required Americans to understand the fact of hegemonic decline and accept it as part of a natural evolution of international politics. To do so, it was argued, would foster a mature adjustment to a complex new reality, and a realistic US foreign policy.

The critics rejected this view of global power and change, refusing to accept its premise: that the world had changed enough to prevent American power from being as effective as it was in the past. The problem of exercising power, they argued, was not primarily a complex, increasingly interdependent world, the rise of new powers in Europe, Japan, China or the Persian Gulf, nor was it a "crisis of democracy" affecting advanced industrial nations around the world. The failure of American power was rooted internally, in a crisis of will. The will to use that power, in light of America's ills and Soviet gains around the world, had been severely diminished, but the possibility for America to be stronger had not been compromised. Jeanne Kirkpatrick argued this in her famous article "Dictatorships and Double Standards," but hers was only the most well-known, not an isolated case. Other advocates of reassertion all made the same assumption: that the world had not grown too complex or unmanageable, that American power could be effectively exercised if the country's leaders and citizens mustered the will.

This judgment, citing lack of will as the source of US complacency and decline, was echoed with great frequency in the years leading up to the election of Ronald Reagan. In addition to Kirkpatrick, there was the Committee on the Present Danger, many of whose members later joined the Reagan Administration, and Norman Podhoretz, one of the earlier neoconservatives, who in 1980 wrote a short book entitled *The Present Danger*, named after the Committee on the Present Danger. In this call to action, "the present danger" was not merely "the forward surge of Soviet imperialism," but the "collapse of American resolve," which was reflected in the subtitle of the book: *Do We Have the Will to Reverse the Decline of American Power?*

When it became increasingly likely that Ronald Reagan would become the next president, one group of conservative policy analysts, which called itself the Committee of Santa Fe, came together in the summer of 1980 to recommend a new US policy for Latin America, one that was soon taken up by the incoming Reagan administration. In it the authors (many of whom were also soon appointed to foreign policy roles in the new government) pointed to the overthrow of Somoza, conflict in El Salvador and Guatemala, the apparent lack of concern that the US had been demonstrating toward Latin America, and the Soviet achievements resulting from this lack of concern to argue for radical change in Washington's policies. Asserting that "US foreign policy is in disarray" and that "the norms of conflict and social change adopted by the Carter Administration are those of the Soviet Union," the group claimed that "the United States appears weak and indecisive," and that "America's inability or unwillingness either to protect or project its basic values and beliefs has led to the present nadir of indecision and impotence and has placed the very existence of the Republic in peril."[11] This argument, like the other portrayals mentioned, not only explained America's troubles, it also contained the particularly attractive element that allowed for these troubles to be easily remedied: by a change of attitude at the highest levels of government.

Many who came into the government with Reagan also asserted their adherence to the same idea, even if they generally characterized the times in a less apocalyptic fashion. Secretary of Defense Caspar Weinberger claimed that, "as ominous developments gathered strength over the last decade, America's confidence in itself was shaken, and America's leadership faltered." The result was that "the perception of our inability to respond adequately and promptly has served to encourage Soviet and Soviet-inspired exploitation of areas of instability."[12] Secretary of State Alexander Haig, who in 1979 had quit his post as the commander of NATO due to his disagreement with Carter's foreign policy, said that when Reagan came to office, "the nation had not yet emerged from its long night of self-doubt." It had been "too distracted to act like a superpower ... paralyzed by the fear of 'another Vietnam,'" even before Carter came to office. Arriving at the same conclusion as Weinberger, Haig clearly saw the consequences of US inaction: "the Soviet Union had been seduced by the weakness of the American will and extended itself."[13] And as Reagan himself represents the period, "during the summer and fall of 1980, there were many problems facing our nation ... But to me none was more serious than the fact that America had lost faith in itself ... our country had begun to abdicate this historical role as the spiritual leader of the Free World and its foremost defender of democracy."[14]

These characterizations of the late 1970s and early 1980s provided the first essential component of the interpretation that Reagan and his supporters made about America's troubles in the world. The source of the problem – what was interpreted as Soviet ascendancy at the expense of the United States – was not a depersonalized history, or unchangeable social forces, or even ultimately the Soviet Union, but the US itself. Rather than assess blame entirely to others in the world, it also was necessary to blame an internal source for the apparent weakness and complacency that afflicted the United States. Mistakes, weakness and self-doubt (and the election of Carter) could be reversed. History, on the other hand, could not.

Part II: Danger

The second element of the perspective that argued for global reassertion was that of imminent danger. Malaise and self-doubt might not be such tremendous problems if the victim of these conditions were not under the continual threat of destruction and defeat. But for a country such as the United States, the self-professed leader of a free world that was in continual danger from the Soviet Union and its allies around the world, such a situation was not merely unfortunate, it was wholly unacceptable. According to this interpretation of recent history, an emboldened and well-armed Soviet Union represented the clearest and most present danger. The objectivity of that danger resulted from, and was dependent upon, a particular telling of Cold War history that privileged certain facts regarding the relationship of the US to communist states.

Two facts stood out, according to what was called the hard-line reading of global confrontation between the superpowers. The first is that the Soviets and their allies were engaged in a continuous and active struggle to spread communism around the world, a struggle that had intensified in the 1970s. The second is that communism was defined as danger and tyranny, and thus a system which could only stand opposed to the United States. The logic that followed was that the interests of this tyranny were furthered by creating political instability in non-communist states vulnerable to communist takeover. In light of the expansion of communism and its sympathizers in Afghanistan, Vietnam, Cambodia, Laos, Angola, Ethiopia, Mozambique, Nicaragua and Grenada, as well as guerrilla movements in El Salvador, Guatemala, Colombia and a variety of other places, the United States was, by 1980, finding itself on the defensive around the world, with the balance of power moving favorably toward the Soviets and their allies. Moreover, as all of these unfriendly governments had come to power through the use of force, and all those vying for power were doing so by employing violence against the state, this was seen to clearly demonstrate that the favored method of expansion for communism involved the use of force. One highly important feature of this situation was that events in each of these countries were not isolated cases. The vast majority of the leftist governments and movements received financial and military support from either directly from the Soviet Union, or indirectly, from its allies. This was an important theme that was continually reiterated. The logic, articulated in the Truman Doctrine, provided the widely accepted assertion that expansionism was the most dangerous feature of totalitarianism. This is what threatened global peace.

Most notable among that group of Soviet allies was Cuba, which was characterized as playing a significant role in supporting communist revolution in Latin America and Africa. In so doing Cuba clashed with the US over military issues several times.[15] Considering Cuban success in Nicaragua, Angola and Ethiopia, and its role in dozens of countries around the world, there was a sense that the United States could not take the Cuban threat lightly. Acting in concert with the Soviet Union, Cuba contributed to the threat faced by the United States and its allies.

This view was forcefully argued by the Committee of Santa Fe, whose report portrayed the danger in the starkest words available to a group addressing a (hopefully) incoming government. Urging a new approach to Latin America, its members issued a warning that "the Americas are under attack," and went on to make a case in which the reader would both recognize the danger and act upon it. The report asserted that the US must think of the Caribbean as a "fourth border" whose security is not being protected by President Carter. "America must seize the initiative or perish," the authors argued. The Caribbean republics, the report read, "situated in our strategic back yard face ... the dedicated, irrepressible activity of a Soviet-backed Cuba to win ultimately total hegemony over this region." Cuba was a "problem [that had] grown to truly dangerous proportions" and would "utilize every available means to overthrow the capitalist order and to transform the world." Moreover, the success of Cuba and the Soviet Union was not merely imminent, it had already occurred in many locations. Claimed the authors: "The Caribbean ... is becoming a Marxist-Leninist lake;" "The Soviet Union is now ensconced in force in the Western Hemisphere;" and "The Caribbean rim and basin are spotted with Soviet surrogates and ringed with socialist states." Their aim, according to the Committee's report, was to strangle the Western industrialized nations by interdicting their oil and ore supplies, create chaos and exploit the opportunities, and "introduce a sterilizing internationalism" into the cultures of Latin America. The Communists had been quite successful, they claimed, as "the annual balance sheet of gains and losses favors the USSR."[16]

The principal foreign policymakers in the Reagan administration, upon entering office, began to react to global events based upon this understanding, and thereby also help to construct and reinforce this view. Secretary of State Alexander Haig stated as a fact that the USSR "possessed greater military power than the United States," and that because of American unwillingness to counter the Soviets, "we were witnessing the conjunction of Soviet ambition and a maturing Soviet global reach." A good part of that reach now extended to Latin America, where the Soviet Union's Cuban surrogate and ally was successfully imitating its benefactor, orchestrating an "assault upon American interests, and upon the safety of legitimate governments and innocent people." "There could not be the slightest doubt," said Haig, "that Cuba was at once the source of supply and the catechist of the Salvadoran insurgency."[17]

UN Ambassador Jeanne Kirkpatrick made a similar assessment, stating that the "period we have now entered is, I believe, an exceedingly dangerous one – perhaps the most dangerous we have faced – and its outcome is far from clear ... The massive, unprecedented, unflagging Soviet military buildup has created what Soviet theoreticians describe as a 'new world correlation of forces.'" The significance of this is seen in "an equally unprecedented Soviet foreign policy – more menacing to the independence and peace of others than at any time since Stalin moved to swallow neighboring states in the period of the Nazi-Soviet pact." The Cuban role in this activity was multifaceted. "In Africa alone," stated Kirkpatrick, Cuba "maintains some 40,000 soldiers ... doing for the Soviet Union what the Gurkha mercenaries did for nineteenth-century England. And in Central America, "Cuba is attempting to export aggression, subvert established governments, and intervene in a most persistent and massive fashion in the internal affairs of more than one country in that region."[18]

Secretary of Defense Weinberger reiterated the danger by stressing the relative strengths of the US and Soviet military establishments: "Soviet expenditures for armaments, in particular strategic arms, grew more rapidly and more steadily during the period called 'detènte' than during the period called the 'cold war.'" It would be "neither reasonable nor prudent to view the Soviet military buildup as defensive in nature ... we have clear evidence of aggressive Soviet activity around the globe." At the same time the Soviet Union was "greatly extending its geo-strategic reach," in the Middle East, Africa, Asia and Latin America, "American and allied access to bases and airspace has declined in many areas of critical concern. America's strategic needs were not being met, and a military buildup on the part of the US was vital, as "there was literally nothing we did not need" in the US armed forces.[19]

Finally, President Reagan too acknowledged his awareness of the manifest and imminent danger resulting from American self-doubt and withdrawal. "Predictably, the Soviets had interpreted our hesitation and reluctance to act and our reduced sense of national self-confidence as a weakness, and had tried to exploit it to the fullest, moving ahead with their agenda to achieve a Communist-dominated world." With such an understanding, there existed no irrelevant place in the world as far as the Cold War is concerned. Any problem was easily made to fit into a larger framework – the effort by America's adversaries to achieve a "Communist-dominated world." In Latin America, then, the problems of social unrest and civil war had clear sources. Reagan wrote that a few days after inauguration, he saw "firm and incontrovertible evidence ... [which] showed that the Soviets and Fidel Castro were targeting all of Central America for a Communist takeover. El Salvador and Nicaragua were only a down payment. Honduras, Guatemala and Costa Rica were next, and then would come Mexico."[20] Left unspoken, and without a need to be spoken, was the obvious implication of Mexico's downfall: that the US was next on the list, and even if we could not be conquered, the communization of Mexico would be a disaster for the US.

This implication was true enough, and therein lay the strength of Reagan's argument and those like it, which postulated that inevitable danger would be the result of opposition to their policies. The logic was seamless, whereby acceptance of the initial premise led to an either/or choice involving a situation where "we shall become second best to the Soviet Union ... [and] our national survival itself would be in peril," or one where "effective action" would "ensure the security and prosperity of this country in peace."[21] The choice was really no choice at all. The assumption seeks to silence debate by making the worst case scenario, communism in Mexico and its concomitant social upheaval, a logical consequence of inaction, which is defined as action that runs contrary to that prescribed.

However, if the peril in a communist Mexico was apparent, it was not equally apparent that dissent from the Reagan policy of global assertion and containment (or rollback) would inevitably lead to such a disastrous conclusion. The Committee of Santa Fe report exhibits some of the problems in upholding this dualistic logic. When the shift was made in the report from issuing generalized alarms to making a case based upon specific instances, the threat from Cuba did not seem as dire as the warnings would have one believe. The dismal picture in the Caribbean which was "becoming a Marxist-Leninist lake," consisted of threats (after Cuba) in Nicaragua, Grenada, Guyana, Jamaica and Panama, none of which has ever been considered strong enough to threaten US security.[22] In each of these places, the authors state, there had been one form or another of cooperation or sympathy with Cuba or left-wing politics. Such evidence was considered damning enough for the governments of these countries to be represented as threats (or possible threats) to the US.

This was another example of the dualisms, often simplistic, that defined the argumentation. The division between 'us' and 'them' was strict, with no room for gray areas. There was little distinction to be made among leftists, socialists, communists and Soviet puppets (witting or unwitting). All were merely variations on the same dangerous theme. Guilt was thus proven by association. Whether one expressed sympathy for Cuba or revolution, or argued for substantial socio-economic change, whether one bought arms from the Soviet bloc, or traded with communist countries, the response from the American right was the same. The alleged offender was in cahoots with the Soviet Union, supported its foreign policy, and was a puppet of the Russians and Cubans. There was a firm refusal to allow the possibility that limited engagement could occur between small, poor states and the Soviet Union, that support for social and political change, massive or even gradual, represented anything less than a desire to advance the interests of global communism, or that arms, advice, or even contact meant anything less than Soviet control over a country receiving such assistance. It may have seemed rather ironic that the United States could be professing fear from these small, poor, relatively powerless countries. However, by recasting them as satellites of Cuba, or of the Soviets, one could then pose their status as obvious threats.

As obvious as Cuba, which to the Committee of Santa Fe, as noted earlier, was a "problem [that had] grown to truly dangerous proportions," and would "utilize every available means to overthrow the capitalist order and to transform the world." With this *a priori* belief about the country, no action could avoid being fit into an interpretation of danger to the US and its allies. Whereas the US might send troops to a country and represent it as aiding an ally in need, no such legitimacy was accorded the same Cuban action, nor could it be by the understanding advanced by the advocates of Reagan's policy. Sending troops to Angola or Yemen could not be examples of aiding allies in need, much the same as the United States or other countries have done for its allies. Instead they were characterized as attempts to further opportunities in "mineral rich south and central Africa and the oil-rich Persian Gulf." Increased spending on armaments was not and could not be a defensive or preemptive action on the part of the Cuban government. Even though an increasingly hostile US was building up its own military forces, the Cuban buildup was not construed as defense, or even as the legitimate juridical and customary right of all states, but only as a "policy of subversion and destabilization in this hemisphere."[23] In this perspective, Cuba's selfish (and sinister) motivations stand in marked contrast to the disinterested exercise of responsibility by the United States.

The Cuba that was the enemy of the Reagan administration (and this phenomenon was not unique to this presidency) was a country, as Michael Shapiro puts it, "imaginatively pre-constituted" in terms of difference.[24] And difference, in this case, is both inherently evil and juxtaposed to what is predicated to be a natural order of things. Actions labeled misdeeds when carried out by Cuba were not so different from the actions of others, including the United States, which were deemed legitimate. Equivalency is eliminated, however, in that each is formulated within an understanding whereby Cuba can enjoy no equality with the US or any other legitimate actor in global politics. The construction of this strict dichotomy between Cuba's illegitimacy and American legitimacy was quickly established in the early 1960s, and easily reinforced, for "to the extent that one accepts and unreflectively reproduces the security oriented geopolitical discursive practice, one engages in implicit acts of recognition of the existing power and authority configurations."[25]

When the Reagan administration rejected deténte in favor of reassertionism, its foreign policy of hostility to Cuba further set the conceptual boundaries within which Cuba's actions lay. The country was returned to the status it held for the US in the 1960s: part of a grave threat to American national security, in which all the attributes of the enemy are defined as dangerous, by virtue of American opposition to them. In other words, foreign policy itself, which entails a process of recognizing and making things "foreign or exotic, and thus different from the self," implicitly includes the practice of "constituting otherness."[26] This provides for the inherent righteousness of American identity, which is established in contradistinction to the inherent evil in communist difference. The Soviets and Cubans are thus foreign, sneaky, subversive, bent on world domination. They do not believe in civil rights, equal rights or human rights. They do not have freedom and democracy. The US, conversely, is defined by the opposite of these things through its words and actions, and therefore, by definition, is not dangerous. Thus it was the exclusion of these attributes, these dangers, anywhere within American purview, which defined and guaranteed American security. As these dangers were also understood to be expanding – metaphors of dominoes falling, or contagions spreading were repeatedly invoked at the time – the issue of their immediate containment became paramount.

As the second component of the Reagan administration's representation of danger, this element of imminent danger served to complete the interpretation of the problems that the US faced in the early 1980s.

Part III: Vulnerability

At this point in the narrative concerning the expansionist drives of the Soviet Union, and their roots in both the inherent tendencies of totalitarianism and the loss of American will, the story's inner logic holds up reasonably well. There are the necessary elements of malaise and danger, combined with the self-importance that the United States is the leader of the free world and thus must act. It is crucial that the problem within the US itself is only lack of will. To correct it requires only a reliance on the collective self. No outsiders are necessary, and not even the whole country has to be convinced and moved for a change to occur, only its leaders. Furthermore, the change in America's fortunes can be rather quick. A change of attitude at the top can be immediate, and the enemy will get the message soon enough. As Reagan said, "there were some new fellows in Washington who had a realistic view of what [the Soviets] were up to and weren't going to let them keep it up."[27] The response was to be swift and sizable.

Still, in order for the Reagan response to fit into this worldview, one more element was needed in the story: the Soviets had to have a weakness that could be exploited, an Achilles heel. In fact, according to the administration, they had two. The first was economic. On one level, according this interpretation, the Soviets were overextended. Their military was consuming ever greater proportions of their GDP, projecting power all over the world, and this could not continue. Reagan states that his "daily National Security Council briefings were revealing tangible evidence that Communism as we knew it was approaching the brink of collapse ... The Soviet economy was being held together with baling wire; it was a basket case, partly because of massive spending on armaments."[28] On a second, deeper level, it was posited in the administration, in the words of Alexander Haig, that "Marxism cannot stimulate economic development; it just does not work."[29]

The second Soviet weakness was political. The communist system was one in which the leaders and the people "were separated from one another by the apparatus of a police state."[30] "All over the world," said Reagan, "there were indications that democracy was on the rise and Communism was near collapse, dying from a terminal disease called tyranny. It could no longer bottle up the energy of the human spirit and man's innate drive to be free ... Of all the millions of refugees we've seen in the modern world, their flight is always away from, not toward, the Communist world."[31]

It is with these weaknesses that the Reagan policy of global reassertion can be considered both logical and necessary. It might be thought fruitless and senseless for the United States to mount a great challenge against a vibrant imperial power, meeting with success whenever and wherever it chose. An overextended, tyrannical empire was a different beast altogether. These were represented as opportunities to be exploited, so on behalf of the Western world, Reagan "wondered how we as a nation could use these cracks in the Soviet system to accelerate the process of collapse." His answer was to employ one of the most powerful weapons capitalism had: money. "The Russians could never win the arms race; we could outspend them forever," and on top of that, "we had the capacity to maintain a technological edge over them forever."[32]

Thus was a coherent representation made of the struggle between the US and the Soviets. The problems were clear, as were their origins. The only logical, correct, necessary and right response to such a situation was Reagan's foreign policy – reassertion, military buildup, taking the hard-line with communism. The choice was made to seem obvious, so obvious that in fact it did not even present itself as a choice, just as the program which needed to be carried out. If the conservative representation offered any choices, its supporters postulated, it was only whether or not to accept it over the "attitude of defeatism, self-doubt, self-denigration, and self-delusion [that] had displaced what had been a distinctly American optimism about the world and our prospects as a nation." If Americans had wanted pessimism, defeat and weakness, they could have re-elected Carter. Since they wanted the opposite (and, in such terms, there would be little reason to reject that future), Reagan assumed the presidency to begin a reversal. Thus his ascent to the presidency became part of the conservative story, "a watershed that marked the end to a period of retreat"[33]

Targeting Central America

Making the world conform to this particular interpretation was more difficult than articulating it, and the Reagan team was never completely successful in its efforts. With regard to the Soviet Union, there was little difficulty for the administration to more firmly place what Reagan termed the "evil empire" into American strategic and moral calculations and to do away with deténte. Prodded by the nation's leaders, the Congress and the public quickly followed into supporting a policy that became characterized as "The Second Cold War."

With regard to Latin America, however, the administration encountered greater difficulty in convincing the country to reimagine a people it already "knew" throughout its history. As has already been discussed, Latin Americans have historically been regarded in the US as peoples identified in terms of underdevelopment, backwardness, or at worst, irresponsible behaviors, all of which presupposed the superiority of the United States. It was the exercise of superiority that had led the US to intervene numerous times in order to restore order and stability. With the exception of Cuba, there had never been a completely successful challenge to US intervention. Central America and the Caribbean seemed to consist of weak nations, no match for American strength and pre-eminence. To remake this part of Latin America into part of a monolithic communist bloc, part of a global network of sophisticated revolutionaries working toward world domination and the defeat of the United States, required the Reagan team to effect a sizable transformation in the popular images Americans held about their southern neighbors. Competency and strength had historically not been emphasized as attributes inherent to Latin American countries.

The most important part of this transformation was the recasting of blame in the fortunes of Latin Americans. If they had not reached the levels of political and economic development attained in the United States (a condition simply labeled backward, underdeveloped or inferior in the past) this was not the direct source of their political troubles, i.e. guerrilla warfare, demands for rapid social change, and the resultant political crackdowns that ensued. These phenomena were only indirectly related. Poverty, inequality, economic modernization, structural change, the lack of democracy, these things were acknowledged as important factors in Latin American society, but in and of themselves, they were not sufficient. As a State Department report said at the time, describing Central America,

> Cuban intervention is, of course, not the sole source of instability. The origins of occasional violent conflict in Latin America lie in histori-cal, social and economic inequities which have generated frustrations among a number of people ... in some countries, particularly the small nations of Central America, dislocations resulting from rapid growth compounded existing tensions, leading to the emergence in several countries of radical movements, which often originated with frustrated elements of the middle class. Subsequent economic reversals have subjected already weak institutions to additional stress, making these countries more vulnerable the appeals of radical groups backed by Cuba ... Cuba is quick to exploit legitimate grievances for its own ends.[34]

This statement acknowledges the counterargument that poverty and inequality are responsible for violence in Central America, but quickly attempts to subsume it in a larger analysis that includes Cuba and the Soviet Union as responsible agents. There is a connection in the statement where legitimate grievances lead to radical movements, but this is irrelevant at the point when they join forces with Cuba, which by definition, has a different, illegitimate agenda: to "exploit legitimate grievances." Social strife and conflict was viewed, as President Reagan noted, merely as opportunities for communists, "Marxist-Leninist bands," "terrorists" or "extremists," who "make no secret of their goal," which is "to exploit human suffering in Central America to strike at the heart of the Western Hemisphere."[35]

In a situation where the enemy's behavior was characterized in these terms, with the sole aim of undermining the US and its legitimate allies, the argument again exhibited a vigorous inner logic: social conditions could only be exploited by those labeled terrorists or extremists, and the advocacy of transformative, rapid, and/or violent social change was labeled terrorist or extremist. As President Reagan characterized El Salvador, "the problem is that an aggressive minority has thrown in its lot with the Communists, looking to the Soviets and their own Cuban henchmen to help them."[36] Therefore, even though the administration acknowledged that "problems of frail government institutions, of poverty, and of underdevelopment ... create vulnerabilities to this form of aggression [Cuban-backed violence]," they could ultimately conclude that social and political upheaval in Latin America resulted from communist adventurism.[37] Without that crucial component in the argumentation, the perspective offered by Reagan could not easily maintain its internal consistency. Such an ordering of the world did not merely allow for a place into which a villainized Castro could easily fit, he (or someone like him) was a necessary component. Again, consistent with the larger argument, the idea that a particular Castro was "invented" does not deny the argument that real threats existed, or that a plausible case cannot be made regarding American interests and principles. What it does imply is that there was a choice that had to be made about what was most important for the United States government to pursue. What followed from that choice was a particular mode of representation – of Castro and the Soviets – that supported those goals.

All that was needed to justify, rationalize and cement an interpretation characterized by imminent danger was communist subversion, "the deliberate use of force to spread tyranny" from Cuba and Nicaragua, and (sometimes only by unspoken, but obvious implication) the Soviet Union.[38] It was readily found by the Reagan administration in each of the societies said to be targeted by communists. First of all, the administration repeatedly announced to the American public that there was a great deal of evidence that Cuba had sent military equipment to aid to several revolutionary movements in the region (a fact which Castro often acknowledged).[39] Second, the policymakers already held the belief before they came to office that Castro's goals were to subvert and destroy legitimate governments in order in inaugurate tyranny, so there was already a bias to interpret Cuban behavior in a manner that supported their view. Thus, they needed only to look at Nicaragua, El Salvador, Guatemala or Colombia, all places where leftist organizations were seeking to oust established governments by means of violence, in order to reach the conclusions that confirmed their presumptions: Castro was supporting insurgencies, arming terrorists or subversives, (they were not described as revolutionaries), and spreading communism. He was "at once the source of supply and the catechist" of Central American upheaval.

Understanding Castro and Cuba in such terms, as dangerous and implacable, and as a necessary part of their foreign policy, the Reagan administration undertook a campaign to delegitimize its Cuban enemy and represent it as threatening. The advice of the Committee of Santa Fe was to establish a Radio Free Cuba and use extensive propaganda against the Cuban government. Should propaganda fail, "a war of national liberation against Castro should be launched."[40] Secretary of State Haig supported this option, but he was apparently the only one in the administration who pushed for such measures.[41] Rather, as the site of unrest, Central America was decided upon as the place for direct confrontation with communism. The task regarding Cuba involved a discussion of danger more that it did military confrontation. The Cuba that had established relations with many nations in the hemisphere and had dealings with the US, including the partial reestablishment of diplomatic relations, had its image partly remade, re-presented once again as the irresponsible firebrand that it was seen as in the 1960s, fomenting revolution and spreading communism. It was an image of danger, terror and subversion, in which Cuba was the source, catalyst and planner of revolutionary activity. This time, however, as opposed to 20 years before, Cuba was to be understood as a country with far more resources at its disposal and far more sophistication than in its previous efforts.

The image

An image, as the term is used here, is more than just a picture, but neither is it so fully-developed as to represent a concrete set of pre-conceived beliefs. They are instead, as Martha Cottam describes in *Images and Intervention*, "perceptual filters that organize our environment and enable us to predict and respond to that environment." Images function very much like stereotypes: they contain "facts" which are held as true, and they contain emotional responses. These things allow for the interpretation of others' behavior in terms of what it is already assumed to be known to an observer. This subsequently informs that observer what should be the response to that behavior.[42] Images help to order a world and make it a much more easily understandable place. At the same time, images are not a conceptual lock; they do not provide only stasis in one's understanding of another, but also reflect adaptation to changing behaviors and environments.

Certain states correspond to certain images, argues Cottam. The most familiar image is that of the enemy, and its most prominent representative in recent history has been the Soviet Union.

> When a state is perceived as an enemy it is attributed with evil intentions, harmful ambitions, and an insatiable desire to dominate and destroy. It and its people are seen as culturally strange and bad but sophisticated enough to be dangerous. The enemy is seen as powerful, as powerful as one's state and, therefore, not easily defeated; its aggression therefore cannot be treated lightly. Enemy regimes are assumed to be run by a cabal of evil geniuses who plan elaborate strategies and who wait patiently for their opportunity to put those plans into effect.[43]

Another image is that of the dependent, or client state, in which the image is that of a childlike people, incapable of making and implementing decisions without guidance from a more advanced, powerful state.[44] Countries of Latin America, as they have been seen over two centuries by American policymakers, correspond to the image of the dependent. Of course, an additional component is that a dependent state might be dependent upon an enemy. In the latter case the dependent harbors malevolence and threatening intentions, and these intentions allow the enemy to expand its influence. And even though the dependent country is restricted not only due to its inferiority, but by the relationship between the enemy and one's own country, its potential to wreak havoc is great. Like a child with matches, a dependent state, with its requisite irresponsibility, provides for the possibility of great danger, especially when it has at its disposal the resources and blessing of an enemy.[45]

Castro's Cuba seems to have been characterized simultaneously by two images: it was understood as both a pawn and a dangerous force in his own right. On the one hand, Castro was often portrayed in US circles as nothing more than a Soviet puppet, the quintessential example of a Moscow stooge. A joint State and Defense Department publication entitled *The Challenge to Democracy in Central America*, claims that Cuba is a "base for the Soviet Union in the Caribbean," and a "training center for would-be Castros." Cuba serves this role in the Soviet cause because "Moscow has delegated to a very willing Castro the task of training the majority of guerrillas and saboteurs" in the "international communist movement."[46] Thoroughly implicated in the efforts of the Kremlin, "Castro has not only been armed ... by his Soviet masters, he has also been inspired and tutored in the methods of totalitarianism by experts in Moscow."[47] Some characterizations went even further, describing Castro as little more than a gun for hire. "Moscow is assisting the activities of its Cuban proxy by underwriting Cuba at a cost of about $4 billion annually."[48] Often depicted as nothing more than a "vassal state," or a "surrogate," which had subordinated itself to the foreign policy goals of the Soviet Union, Cuba, by such formulations, was virtually freed from almost all responsibility for its actions. It was willingly under the control of an outside, powerful force. Understood in terms of an irresponsible but irrepressible inferior, the potential danger emanating from the island was perceived to be immense. It was at once in conflict with the US, well-supplied, and backward enough to be susceptible to the evil machinations of its patron and not use its capabilities responsibly. As the dependent of an even more powerful enemy, Cuba could be seen to have at its disposal all the resources of the Soviet Union, and hardly any of the restraints.

At the same time, however, if Cuba was considered a danger by virtue of its role at a Soviet pawn, this was only ever a temporary distinction that rarely seemed to last through a single speech or position paper. In many of the same State Department documents that call Castro a puppet, there is a seemingly unselfconscious shift from the representation of Castro as pawn to one of Castro as agent, in which he was attributed a great deal of responsibility for Cuban actions. Consequently, the American response necessarily had to be directed at Cuba. When Reagan came to office, the administration's efforts to "go to the source" of unrest in Central America were directed at Cuba, not the Soviet Union. While the Soviet Union no doubt approved of Cuban actions, they were most certainly viewed as *Cuba's* actions, or Castro's, who had been characterized and understood as an independent actor, a responsible agent capable of making decisions and carrying them out successfully.

If civil wars and social unrest in Central America were not considered, by definition, homegrown phenomena, then there had to be a responsible outside agent. As often as not, that provocateur was found in Cuba, not the USSR. For Cuba to be such a central focus of US hostility, it was necessary for Castro to be seen as a terrible and dangerous foe, to have his (undoubtedly scandalous) reputation precede him. Castro the international outlaw had to be properly constructed in order for him to occupy the appropriate place assigned to him by the Reagan team. What, from the US point of view, would be the logic in being so concerned with the puppet? A sensible policy would be focused upon the agent in control. Thus to be a legitimate target of US foreign policy, Castro had to also be an agent capable of making decisions and taking actions that were dangerous and threatening to the US. So while he may have been a workhorse for the Soviet Union, his perceived strength and success also made him an important player and his country a sizable power, and, subsequently, a target. It is not a weak pawn that is imagined as a Hitler, but a genuine threat, a worthy foe whose actions necessitate a swift, strong, uncompromising response, such as diplomatic isolation and economic embargo. As the State Department said in 1983, "The United States enjoys normal relations with many other nations which declare themselves to be Marxist-Leninist. We engage in trade with the Soviet Union ... our embargo policy has been and remains a correct and necessary instrument for containing the real challenge to the hemisphere which Cuba represents."[49] In these representations Cuba acquired the status of enemy: one who is seen as different in domestic polity and culture, evil in motivation, inflexible, and completely incompatible with the goals of the US.

The Kremlin was, by no means, innocent, but it was often marginalized. If Moscow was ultimately behind the better part of the world's mischief, it was not necessarily always in the lead. Plenty of examples sufficed to make the case, the most important being that the export of revolution in the Americas and in Africa was regarded as a Cuban initiative as much as it has a Soviet one.[50] The response to this was the assertion that Moscow helped Cuba with the "foreign policy mission that Castro was determined to carry out."[51] In this case it was Castro's mission, not the Soviet's. The State Department issued several reports with titles such as "Cuba's Renewed Support for Violence in Latin America" and "Dealing with the Reality of Cuba," in which the Soviet Union is given a supporting role in the distinctly Cuban efforts aimed at subversion. The fact that it is Cuba who is privileged as the foe in these documents lends further support to the notion that Cuba is a responsible agent. The words in the documents themselves also attribute various actions to Cuba. For example, "Castro is actively engaged in converting Nicaragua into another Cuba ... In El Salvador, Cuba acted to organize the groups of the far left."[52] "Castro has counseled the Sandinistas ... Cuba has orchestrated propaganda."[53] And "Cuba is manipulating and feeding violence in El Salvador."[54] Furthermore, the country is acknowledged as a "would-be foreign policy giant ceaselessly projecting political-military influence far beyond its borders."[55] The "Cuban campaign to promote insurgencies" is "planned and coordinated by the America Department of the Cuban Communist Party." And it is the Cubans, not the Soviets, who are charged with: uniting traditionally splintered radical groups, training ideologically committed cadres, supplying weapons to support the Cuban-trained cadres' efforts to assume power by force, encouraging terrorism, and using military aid and advisors to gain influence over radical governments through armed pro-Cuban Marxists.[56] Castro, in these representations, is the perfect example of an "evil genius who plans elaborate strategies" against the US. He has earned the distinction not merely because of the company he keeps, but by his own credentials as well. The Soviets get little credit (or blame) for these operations. With regard to places such as Nicaragua and El Salvador, Cuba is blamed for revolution much in the same way that the Soviets were often held responsible for Cuba. Occupying a conceptual space where it is both agent and puppet, the regime lies in an ambiguous place for American governments: somewhere between the perfect enemy and the perfect dependent.

Making the image stick

One of the first attempts the Reagan administration made with regard to instilling particular images about Central America came in its White Paper of February 1981, in which the new government sought to display the evidence against Cuba and its communist allies, to show how the international communist movement worked, and to use the example of El Salvador as a textbook case of communist subversion.[57] The White Paper not only reiterated the same assertions that Reagan and others did regarding the advance of communism, but in issuing it from the State Department, the new Reagan administration attempted to confer upon the views expressed an aura of institutional legitimacy. Authorship of the interpretation of global politics that had been emerging for a few years was now not merely personal, or in the minority, it had the weight and power of the United States government behind it. This was of great importance, as authority is often derived from one's institutional placement. Even more than that, leveling accusations of communist subversion from the halls of government allows the accusers to hide their sources and their evidence in the name of national security. Those who might ask for such evidence can be easily ignored or silenced with seemingly knowledgeable admonitions to trust those in positions of legitimate authority.

Perhaps the authors of the White Paper understood this too well, and did too little to make a reasonably convincing case that what they documented was indeed a "textbook case of indirect armed aggression by communist powers through Cuba." While it was claimed numerous times that communists are providing arms, training, direction and a "global propaganda campaign" in support of the Salvadoran insurgency, there is little actual evidence provided in the paper to support the claim. The bulk of what the document terms evidence is concerned with the trip of an anonymous person through Eastern Europe, Vietnam and Ethiopia, but assumed to be the leader of the Salvadoran Communist Party on a trip to procure arms. The information, considered "incontrovertible," was said to reveal "a highly disturbing pattern of parallel and coordinated action by a number of Communist and some radical countries" to overthrow the government of El Salvador. With an attempt to make a damning case in formalistic, bureaucratic sounding prose, yet with all the fervor marking the Reagan administration at the time, the document attributes such activities to "extremists" and "terrorists" who are coordinated and supported by their Cuban and Soviet allies, as well as "East Germany, Vietnam, and other communist states," and who are served by communist "worldwide propaganda networks."[58]

Several refutations of the White Paper were made in newspapers, periodicals and academic journals, each of them pointing to a variety of deficiencies in the document. Critics of the White Paper claimed that it did not at all substantiate the claim that "Cuba, the Soviet Union and other Communist states ... are carrying out what is clearly a well-coordinated, covert effort to bring about the overthrow of El Salvador's established government."[59] Instead, it resembled, in James Petras' words, "a political frame-up in which inconvenient facts are overlooked and innuendoes and unwarranted inferences are made at crucial points in the argument."[60] However, rather than reproduce the debate here and declare the critics winners once again, it suffices to say that, like the soldiers in Vietnam who were said to have never lost in a battle with the enemy, victory for the critics was irrelevant.

The White Paper is not a presentation of evidence, and may not have ever really been intended for that purpose. It is instead an effort aimed at the representation of communism in the attempt to help construct a world that fit the preconceptions held in the Reagan administration. Though it presents itself as the proof of Cuban subversion in Central America, what it really does is serve as an accusation. This is not to suggest that there was no connection, involvement or sympathy given the Salvadoran guerrillas by Castro. A great deal of military, financial and organizational aid was provided by Castro to the Nicaraguan government and the FMLN in El Salvador, and the interested parties have long since admitted their respective roles. However, the White Paper did not really have to portray an interest in the complex dealings of Central American strife so much as it had to tell a particular story about Cuban and Soviet subversion. The facts of the case could be assumed, implied or ignored, within limits. Thus there is no mention of the numerous social, political and civic movements that arose in El Salvador in the 1960s and 70s. Nor is any discussion made of the widespread poverty, inequality and repression that found its responses in a variety of organizations, among them the guerrillas. This is not surprising. These things did not fit into a story that necessarily dealt with communist subversion.

Still, this was not essential in the language that informed the White Paper. The task of the White Paper was not to reveal a problem, but to construct a problem that could be solved by the adaptation of policies the Reagan administration advocated. The Reagan Administration not only saw subversion, it sought it. Subversion was a necessary component for their understandings and actions. This is not to say that the Reagan team went looking for trouble, but that war in El Salvador could only be understood a problem of Cuban subversion and global communism once the American government made it one. As David Campbell describes, "danger is not an objective condition. It [sic] is not a thing which exists independently of those to whom it may become a threat ... Danger bears no essential necessary or unproblematic relation to the action or event from which it is said to derive." Ultimately, "danger is an effect of interpretation."[61] By Reagan's interpretation, the struggle against Cuba could be nothing other than a part of the struggle with the Soviet Union. The situation as the Reagan administration saw/sought it was one in which the Cubans, surviving only due to the Soviets, had taken a leading role in promoting subversion in Central America. The Soviets had no need to be overly involved except to deliver weapons because their proxy in the Western Hemisphere was coordinating the effort.

The Cuban threat

If the White Paper failed as evidence of communist subversion, it did serve the Reagan administration well in that it helped to set the parameters of the debate about Cuba, communism and the Soviet Union. It worked to place the Cubans more completely into the international communist movement as examples of the communist threat that had to be combated in the Cold War. The presence of this adversary necessitated perpetual vigilance, which required a continual telling and retelling of the story of the US and its Cuban enemy in order to normalize and naturalize the distinctions and the enmity. It was up to the US government not only to battle such an enemy, but to continually imagine and produce an enemy worth such attention and effort. There was rarely a kind or compromising word to be uttered regarding Cuba. The country was defined and produced as a threat by both a hostile American policy and by the use of a language of difference, in which Cuba represented entirely the opposite of all the United States embodied.

What emerged and eventually stabilized as the picture of Cuba was a country that was the "only" one in the hemisphere that rejected the principles "fundamental to a peaceful order." These principles, as articulated by then-Vice President Bush, included: respect for national sovereignty and self-determination, respect for the rights of people in a free society, noninterference in internal affairs, and collective defense against aggression. Instead, it brought to the hemisphere "the ideology of the Soviet Union with a commitment to spread totalitarianism in its own image."[62] Using "great subtlety and sophistication" to "destabilize fragile governments," Cuba "has been systematically creating a machine for the destruction of established institutions and governments."[63] The repetition of these kinds of words, the continual rearticulation of Cuba as evil enemy, contributed to the production and perpetuation of the stark dichotomy necessary for the successful portrayal of a Cuba without any redeeming qualities and thus deserving of American hostility.

A closer look at this type of representation reveals several assumptions and implications that are implicit in the language. The use of the word "only" serves to set Cuba apart from all other nations in the region. Isolated in the Western Hemisphere – where freedom "is the birthright of the people," where, as President Reagan proclaimed, the people "share the fundamental values of G-d, family, work, freedom, democracy and justice" and a healthy dislike for foreign ideologies – Cuba, and its disregard for the principles "fundamental to a peaceful order," is juxtaposed to all those labeled as free, peace loving democracies in the region.[64] The unspoken implication of representing Cuba as a solitary actor is clear: there is no legitimacy in solitude. A country that stands alone does so for a reason. No one wants to befriend a rotten regime. Thus Cuba stands not simply against the United States, but all the Americas.

This characterization of Cuba as alone is curious because at the time this statement was made, the Cubans had a close ally in the Sandinista government in Nicaragua. This troublesome detail – a Cuban ally in the hemisphere – provided additional participants in the enemy camp, hampering the ability to portray Cuba as evil by virtue of its obvious isolation. However, it was possible for the Reagan team to rewrite the role of Nicaragua when this served the necessary purpose. Rather than characterize the country as an ally or an equal to Cuba, much less a sovereign entity with the same international rights as the United States, the administration rhetorically converted Nicaragua into a lesser entity, "a forward base of operations," a "territory to provide training and other facilities to guerrillas active in neighboring countries," and a "staging site for a massive Cuban-directed flow of arms to Salvadoran guerrillas."[65] Nicaragua's purpose seemed most often to be, according to the United States, to serve the interests of Cuba and the international communist movement. The Nicaraguan government was represented here as at best, as a puppet, or worse, nonexistent, in similar ways that Castro and Cuba were sometimes portrayed with respect to the Soviet Union. With Nicaragua, the country, swept aside in favor of Nicaragua, the staging site, "only" Cuba is left as the sole agent in the enemy camp in this conflict. (However, when portraying the strength of the enemy was of paramount concern, Nicaragua was included as more of an equal member of the enemy camp, right alongside not only Cuba, but the Soviet Union. If it was the case that Nicaragua would be elevated from the level of "base" or "staging site," it usually received a sizable promotion. In a single speech by Reagan, he speaks of Nicaragua as a "base" for "the Soviets and their own Cuban henchmen," and of "Nicaraguan intimidation" of Costa Rica, completely ignoring the shift in the status of Nicaragua.[66]

Of course, Cuba was not completely alone. The country was not nearly strong and capable enough to withstand the collective challenge from all the Americas without its Soviet sponsor. Castro had imported "the ideology of the Soviet Union with a commitment to spread totalitarianism." It had to, by definition, be an import, because no such thing as 'American' communism was acknowledged to exist. The implicit consequence of speaking about communism as a foreign import speaks to a suspicion, often aroused in the United States, of things that are foreign, which are often suspect simply because of their foreign-ness. By locating the sources of communism outside of the United States and outside the Western Hemisphere, its status as the most obvious and dangerous of all imports is fortified. Thus it becomes as deserving of at least as much scorn as any other product dumped into the American market.

Furthermore, in this imagining communism could only have met with success in the Americas with the help of an outside agent. The idea that troubles are caused by an external force has been a consistent theme in American politics. The assumption is that people who are left to their own devices, save rabble-rousers and scoundrels, have no natural antagonism or conflict of interest with the US. As former Secretary of State Dean Rusk said, "if every nation were genuinely independent, and left alone to work out its relations with its neighbors by common agreement, the tensions between Washington and Moscow would vanish overnight."[67] However as Richard Drinnon points out in *Facing West*, Moscow has been only one of many devils confronting Americans in their history. If it was not the devil himself at the root of bad behavior in the colonial and federal periods, then it was the French or the British. Their most pernicious influence was on the Native Americans, who like Cubans after them, were considered by white Americans to be inferior and childlike. Content and incapable of self-assertion, their stirrings could only have been the result of meddling, interference and manipulation by outside agitators.[68] Children, inferiors and dependent countries are supposed to do what is expected of them. When they act in an unexpected, unfamiliar or rebellious way, the assumption in the US has often been to attribute the cause of that behavior to some third party who has managed to dupe and thus control them.[69] According to this image, troublesome children are incapable of possessing their own self-will and determination. They are almost always pawns of some greater power, whose intelligence is superior, and whose intentions are, without question, sinister.

The foreign-ness of communism serves an additional task as well: it takes the burden of responsibility off of Cuba, or more accurately, off of the general population of Cuba. If communism is not intrinsic to the Western Hemisphere, if it would never arise here itself, then it must be imposed to take hold. And this in turn implies its illegitimacy, for it would never have to be imposed were it accepted and acceptable. It would have developed on its own were that the case, as an expression of the popular will and democratic efforts. Thus Ronald Reagan and US presidents from Eisenhower to Obama have spoken of "the Cuban people" as an entity distinct from "the Castro regime" or "the communist-controlled government." When President Eisenhower cut off diplomatic relations with Cuba in 1960, he stated that his "sympathy goes out to the people of Cuba now suffering under the yoke of a dictator."[70] Two years later Dean Rusk told the Organization of American States (OAS) that "we have no quarrel with the people of Cuba ... we look forward to the day when a free and progressive government will flourish in Havana, and the Cuban people can join with us in the common undertakings of the hemisphere."[71] And still, 20 years later, in spite of Castro's continued effectiveness in arousing nationalist-inspired sympathy for his government, President Reagan stated that we would "pledge ourselves to the freedom of the noble, long-suffering, Cuban people."[72]

The implication is apparent: true 'Americans' do not believe in communism, they do not support it, and any 'American' who lives under it does so against his will. All 'Americans' are alike in their preferences for freedom, democracy and liberty, as the US defines them. Even Castro's tyranny cannot undo this. As President Reagan claimed, "over two decades of communism have not eradicated the traditional Cuban love of liberty and tolerance for diversity which is part of the hemisphere's common Western heritage."[73] The assumption made here is that if the Cuban people were free to choose their own government, they would choose a US-style democracy with a leader friendly to the US because the interests and desires of the people of the US and of Cuba are identical. It was thus axiomatic in the Reagan administration that the Cuban people were antagonistic to the Castro regime.

If the people of Cuba had no interest in the spread of communism according to the US portrayal of the situation, then the enemy was further narrowed. It lay not really in all of Cuba, but in the government, or ultimately with Castro. As the leader of Cuba and the small, unelected government of extremists, he had delivered an unsuspecting country to the communists. Cuba, by such formulations, was not an independent country. It was not free. Rather, it was controlled by those who were "armed and directed by a faraway power, seek[ing] to impose a philosophy that is alien to everything in which we believe."[74] Nothing about the Cuban revolution is given any standing as a local, home-grown phenomenon. It is simply an outgrowth of the Soviet Union, "with a commitment to spread totalitarianism in its own image." Imposed by extremists, wedded to a foreign ideology, and supported by the Soviets, it is understood in such a way that it is prohibited from maintaining a legitimate standing in the Western Hemisphere.

Instead, Cuban communism is represented nothing less than "a new colonialism" that had to be removed from the Americas as was the old colonialism.[75] Castro may have been a native Cuban, but he was not an 'American.' He was wedded only by nationality to other 'Americans,' but that was the point where any affinity ended. Ideologically, where it mattered most to the US government, he was attached to the Soviet Union. Instead, Castro himself was considered a colonizer, and his far-flung adventures were called "Castroite colonial expansion." As this hemisphere had long since been declared closed to further colonization, such a characterization of Castro and the Soviets led to the logical conclusion, embodied in the text and the spirit of the Monroe Doctrine, that they and their influence must be removed.

Removing such an enemy was not deemed to be an easy task. As much as the US government went at length to discuss communist societies as failures, highlighting themes of political illegitimacy, economic weakness, and the need to continually be involved in expansion as a way of preventing internal contradictions from undermining the regime, it had to emphasize with equal or greater urgency the strengths of these societies. This is the paradox embodied in the picture discussed at the beginning of the chapter. Strength in the enemy was just as necessary as weakness. Otherwise US policy would seem pointless.

As a result the enemy was attributed with "great subtlety and sophistication." The Cubans were said to maintain a "large and sophisticated propaganda network," and to employ "a sophisticated strategy" for overthrowing governments. Generally, these kinds of statements were made without elaboration. Reference to an enemy who "unleashes its global propaganda machine" creates a greater threat than listing specifics, much as the Committee of Santa Fe report enjoyed greater rhetorical force by emphasizing the danger from a regional communist network as opposed to the danger from Guyana, Jamaica and Grenada. Nonetheless, the details that are provided were well-scripted to have the maximum effect. For example, in documents produced during the Reagan era, Cuba "tailors" sports competitions, youth and cultural festivals, and special scholarships for the purpose of providing "channels to identify potential agents for intelligence and propaganda operations." It "uses Mexico as a base for coordination of propaganda on behalf of insurgents." The Soviets help in the efforts by employing its "extensive propaganda network selectively to discredit governments." In addition, the Cubans provide political training at a variety of their schools in which "carefully selected foreign students" are admitted for "indoctrination." Insurgents are given military training in Cuba at camps "dedicated specifically" to such activities, and some Cubans are trained to conduct "clandestine operations." All these things are said to show that Cuba's "infrastructure for intensified revolutionary agitation in Latin America is a multifaceted yet carefully coordinated mechanism."[76]

The language of the mechanism, or the "machine for the destruction of established institutions and governments everywhere" further underscores the potential evil. It appeals to a sense of the machine as cold, unfeeling, threatening, and increasingly able to take control away from the individual. Ultimately, in the form of nuclear weapons, it can destroy all human life. This imagery gives the impression that the Cubans and the Soviets have created a power that is strong, impersonal, relentless and yet still adjustable, with an aim to destroy that which is legitimate, and thus worthy of preservation.

Moreover, these actions became conflated into even greater travesties and dangers due to their characterization as premeditated acts of a foe who is completely aware of what he is doing and why he is doing it. The enemy is given added attributes of evil as one who has known his goals all along and has engineered strategies to achieve them.[77] As the manifestation of this image, the Soviets and their allies are seen to have been patient, waiting for the right opportunity, the moment of weakness (much of the 1970s) to act. This is what makes for "great subtlety and sophistication." At the same time, these two attributes reinforce the idea of the enemy's self-awareness. In other words, self-awareness implies sophistication, while sophistication in turn implies self-awareness. By contrast, American actions (or the lack of them) were characterized in terms of naiveté, resulting simply from innocence, the fact that the United States does not possess the same kind of evil intentions which are the hallmark of the other side. The United States of the 1970s and 1980s is represented as either complacent or unsuspecting, while the enemy is busy at work, establishing, in President Reagan's words, a "hostile military presence on our border." As Reagan said to emphasize the danger, "they know this. They have written about this. We have been slow to understand that the defense of the Caribbean and Central America against Marxist-Leninist takeover is vital to our national security in ways we're not accustomed to thinking about."[78]

The tables have been turned here, whereby the United States is described as the victim of an adversary who is, in another formulation, ultimately destined to succumb to American strength and the institutions of freedom. This understanding is completely contradictory to the notion that the United States is advanced and that Cuba is backward or underdeveloped. However, it is not unusual. As Richard Drinnon points out in another example of what he called an "innate illogic," the same contradictory characteristics were bestowed upon the Vietcong and enemies of the US going all the way back to the first Indian wars.[79] It is a necessary contradiction though, and one that must be ignored for the US to carry out its policies. Without the cabal of evil geniuses carefully plotting the overthrow of the free world, the enemy stands a chance of not appearing dangerous enough.

If "subtlety and sophistication" were not enough to convince, then heavier, more blunt instruments could be used to convey the extent to which danger was present. One of these instruments was to refer to the connection between the Soviet Union and Cuba as the "Moscow-Havana Axis."[80] An invention wholly of the Reagan administration's making, it was the next logical step beyond the Munich analogy: going from imagining the Communists as being very much like Nazis to imagining them actually as Nazis.[81] This completes the argument, taking us back to the beginning of the chapter and the photograph of Castro. In addition to the characterizations of communism as a threat in its own right, on top of all the imagery and language of Russians, Marxists and Communists, there was also the not-so-subtle association of communism with Nazism. As Cuba was part of an axis, and Castro saluted like Hitler, it signified that Castro's placement in the enemy camp was total. He could possess no redeeming values. The attempt to make the connection to Nazism represented a further attempt to marginalize dissent and define the terms of debate. If, during the Reagan administration, there existed no clear consensus on the extent of the danger emanating from the Soviet bloc, there was a consensus about the danger faced during what has been called "the good war." No convincing argument could be made that fighting against the Nazis was a mistake. Therefore anyone who was, or acted like, or could be associated with a Nazi was worthy of American enmity and a hostile US policy.

The dual challenge to the United States

This characterization of Cuba as it existed to those in the Reagan administration serves to furnish a set of attitudes, prejudices, representations and constructions of respective US and Cuban identities as they have been predominantly understood in the United States in the context of the Cold War and anti-communism. The representations of Cuba as a communist nation form the second of the two domains in which Cuba has existed as an object of American foreign policy. Since Castro came to power, the island has occupied a particular conceptual space with regard to two overarching themes: US dominance in Latin America and Cold War anti-communism. While these two sites of political contestation have been represented here as different spheres of American foreign policy, they have been by no means mutually exclusive. Rather, since the end of World War II, they have often converged to produce an especially sharp US reaction in places such as Guatemala, the Dominican Republic, Chile, Nicaragua, Grenada and especially Cuba.

Communism in a Latin American country, or at least the perception of it, was seen to present a problem of special significance for the US. Regardless of the fact that this was an age of nuclear missiles, in which there was the possibility of immediate, assured destruction regardless of a missile's origin, the establishment of a communist government in the Western Hemisphere, an ideological soulmate to the greatest American adversary in history, was something considered to be far less tolerable than a communist government in other parts of the world. Even if nuclear annihilation could be avoided, the neighborhood would still be threatened. A more traditional idea of security, that which emphasizes proximity and the possibilities for harm based on that proximity, held sway throughout the Cold War with regard to Latin America. Compounding security concerns were America's ideological leanings. Anti-communism easily maintained its strength as long as there were communists to confront. Also, by the post-war era Monroe's Doctrine of a common Western Hemisphere was historically enshrined as virtually immutable, even if great transformations in global politics had rendered it unusable as a working policy. There was little during the Cold War to challenge the special status of Latin America in the eyes of US policymakers.

While the anti-communist inclination was the most prevalent feature of American foreign policy since World War II, America's Cold War and imperialist outlooks simultaneously contained and subsumed one another. Each could be made to fit comfortably within the framework of the other. When they combined for the first time in Guatemala, President Eisenhower and Secretary of State John Foster Dulles objected to a "Communist-type reign of terror," but especially to one "on this continent."[82] Kennedy pointed to the problems in Cuba in which "Communist agents seeking to exploit that region's peaceful revolution of hope have established a base on Cuba," and made clear that "Communist domination in this hemisphere can never be negotiated."[83] Ronald Reagan was especially adamant about the spread of communism in the region, saying of Nicaragua that "the United States must deny the Soviets a beachhead in North America," as "the Soviets and the Cubans [could] become the dominant power in the crucial corridor between North and South America. Established there, they will be in a position to threaten the Panama Canal, interdict our Caribbean sea lanes, and ultimately, move against Mexico."[84]

These interwoven concerns reflect both the assumption of regional hegemony and the commitment to anti-communism. Communism is seen as an immediate threat to US security and well-being *because* of its presence in the hemisphere. It is spreading on *this* continent, establishing a beachhead in North America, finding a nearby base. Whether the scenarios envisioned by President Reagan and others were likely or not, the American government treated them as possibilities to be averted. The undesirability of communism in Latin America was taken for granted, but the particular cause for alarm came from its proximity, from the fact that the potential for mischief was so close, "on our doorstep." Hence, it was the job of the United States to rid the region of this threat as the US had done in the past with a variety of other menaces.

At the same time, one can read these statements and see communism as the overriding concern. US foreign policy speeches and documents during the Cold War made reference to the Soviet Union and communism with great frequency. Since US security was a function of political developments around the globe, not confined to one region or country, Latin America was just another place, albeit a special one, where the battle was fought. Enemies in this hemisphere were certainly a problem, but communist enemies in particular were not to be tolerated simply because they were communist and, by definition, sympathetic to the Soviet Union.

These two considerable strains in American foreign policy, anti-communism and regional hegemony, left little room for challenges. There was scant precedent for US restraint in its relations with the rest of the hemisphere even before the Soviet Union was identified as a threat. When these two overriding concerns became joined as part of US efforts to stop the spread of communism in Latin America, the prospects for the US tolerating a challenge diminished even further.

This is precisely what has happened in Cuba. These two themes intersected. The US found itself faced with two simultaneous adversaries in one Cuban government: a Soviet client state and ally, and an independent and troublesome neighbor. Castro's success in challenging US hegemony in Cuba while turning to communism and the Soviets provided the United States with a single location where the attributes that secured American superiority in the region meshed with those that were central to the struggle against communism. Cuba was simultaneously inferior, underdeveloped, dangerous and illegitimate. Castro leads the only government that ever successfully challenged the US simultaneously in the Cold War and in the regional hierarchy. By violating the limits of hemispheric intransigence to the US and transforming Cuba into a communist state allied with the Soviet Union, Castro made a double challenge distinct in its completeness. He snubbed the United States in the two areas, which combined, could "never be negotiated." The result of this convergence, and what serves to elucidate the intense and unyielding reaction on the part of the US, was an amplification of US hostility and intolerance, producing in Cuba a new entity, often termed "the Cuban problem." While the US confrontation with Cuba took place within the context of the Cold War, it was at the same time its own battle, coloring American policies toward Cuba in ways that were absent in policies toward other Marxist regimes in Europe, Asia and Africa.

An understanding of the relationship between the United States and Cuba as a combination or intersection of these two themes serves to clarify how this bitter and intense confrontation has characterized US-Cuban relations since the ascendancy of Fidel Castro. This reading of two American histories shows how the "mythical speech" had already established the boundaries of this territory, providing the possibilities for such an acute reaction. There were particular understandings of America's role in the world, spelled out in speeches and official documents, regarding both Latin America and the Soviets. The vigorous and simultaneous challenge of these two world views by Cuba placed Castro's government in a position vis-á-vis the United States that has not been paralleled (in scope and length of time) by any other regime in the world.

Furthermore, the unyielding hostility that this circumstance generated has not vanished despite of the end of the Cold War. Rather, the image of Castro and the Cuban revolution constructed by the Reagan administration continues to exhibit many of the same elements in the post-Cold War era, even though what seems to have been one of the major determinants of American policy has ceased to exist.

5   Waiting for Fidel ... and now Raúl

The Castro dictatorship cannot and will not survive.

President George H.W. Bush[1]

He can't last forever. Nobody lives forever.

President Bill Clinton[2]

The reports of my death are greatly exaggerated.

Mark Twain

"What's the difference?" goes the punchline to a Cuban joke concerning Fidel's exhortations of "Socialism or death!" Aside from the gallows humor in pointing out the dire straits that many Cubans have found themselves in amidst shortages and economic hardship, the joke serves to remind one that, even if socialism is death, it is still the case that socialism is not quite dead yet. Proclamations by presidents Bush, Clinton, Bush and Obama notwithstanding, in addition to many members of Congress and a large number of Cuban-Americans, reports of the Cuban revolution's demise have been greatly exaggerated for years.

The response of the US government to Castro's endurance, and his regime, which has been led by Raúl Castro since 2006, is to not only continue doing what it has done for decades, but up until the arrival of President Obama, to intensify the efforts. Seeking to outlast Fidel Castro and the Cuban revolution, while also attempting to hasten its collapse, the US continues to enforce the economic embargo while passing legislation to strengthen it. It has further limited the amount of money that people in the United States can send to relatives in Cuba. It has tightened the travel ban. It has pursued the diplomatic isolation of Cuba by calling on third countries to cut off trade and friendly relations. And it maintains a war of words, representing the Cuban revolution as anathema to the United States. The exception to this effort has been to allow shipments of food and medicine to Cuba.

In particular, the goal has been to try and fatally weaken the Cuban economy and by extension the Cuban government, which seemed all the more possible with the disappearance of the Soviet Union. The logic, as formulated in Washington, is that an "influx of hard currency from the United States [or anywhere, for that matter] could allow the regime to resist change and stay afloat for years longer."[3] This was the rationale for the adoption of the *Cuban Democracy Act of 1992,* the *Cuban Liberty and Democratic Solidarity (Libertad) Act of 1996,* (also known as the Helms-Burton Act), and a variety of restrictions on travel and remittances over the years. Each of these measures have tried to further cut off any assistance to Cuba by ending trade between Cuba and subsidiaries of US companies in third countries, by punishing companies around the globe that do business with Cuba, and by limiting the flow of dollars coming to Cuba from the US. The two laws passed in the 1990's tried to force companies to either do business with Cuba or the United States, knowing that companies do not want to be excluded from the US market. As President George H.W. Bush said in his support of the *Cuban Democracy Act,* "I'm not going to let others prop up Castro with aid or some sweetheart trade deal."[4]

President Obama (whose policies toward Cuba will be addressed in the next chapter) is the eleventh US president to confront the Cuban revolution, the latest in a succession of American administrations simply waiting for Fidel, and now Raúl, to finally fall under the weight of American pressure, if not the weight of communism itself. Perhaps it seems certain that the Cuban regime will finally fall, but such certainty has been repeatedly proven wrong over the years.[5] A cartoon that appeared in *Newsweek* seemed to best capture the nature of the American dilemma with regard to the island. It depicts a caricature of every president from Eisenhower to Clinton, each reciting one word in the sentence, "Don't worry, Fidel Castro will fall any minute now."[6] If Castro dutifully, and predictably, followed the Soviet and Eastern European lead for many years, his refusal to do in the wake of their demise has been a source of consternation to many in the US who wish to rid the world of one of the last remaining communist regimes.

Critics of the US have asked what the point is in seeking to further injure a regime that poses no imaginable physical threat to the United States, and in which the people are suffering from severe economic adversity. They argue that there is no tangible American interest that this policy serves other than punishment of Cuba or, more importantly, electoral support from Florida. As Rubén Berríos argued in plain terms several years ago, "the only barrier that has discouraged the lifting of the embargo is a Cuban-American constituency that votes and has given political donations to the past five administrations," and his argument still rings true to this day among opponents of US policy.[7] Moreover, this critique submits that the continuation of American policy serves to ultimately undermine America's real interests in the region: the promotion of democracy and the prevention of social chaos, which could result in a refugee crisis in South Florida. Walter Russell Mead has made this argument, noting that "before and since Castro took power, Washington's Cuba policy has, except in times of crisis, been left in the hands of special interest groups whose agendas were not always in the interests of either country." He concluded that "US policy toward Cuba is increasing the chances for a volcanic future and decreasing what is already a marginal chance for the emergence of stable democracy," and that "violence and instability on the island will provoke similar problems in Florida."[8] Or as Louis Perez has observed, even though "the purpose of sanctions has been to politicize hunger and to foment popular disaffection in the hope that ... Cubans would rise up against their government," and that sanctions have worked in creating hardship, it is also the case that this has not led to revolt, but to a situation where, "a people utterly prostrate, preoccupied with matters of survival as the overriding reality of daily life, are not readily disposed to think about elections."[9]

As has been emphasized earlier, to say that US policy toward Cuba reflects the significance of domestic politics is correct, but only partially so. Such critiques stop short of addressing what has been posited here as central to an understanding of American foreign policy. If interests reflect what one wants, what one wants depends upon who one is, and who one is concerns the establishment and continual affirmation of identity in contrast to the differences of another. The two, identity and difference, are inseparable. This dichotomous understanding of oneself and one's adversaries has been skillfully deployed in the United States by American political leaders and elements of the Cuban community who advocate the use of economic sanctions in order to weaken Castro and the Cuban revolution. As President George W. Bush stated in his announcement in 2004 of a new "Freedom Fund" for a transition to democracy, "Trade with Cuba under the current regime would merely enrich the elites in power and strengthen their grip. Congress should show their support and solidarity for fundamental change in Cuba by maintaining our embargo on the dictatorship until that change comes."[10] Characterizing their efforts as a struggle for democracy, liberty and free enterprise, they have successfully appropriated some of the most powerful attributes of American identity as their own. At the same time, these advocates have been equally successful in representing their opponents as apologists of Castro, unwitting defenders of communism, or obstacles to the attainment of democracy in Cuba. According to such formulations, to reach an accommodation with Fidel or Raúl, to restore full relations, to end the embargo, to recognize the Cuban revolution as legitimate, is to challenge a particular understanding of an American identity, and thus American interests.

A focus on this interpretation of US-Cuban relations and the representations that nourish it does not submit that the concerns of establishing and maintaining identity are distinct from the dynamics of American domestic politics, and that such a focus provides a better explanation of American foreign policy. Rather, it suggests that the aims of domestic politics – raising campaign contributions and winning votes – are not only ends in and of themselves, but are also manifestations of an American politics, international and domestic, that is grounded in a language of ideals, rights, democracy and American strength. Addressing the dynamics of domestic politics does not represent a faulty mode of analysis of US foreign policy, only a limited focus on certain features of politics characterized by the themes addressed earlier (exceptionalism, democratic ideals, inter-American solidarity, developmentalism, and anti-communism). It does not address how these themes have bolstered a powerful mode of representation in American domestic and foreign policy.

An example of this point is that some of the greatest sources of support for taking greater action to undermine Castro have come from Congress. Yet many of the members who are the greatest opponents of Castro come not from Florida, but from regions with few Cuban-American voters. Congressman Robert Torricelli, a sponsor of The Cuban Democracy Act of 1992, which was directed at tightening the embargo on Cuba, served a district with few Cuban-American residents. The same was true of North Carolina's Senator Jesse Helms, another sponsor of such legislation, the *Cuban Liberty and Democratic Solidarity (Libertad) Act of 1996*. More recent, and less well-known examples, include the 2009 resolution calling for democracy in Cuba, introduced in the House of Representatives by Congressman Todd Tiahrt of Kansas, and legislation offered by Senator John Ensign of Nevada to approve the Cuba Transition Act of 2006.[11] Whether these and other members of Congress were truly convinced that Castro's government represents the evil they depict or were only cynical manipulators who said the right things to obtain money from supporters is not considered here to be of the utmost significance. What is significant is that they are drawing from, and adding to, a discourse inclusive of meanings and assumptions that are deeply embedded in prevalent understandings of American identity, in which "Americans think of themselves as a people who enjoy freedom, opportunity, and all the institutions of representative government and rights provided by the Constitution," and that "American security is dependent on propagating democracy."[12] The rhetoric of American values, democracy, exceptionalism, and opposition to communism or totalitarianism continues to be effective in American politics, as these ideals occupy a central place in the political discourse of United States, embracing what Michael Shapiro calls the "operational terms of the powerful."[13]

The pervasiveness and embeddedness of these representations of Cuba reinforces a continuity in US policy after the Cold War. American foreign policy may indeed involve a "struggle related to the production and reproduction of identity." However, it is not inevitable that the end of the Cold War has involved a reappraisal of that struggle. As Campbell notes, "while the objects of established post-1945 strategies of otherness may no longer be plausible candidates for enmity, their transformation has not by itself altered the entailments of identity which they satisfied."[14] In fact, that identity was strengthened by the collapse of the Soviet Union, an event that fostered a representation of a successful United States that won the Cold War. It vindicated the view that the outcome of the Cold War signified a victory for democracy, freedom, liberty, capitalism, free markets, individualism, anti-communism and American strength and leadership, all in ways that the United States has historically interpreted these things. It is not necessary for these identifications to be altered in order for them to be successfully redeployed against new or lingering examples of global danger.

If the entailments of American identity have not changed since the end of the Cold War, neither have the characteristics that constitute Cuban differences. With respect to both inter-American relations and the confrontation with communism, Cuba maintains a consistent relationship to the United States. As was discussed in earlier chapters, Latin America, and Cuba in particular, continue to be represented and engaged as an inferior relation to the United States. In addition, Cuba is still represented in terms that emphasize its illegitimacy. Therefore it remains an entity that is viewed in the US as an obstacle and a threat to democracy, human rights and the realization of legitimate international norms.

It follows from these considerations (that the characteristic features of American and Cuban identities have not been altered) that a fundamental reorientation of American foreign policy is not necessary after the politics of the Cold War. As American leaders have interpreted the US role in a post-Soviet world, danger involves new sources such as Iran and North Korea (and Iraq up until 2003). These places have taken the place of Soviet communism as a threat to American interests and values. At the same time, these new enemies from which danger emanates are not entirely new, only a redefinition of earlier dangers. David Campbell notes how this process evolves, stating that in the US, "there has always been more than one referent around which danger has crystallized. What appears as new is more often than not the emergence to the fore of something previously obscured by that which has faded away or become less salient."[15] If communism was seen in the US as the greatest threat to the world for almost 50 years, it was also understood as only one particular kind of the greater threat to global peace: non-democracy. The absence of a liberal order in the form of communism was dangerous, according to the premises of US policy, but so too was the fascist threat before it. Now, with the disappearance of a communist threat, that same absence in any other form continues to represent dangerous possibilities, be they in Iraq, North Korea, Russia, the Balkans, China, Iran or Cuba. Grounded in this post-Cold War understanding of threats that are both old and new, American foreign policy, as a set of practices which serve to constitute and secure identity through the negation of differences, is made to seem consistent by policymakers, allowing for continuity in its representation.

Cuban illegitimacy – The focal point of US policy

Cuba fares especially poorly in the post-Cold War era, as the revolution represents both the old enemy in the threat from communism, and the new one in which it is readily subsumed as an example of a non-democratic nation that provides no freedom for its citizens and seeks to undermine the norms governing international relations. Thus, in the rhetoric of US leaders, there are elements of both old and new. Statements by American officials may rarely use the word communism anymore, but this is because the practice is not necessary for characterizing difference. One State Department publication, released not long after the fall of the Soviet Union, stated that "our policy toward Cuba remains consistent with our worldwide policy of support for democracy and human rights."[16] The shift in language began soon after the Cold War ended, and has remained consistent. A review of several speeches and statements on Cuba by Presidents Obama and George W. Bush found that the two repeatedly used terms such as freedom, human rights and democracy. However, the words communist or communism appeared only once in their remarks.[17] The US is not, in this formulation, fighting an old, perhaps unnecessary battle, it is engaged in the same struggle that characterizes US policy in many other places around the world, in defense of principles and objectives few could argue with. This representation is intended to sustain the placement of Castro and his revolution in a category that includes regimes considered to be illegitimate.

The idea that Castro's revolution is illegitimate maintains special importance after the Cold War, as it has become the focal point of US opposition and hostility, its central organizing principle. The Cuban government is understood as illegitimate and denying the freedom to its citizens, while US policy seeks a virtuous and just alternative. In the United States, the idea of illegitimacy has historically been grounded in two places. The first site involves the institutions of representative constitutional democracy, "in which the state is accountable to its citizens and the citizens have rights against the state." This is expressed in a "concern with human rights, freedom, the entitlements of citizenship, and competitive elections."[18] The second of these sites can be referred to, in simple terms, as "the free market" which valorizes a liberal, capitalist economic order. The success inherent in their combination has been considered axiomatic in official discourse, as both are said to involve "the true political and economic empowerment of the people themselves."[19] Moreover, these sources of legitimacy not only characterize the domestic concerns of American leaders, but international politics as well, a condition labeled by Sheldon Wolin as "Operation Democracy." As Wolin notes, "ever since World War I, when Woodrow Wilson justified America's entrance into the war under the slogan of 'making the world safe for democracy,' it has been commonplace for American presidents and political leaders to claim democracy both as an objective or end that justifies the use of state power and as a subject or agent whose will – because it is a democratic will – legitimates that end."[20]

This set of assumptions has been at the center of the American inclination to "export democracy," to encourage others, by suasion or coercion, to "elect good men" who would pursue a whole set of practices beneficial or advantageous to the United States.[21] For in these practices, involving the maintenance of political and economic liberalism, lie legitimacy. Their absence, by contrast, are considered to be signs of illegitimacy. In the case of Cuba, this absence is particularly important in the post-Cold War era, for the lack of a physical threat to the US from anything Cuban other than refugees has propelled representations of Castro's illegitimacy to the fore, whereby they became more significant than Cuba's status as a security risk. In other words, the Cuban problem after the Cold War has consisted less in what Castro did than in what he, and now his brother, are. In this construction of a Cuban identity, which justifies hostile US action, the idea of what is threatening takes on an added dimension. "The threat is posed not merely by *actions* the other might take to injure or defeat … but by the very visibility of its mode of *being* as other."[22] This threat is clearly not physical, but it is still a political one. The revolution's durability, by its very survival, continues to represent a challenge to the United States, and to an American understanding of the proper place of each country in hemispheric and global politics.

Cuba's perceived mode of being – which includes those characteristics that are regarded in the US as the signs of the revolution's illegitimacy – revolves around two themes. The first concerns the practices of the regime itself, specifically, the idea that the government is totalitarian, denying the freedoms and human rights of its citizens. The second indicator of illegitimacy involves the characteristics of the regime. These qualities, three of which are examined here, reflect the circumstances of a post-Cold War setting. They include the representations that the Cuban revolution is dying entity, a failed experiment that is destined to fail like other communist regimes, and a country isolated from the rest of the world, which has increasingly turned toward liberal democracy.

Castro's crimes

Prior to the 1990s, the United States identified its differences with the Cuban revolution primarily in terms of the country's foreign policy – Cuban communism was viewed as a threat to American global interests. In the 1960s, the two greatest impediments to an improved relationship with the US were Cuba's support for revolutionary movements around the globe, especially in Latin America and the Caribbean, and Cuba's ties to the Soviet Union. In the 1970s, two more conditions were added to the list. Cuban troops had to be removed from Africa (Angola and Ethiopia) where Cuban forces were "used as a surrogate for Soviet geopolitical objectives."[23] And finally, the Cuban government had to make improvements on respecting its citizens' human rights, a condition added by the Carter administration, and the only one which did not specifically address Cuban foreign policy.

In 1994, the State Department's *Background Notes* on Cuba, a document published as an impartial profile of the country, yet which generally sought to portray Cuba in the worst light possible, stated that, "In the late 1980's … Cuba unilaterally removed its forces from Ethiopia [and] met the timetable of the 1988 Angola-Namibia accords by completing the withdrawal of its forces from Angola before July of 1991." The report also noted that

"Cuba's special relationship with the Soviet Union ended with the dissolution of the Soviet Union in 1991." And it also conceded its belief in Castro's statement made in January 1992, following the peace agreement in El Salvador that, "Cuban support for insurgents was a thing of the past."[24] In other words, in the State Department's own publication there was acknowledgment that the United States had achieved most of its objectives.

These changes, however, did not prompt an alteration in American policy toward Cuba. As the Cubans began to meet the US criteria for normalizing relations, greater emphasis was placed on the last condition: respect for human rights. Whereas President Carter equated respect for human rights with the release of political prisoners, during the George H.W. Bush administration, the idea of what human rights entailed expanded, and two more conditions were added to the list that had to be met before the US would normalize relations with Cuba. They were, and are, that Cuba must hold free and fair elections under international supervision, and that Cuba must adopt a market economy. The focus upon these aspects of the Cuban revolution is what currently characterizes the official American understanding and construction of Cuba, a view in which the greatest concern to American policymakers involves what are normally considered to be the domain of domestic politics and usually out the purview of foreign concern. Until both of these transformations occur, Fidel and Raúl Castro are accused of denying Cuban citizens their freedom and basic human rights. For these abuses, the Cuban revolution and government are portrayed, constructed and understood as illegitimate.

As Wayne Smith put it, referring to this situation, "one might have accused the US government of moving the goalposts."[25] Washington's major concerns with Cuba now have to do with its internal arrangements, arrangements that are represented as being so fundamental to international norms that they cannot be ignored. While such concerns regarding Cuba have been prominent since 1959, they are now the only ones available to American opponents of improving and normalizing relations with Cuba. As a result, understandings that feature totalitarianism and human rights abuses are featured as the most important elements of the Cuban threat. (This critique, of course, does not suggest that there are no human rights abuses in Cuba, or that the government is democratic. It simply examines the political consequences of a mode of representation that makes Cuba an object of hostility and enmity in US foreign policy.) Carried over from Cold War discourse and applied to a changed international setting, they represent "surviving textual practices," that continue to abet the "systems of meaning and value from which actions and policies are derived and legitimated."[26]

Dictatorship, freedom, and human rights abuses

The primary point from which US policy toward Cuba emanates is that the country is a totalitarian dictatorship that denies freedom and human rights to its citizens. Until Raúl Castro's ascent to the top spot, the country had been described by the US State Department as, "a totalitarian state dominated by Fidel Castro ... [who] exercises control over nearly all aspects of Cuban life." "To an extent almost unique in world politics," it is established, "the Cuban state is dominated by one person."[27] Current assessments say instead that, "Cuba is a totalitarian communist state headed by General Raúl Castro and a cadre of party loyalists. Castro replaced his brother Fidel Castro as chief of state, president of Cuba, and commander-in-chief of the armed forces on February 24, 2008. Fidel Castro retains the position of First Secretary of the Cuban Communist Party (PCC) ... Cuba's government controls all aspects of life through the Communist Party and its affiliated mass organizations."[28] The government has maintained control by using "a network of directorates," most notably, the ministry of the interior, which "ensures political and social conformity as well as internal security, [and] maintains pervasive vigilance through a network of informers and 80,000 block committees."[29] Or, more pointedly, in the words of President George H.W. Bush, "he [Castro] is a dictator, a totalitarian dictator."[30] All else is seen to follow from that, from the country's domestic and foreign policies, to the US responses which are said to necessarily result from such provocations. After all, as a succession of post-Cold War presidents have stated, the problem between the US and Cuba continues to be Castro's refusal to change, not the United States'.[31] In this understanding the illegitimacy of the Cuban government is self-evident, as is the need to bring about its demise. If "ten million of our neighbors have withstood three decades of a one-man, one-party state," then "that is a tragedy which must end."[32] No other reasons need to be provided in order to justify US action. Or as President George W. Bush said, "We love freedom. We love what freedom means. It is the cornerstone of our country, and therefore, we will never stop in our search for ways to advance freedom in Cuba."[33]

In the State Department's *Background Notes*, as well as other documents such as the *2009 Country Report on Human Rights Practices*, the description of the country also serves as a condemnation, which makes the condemnation seem reasonable and logical, and thus removed from criticism. In 1994, the *Background Notes* stated that "Cuba is a totalitarian state dominated by Fidel Castro," and that in addition to him the "principal government officials" are his brother Raúl, head of the armed forces, Roberto Robiana, minister of foreign relations, and Fernando Remirez, Ambassador to the UN. Only four people were characterized as "principal officials." No others merited mention at the time, not even the minister of the interior, whose office exists to "ensure political and social conformity." The exclusion of all other names and offices represents a significant absence. However, this absence is meant to be noticed. As a rhetorical strategy, the emphasis on the number of decision makers serves to demonstrate the undemocratic nature of the regime, that very few have access to or influence upon the highest levels of authority. As an element of the case made against Castro in the document, there can be no better evidence of totalitarian dictatorship than having only four principal officials.

The portrayal of totalitarian dictatorship is echoed in the US Congress, where members have spoken of Cuba as "one of the few countries of the world in which the struggle against totalitarianism has not yet been won," and as a place where "this regime for now almost half a century has brutalized its people with totalitarian rule."[34] Such language has appeared not only in the rhetoric of floor debate, committee hearings, and press conferences, but in legislation. For example, in seeking to strengthen the US embargo on Cuba, the *Cuban Liberty and Democratic Solidarity (Libertad) Act of 1996* says that the embargo can only be eased when the government "is demonstrably in transition from communist totalitarian dictatorship to representative democracy."[35] Excluding little criticism of the Cuban regime, the law identifies these three qualities which make better relations impossible, so that it is not only communism, or totalitarianism, or dictatorship, but all three which mark Cuba.

The implication of this is that any regime possessive of all these qualities is necessarily deserving of the treatment it receives from the United States. The description seeks to make the response self-evident, for, in the words of Michael Shapiro, "to the extent that the Other is regarded as something not occupying the same natural/moral space as the self, conduct toward the Other becomes more exploitive."[36] Or in this case, more hostile. As a totalitarian state, rhetorically represented as an entity that is, politically, the polar opposite of the United States, Cuba is not accorded the status of an equal to the United States.

The label totalitarian, inclusive of the denial of freedom and the violation of human rights, is accompanied in that discourse by specific charges against the Cuban revolution regarding its own record on human rights. In the current understanding of what is included under the label human rights, the US lists freedom from political killings, disappearances, torture and other cruel, inhuman, or degrading treatment or punishment, arbitrary arrest, detention or exile, denial of a fair public trial, arbitrary interference with privacy, family, home or correspondence, as well as freedom of speech, press and religion, freedom of assembly and association, freedom of movement within the country, foreign travel, emigration, repatriation, and of course, the right to elections and political participation. In the State Department's *2009 Country Reports on Human Rights Practices*, the Cuban government is found wanting with respect to all but the first two of these items, repeatedly engaging in a number of well-documented violations of human rights.[37]

Human rights violations clearly speak to the point to the infringement of freedom and the illegitimacy of the Cuban government, and they are repeatedly invoked in American political discourse. What's more, maintaining the focus on Cuban lack of freedom and illegitimacy is not only effected by the repetition of condemnation, it is dependent upon such repetition. There must always be new stories and new examples of abuse that continually reinforce the same representations of Cuba and Castro, for the security of identity and the negations of difference are not constituted through a founding act, but through a stylized repetition of acts.[38] This partly explains why anecdotal evidence serves the strongest condemnations. The testimony of an individual, recited before a Congressional audience, becomes one act in "a series of ritualized performances," each of which constitutes both a foundation for action and an augmentation to previous acts.[39] Because of the unstated assumption that a single story is exemplary of an entire population, the anecdote or testimonial attempts to personalize the pain and anguish of a people in whose name the US claims to act. For example President Clinton once noted in a news conference that, "just in the last few days, someone in Cuba was sentenced to several years in prison for simply talking to a foreign journalist."[40] Though it was cited by the president as a single example of Castro's abuse of human rights, the implication was that this instance was merely one of numerous accounts. Such practice is suggested to be standard daily practice in Cuba, as the president mentioned that this happened "just in the last few days." The president also informed his audience that this happened to "someone." The person's anonymity is important here because it reinforces the understanding that individuals do not matter in Cuba, that people are frequently arrested and imprisoned for such offenses, and that for the president or anyone in the US to keep track of all such occurrences is difficult, if not impossible.

While the anonymous victim evokes both sympathy and outrage, the known victim is an even more powerful weapon against the Cuban government. There are a sufficient number of victims who have come to the United States such that a multitude of testimonials have been given, recounting the Cuban regime's brutality.[41] US Senators and Representatives commonly tell stories or read letters and testimonials about Castro's victims, giving voice to stories of persecution and tragedy. On the Senate floor in May 2008, Senator Menendez, in supporting a resolution recognizing "Cuba Solidarity Day," described the arrest of 70 people, pointing out that they were "arrested, detained, and harassed. These 70 Cubans, according to the Cuban regime, had committed the crime of peaceful assembly ... while they were peacefully walking, they had on their arms this wristband. The simple white wristband says one word: cambio [change]."[42] Senator Helms and others have read letters on the floor of the Senate, providing detailed descriptions of life in Cuban prisons during debate on the *Libertad Act*. Witnesses who were once political prisoners in Cuba were even called to testify at the Congressional hearings.[43] Their presence in such proceedings is reminiscent of the practice used in presidential speeches of identifying a member of the audience, and singling out that person as someone who embodies the values and ideals appealed to in the address. By recognizing a real person to attach to ones words, it makes those words all the more real. By the same token, when Castro's detractors in the Congress include in their proceedings a living example of Castro's injustice, it brings added weight to the evil representations of Castro, and pays homage to Stalin's dictum that the death of one is a tragedy, but that the death of a thousand is a statistic.

Through the continual discussion of totalitarianism in Cuba and Castro's violations of human rights, the image is sustained in which the Cuban people are not imagined as a free people, but enslaved, where totalitarian government denies basic human rights to an innocent population, and forbids economic and political freedom. People are characterized as living in a world where they cannot speak freely, or meet and organize freely. They are in prison, in servitude. These understandings of the Cuban government and its citizens are not considered to be false. The denial of political and economic freedom that Cubans experience is of course, beyond dispute. Current US policy toward Cuba, however, does not naturally have to follow from these understandings. Rather, these types of representations have two effects that reinforce the foundations of American policy. First of all, as textual practices that bridge two global settings understood to be quite different (the Cold War and post-Cold War era), they continue to demarcate the discursive territory by which democracy and its antithesis are divided and recognized. As Shapiro points out, to the extent that one accepts and reproduces a discursive practice, one engages in acts of recognition of existing arrangements of power and authority. Even if one acts in an unselfconscious manner, there is an implicit act of acknowledgment taking place.[44] In the case of Cuba and the US, this dynamic remains unbroken. The language of communism, freedom, human rights, totalitarianism and dictatorship communicates to American officials the role Cuba has played and shall continue to play with respect to the US, whereby the boundaries of legitimate speech regarding acceptable interpretations of Castro and Cuba are sustained.

Second, representations whose focus on these particular features serve to denote a clear difference between the government and the population. As has already been discussed, this involves the establishment of a dichotomy in the official discourse, such that "the United States has no quarrel with the Cuban people," an entity imagined as monolithic and innocent, denied freedom for no reason other than to serve "the Castro regime."[45] With the people juxtaposed to the Castro regime, a totalitarian violator of human rights, the problem and the solution are supposed to come into focus. A people that wants democracy and freedom is being denied by its government, and that makes the government illegitimate. This, in turn, serves as the justification which makes it permissible for the US to try and remove that government. As the legitimate sovereign authority of a state is said to reside in its people, a claim that has been made by governments of various types for decades, it does not follow that US efforts to depose Castro constitute intervention.[46] Nor does it constitute an illegal or immoral action. It is only an "act of assistance performed by one sovereign state on behalf of the people of another sovereign state."[47] Castro is in power, by definition, against the will of the people, and therefore, the US government makes the assumption that it can speak for them. For example, President George H.W.

Bush expressed his "firm solidarity with the Cuban people as they strive to bring peaceful, democratic change to Cuba."[48] Susan Rice, US Ambassador to the United Nations, made the same case almost two decades later, stating that "the United States, like most Member States, is firmly committed to supporting the desire of the Cuban people to determine freely their country's future."[49] Without consulting the Cuban people, and often without any particular event in Cuba prompting such statements, officials of the US government frequently reference the desires of the Cuban people and American objective to fulfill them.

This practice is an example of what Cynthia Weber terms the simulation of sovereignty, in which American leaders cannot justifiably claim to represent the will of a foreign people and must therefore simulate their sovereignty in order to act on their behalf. As Weber points out, United States intervention discourse since Woodrow Wilson has made a consistent claim that US military action does not constitute intervention. "The US maintains that its action does not ... violate the sovereignty of the target state because a discursive distinction has been drawn between a repressive government with no legitimate claim to sovereign authority and the people of the state who are sovereign." This particular understanding is based upon the added element that the government of the United States is "represented as the center of judgment about who the sovereign people are."[50] It is only the case that an American government can presume to speak for the Cuban people if it assumes the role as the "community of judgment" regarding a) who exercises sovereignty in Cuba, and b) what the wishes of that sovereign people are.

These judgments are presupposed, completed by virtue of those representations which render a single 'America' out of the Western Hemisphere, postulating that all 'Americans' desire US-style liberal democracy and that the United States harbors responsibility for encouraging and realizing it. As this is understood as a premise for US action, a foundation upon which American policy rests, one can even go so far as an American congressman did, asserting that US policy toward Cuba "is not a political issue."[51] In other words, what is arguable, what is debatable, what is desirable, and what is right, have been presupposed. These issues have already been decided by such a formulation, implying that the solution is equally clear. All that can be said to remain is the administrative or executive problem of carrying out the appropriate policy, which will result in Castro's already agreed-upon removal. The politics of the American confrontation with Cuba are, in effect, written out of existence, while the language of freedom, human rights and illegitimacy is highlighted.

Castro's qualities

In addition to the identification of the Cuban regime's wrongdoing, which includes not only Fidel and Raúl's actions against Cuban citizens, but a mode of being that is considered anathema to contemporary international norms, there has also been in the United States a variety of metaphorical representations that have been used to illustrate the illegitimacy of the Cuban government. In contrast to understandings that emphasize the endurance of communist practices, these representations involve qualities that are peculiar to the post-Cold War era. However, as the images and understandings they engender are rooted in an unbroken opposition to Cuban communism, they maintain their link to the past and do not imply a rupture in American policy, only a modification warranted by specific circumstances. As David Campbell points out, if "the objects of concern change over time, the techniques and exclusions by which those objects are constituted as dangers [may] persist."[52] Thus can the qualities of continuity and adaptive change come together in these instances to allow US policy to be directed at an incompletely altered Cuba.

These post-Cold War representations, employed in the service of US policy, suggest as metaphors are intended to do, "the condition of possibility" and "a range of reasonable inferences intended to inform opinion and influence behavior."[53] They offer a path to several conclusions: that the Cuban revolution is an entity whose relevance and strength has passed, that there is little possibility that the communist regime will continue to survive, and that the United States can simply wait out the Cuban Revolution, which cannot survive the deaths of Fidel and Raúl Castro. Three of these metaphors, which are addressed here, have been employed since the end of the Cold War. They emerged in the official US discourse not only as evidence against Cuba, but as a premise upon which Castro's ouster rests as a logical consequence. The first concerns the metaphor of death, whereby Cuba has been represented as a dying regime, inexorably directed toward the same death that other communist states suffered. The second entails the appropriation of a metaphor of experimentation, in which the revolution is represented not as part of an evolution of history and contingency, but as an unnatural experiment imposed upon an unwilling society. Furthermore, it is an experiment that has already proven to be a failure in other societies and thus must necessarily fail in Cuba. The third addresses the idea that the Cuban revolution is isolated in the world, that it stands alone in the face of great historical change which, in the Western Hemisphere, only Cuba resists.

The use of these representations since the end of the Cold War suggests that Cuba has gone from being a relatively strong and able actor in world politics (even if that strength was entirely dependent upon Soviet support) to a "decaying cadaver" whose death is imminent.[54] At the same time, the connection of these qualities to those of communism and its stated inherent illegitimacy provide for an American policy that is based upon completing the task of eliminating the Cuban revolution, and in particular the rule of Fidel and Raúl Castro, rather than understanding their presence or absence to be irrelevant.

The dead and the dying

Language that characterizes communism in Cuba in terms of death and dying, which highlights the passing nature of communism, has been employed since the early 1990s in the US, especially in the years immediately after the fall of the Berlin Wall. This image suggests, first of all, that there is a teleological view of the Cuban revolution, that there is and must be an ending and a new beginning after it. Second, this language suggests that there is only a single possible outcome for the revolution. In this discourse, the finality of the Cuban revolution is not seriously questioned. What is contested is how and when it will collapse.

After the fall of the Berlin Wall, and especially after the collapse of the Soviet Union, metaphors of death and dying were sometimes invoked with respect to Cuba. There were several articles published that discussed the prospect of Cuban communism being next in line to fall (cited earlier in this chapter). President George H.W. Bush repeatedly spoke the language of inevitable death for Castro's Cuba, saying that his "dictatorship will not survive," and that "the man [Castro] cannot sustain." The president also stated that "he's a has-been," there is "no hope for him. It's a dead end."[55] This representation was continued by president Clinton, who, in spite of differing party affiliations, maintained continuity with his predecessor, declaring Cuba's system to be "at a dead end politically, economically, and spiritually." State Department officials under Clinton made the same pronouncements, saying that, "Cuba is a country at a dead-end."[56] These characterizations tended to diminish after a few years, as the Cuban revolution refused to collapse in line with American expectations and hopes. Still, in spite of the Cuban government's unexpected longevity, this representation is sometimes used in current formulations, such that Cuba's economic relationship with Venezuela, which involves an exchange of Venezuelan oil for Cuban goods and services, is characterized as "a lifeline for Cuba," preventing its otherwise preordained death.[57] The view these statements embody, that there is a final, and fatal aspect of the Cuban revolution which must necessarily be played out at some future date, has not diminished.

Part of this teleological understanding is purely definitional. By equating the revolution with Fidel (and now Raúl) Castro, US officials who are awaiting a new relationship with Cuba can be satisfied by the removal of the Castro brothers enough to begin that new relationship. As Former Congressman Robert Torricelli has said, "there is every opportunity for every citizen in Cuba, save two, Fidel and Raúl, to join the forces of freedom."[58] In fact, the bill language in the Helms-Burton Act specifically states that the US cannot provide any opening to a government in Cuba that includes Fidel or Raúl Castro. As these two cannot live forever, a strategy of waiting provides one (eventually effective) strategy for combating the Cuban revolution.

Yet the belief in the imminent demise of the revolution includes more than a fixation upon personalities. It is reflected in a particular telling of the end of the Cold War, which the US is said to have won due to superior values, strength and steadfast determination to withstand the efforts made by the Soviet Union to foster global revolution. As President Bush argued in 1992, "steadfast and sure, generations of Americans stood in the path of the Soviet advance ... The qualities that enabled us to triumph in that struggle [were] faith, strength, unity, and above all, American leadership."[59] In this telling, the end of the Cold War is rooted in American foreign policy, the strength of liberalism, and the power of global capitalism, rather than any of the internal characteristics of the regimes in Eastern Europe and the Soviet Union. This forgetting, this marginalization of domestic politics in Eastern Europe, allows for a Cuba that is equally vulnerable to failure as the USSR. The logic is that if the Soviets, a global superpower, could not ultimately withstand the challenge of the United States and the Western world, then there is, by extension, little reason to expect that Cuba, a poor, weak and crisis-ridden nation, can withstand that same challenge. By such reasoning, the Cuban revolution cannot be anything but a dying entity.

Two particularly interesting examples illustrate the view that the demise of the Cuban revolution is inevitable, like death. A study by the RAND Corporation conducted for the Defense Department in 1994, entitled *Storm Warnings for Cuba*, reproduced this view.[60] In examining the prospects for change in Cuba, what form it might take, and how the US should respond, the authors referred to the possible changes in Cuba as "endgames." Several possibilities were offered, ranging from the continued rule of Castro, to violent social upheaval resulting in the overthrow of the government. Yet the unfolding of events in Cuba was not characterized as an unfolding, an evolution, a change in course, or anything else that implies a process without end. The representations of Cuba that they deploy all have an outcome. Even the continuation of Castro's rule is dubbed an endgame by the RAND authors. As the authors state, "the Castro regime may survive, as in Endgames I and II. If so, it will probably remain in a lingering, prolonged, but controlled state of crisis for many years."[61]

An endgame can last for "many years" because there is a teleology at work in the representation of Cuba and the revolution. There has been an elimination of any characterizations that imagine a Cuba not at the end of its revolution. It is assumed that there is an end that will soon be reached. With this assumption safely established, it becomes possible for the RAND study to represent Castro in a manner that he too may participate, for many years, in an endgame, even if this endgame is characterized by stability and continuity in Castro's government. Cuba is thus identified as a country that will, upon the completion of its endgame, reemerge in order to start a new beginning under conditions assumed to be normal or natural.

Another, more recent example of how this thinking is reflected in US policy involves the creation by President Bush in 2003 of the Commission for Assistance to a Free Cuba. The second report of this commission, released in 2006, offers a detailed plan of how to prepare for a transitional Cuban government, one that is acceptable to the United States. Among the recommendations it makes are: designate a US agency to provide technical assistance – within two weeks of determining a transition government is in place – to help hold elections; inventory the obstacles in Cuban law to holding free and fair elections; select an agency to provide assistance to Cuban police in the "potentially chaotic moments following a transition;" hire on retainer qualified partners who will "ensure that, when the moment comes, the U.S. Government will have in place both plans and personnel ready to deploy" inside Cuba; and "direct the Department of Commerce, Agriculture, the U.S. Trade Representative, and the Department of State to undertake a series of seminars with U.S. companies in order to initiate planning for ... doing business with a free, democratic Cuba."[62]

What is notable about this report and the Commission that wrote it is not that the US government is recommending that detailed contingency plans be developed to respond to developments overseas. This is a common practice. Rather, it is the mere existence of the commission and its report. The level of presumption they reflect is remarkable – a presumption that it will be the purview of the United States government to help manage a change in Cuban governance, a presumption that it is right and appropriate for the US government to prepare for this role, a presumption that US involvement of this type will be welcomed or requested, and a presumption that the Commission and its work are necessary because the Cuban revolution is understood as an entity that is expected to come to an end.

The unquestioned repetition of the assumption of a coming (or current) endgame or transition in Cuba seeks to diminish possibilities for alternative understandings of Cuba and serves to reinforce the continuation of American policies of political and economic isolation. Such logic suggests that there is little reason to alter policy now that the end is near.[63] However, the idea of the inevitable endgame or transition is not necessarily a fact. The Cuba that is seen as entering the death throes of its revolution is a construction, a story, a representation, a favored way of talking and thinking about Cuba.

A failed experiment

In addition to the deployment of metaphors regarding Cuba's death, there is also the reference to the Cuban revolution as "a failed experiment." Something that is an experiment is supposed to reveal a truth that was there before the experiment began, only unknown. Its fate is predetermined and cannot be altered. Moreover, experiments are repeatable. The results, under the same circumstances, will be replicated. In consideration of the fate of the Soviet Union and the communist regimes of Eastern Europe, the representation of communism as a failed experiment provides for an understanding that it is something that must necessarily have a particular outcome. For Cuba, then, this understanding encourages the metaphor of the endgame, in which the primary concern is the length of time the regime will be able to survive.

The truth of communism has been revealed in other experiments. It is not merely the Cuban revolution that has failed, but communism itself which is understood as "the failed statist model."[64]

In recalling the resignation of Mikhail Gorbachev and the end of the Soviet Union, Secretary of State James Baker stated that, "the experiment begun by Karl Marx and Vladmir Lenin, and carried on by Joseph Stalin and others, had failed."[65] Even if communism at one time was represented as threat or a danger, or even if it was, according to others, an overstated or nonexistent threat that diverted American attention and resources from other, more valuable enterprises, such understandings have become, to a great extent, irrelevant. A teleological history, by which the past is judged in terms of the present, and which marks a widespread view of the end of the Cold War in the US, makes relevant only the most recent understanding of the Soviet Union and communism: that of abject failure.

The Cuban revolution is represented as a part of that failed experiment, in spite of the fact that it has survived many years after the collapse of the Soviet Union and the governments of Eastern Europe. The verdict has already been decided in the United States. "Castro's vision of the future," stated George H.W. Bush in 1992, "is to cling to a failed past."[66] This view of Cuban failure has been repeated often over the past several years. President Clinton observed that "the person in the whole world that least want[s] the embargo lifted [is] Fidel Castro ... because as long as that embargo is there, he's got an excuse for the failures of his regime."[67] And George W. Bush echoed the same words, calling on Fidel Castro to "cast aside old and failed ideas," and telling the Cuban people, in an address broadcast on Radio Marti into Cuba, "You may have once believed in the revolution. Now you can see its failure."[68]

The failures that this succession of US presidents refers to are disputable. After all, Cuba's many successes – becoming a respected leader of developing and "non-aligned" countries, withstanding a continuous challenge from the United States, bringing education, health care and an end to poverty for many people – could be argued to be as strong as its failures. Furthermore, it can be argued not that the Cuban revolution or Castro is a failure, but that their allies were. Considering that Cuba's allies were overthrown and that the successor governments broke the agreements they made with Cuba, it is not surprising that Cuba received a severe economic setback and has tried to recover through the long "special period." Castro may have chosen unreliable friends, but his perseverance over the past two decades and his ability to avoid a similar fate may be testament not to his failure, but rather to his success.

Yet in the current climate, one in which Cuba continues to face economic hardship, its opponents in the US wait to finally see the end of the revolution, these alternative understandings are marginalized in order to bolster an understanding that Cuba's "economic and political systems have failed."[69] Even those who criticize US policy may concur on this characterization.

Senator Christopher Dodd, a longtime opponent of the embargo, has argued that he opposed any policy that would "let Castro off the hook for his failed economic system by allowing him to blame the United States" for such failure.[70]

There are two assumptions made in regarding the proclamation that the Cuban revolution is a failed experiment which are problematic upon closer examination. The first has to do with the timing of the act, that one's ability to declare success or failure depends greatly upon when one decides to pass judgment. It would be difficult to say that the Cuban revolution was a failure in 1959, or in 1961 after educational and land reforms had already been established, and Cuba's armed forces had repelled the US-backed invasion at the Bay of Pigs. It would be equally difficult to argue failure in the mid-1970s when Cuba had intervened successfully in Angola and Ethiopia, was highly regarded around the world, and was elected leader of the Non-Aligned Movement.[71] In order to make a definitive statement about the success or failure of a country or a government, it is necessary not only to ignore and emphasize selected parts of the past, but to remain silent about the fact that history unfolds beyond the particular time one passes judgment.

The second assumption made in the efforts to brand Castro a failure stems from an "end of history" argument in which American, and Western, liberal democracy is placed at the pinnacle of a global political development where history is meant to arrive.[72] Just as an imagined endpoint in the unfolding of history provided for a superior America juxtaposed to a failed Cuba, so too does this exist with regard to the evolution of political systems and the ideas that support them. In spite of arguments against this thesis, it has been increasingly embraced in the official discourse of American foreign policy.[73] In the aftermath of the Cold War President Clinton declared that "freedom has been won," while before him George H.W. Bush claimed that "freedom has carried the day."[74]

It follows from this understanding that Cuba resists the historical evolution toward democracy that the rest of the world embraces, that it "swims against the tide."[75] Yet this assumes that the rest of the world, which represents "the tide," is pursuing a natural path, one that spontaneously evolves if democracy, liberty and freedom are allowed to flourish, and if "experiments," i.e., communism, are not imposed upon an otherwise natural order. While communism is represented as an experiment, democracy and free market capitalism are the purview of nature.

The primary exemplars of what lies at the end of that path are assumed, in such a reading, to be the liberal democracies of the West, particularly the United States. As President Clinton stated, "the ideas we [Americans] struggle for, democracy, freedom – freedom of religion, freedom of speech, freedom of assembly, open markets, respect for diversity – these ideas are more and more the ideals of the world."[76] Alternative political orders at this point in history are represented as arrangements that are something unnatural and therefore less than democracy, be they Castro's revolution,

Saddam Hussein's Iraq, Islamic Iran, or another communist holdout, North Korea.[77] These countries are represented as the result of political efforts that did not arise from popular will, but a small minority, political systems that had to be imposed upon a population and maintained only through force, terror, surveillance and the continual threat of punishment. Understood as possessive of these characteristics, the Cuban regime is to be further delegitimized.

Isolation

The understanding in the United States of a Cuba that is dying, in the endgame of a revolution, and that is a "failed experiment" is aided further by the attempts to portray a Cuba that is isolated. The demise of communism almost everywhere else in the world is used to build an image that provides a clear picture of Cuba's similar fate: Cuba lost its friends and allies, and this isolation is a further sign of the illegitimacy of the government and the revolution.

In the immediate years after the Cold War, the general argument was as follows. The withdrawal of Soviet and then Russian support "means that Cuba can no longer support insurgency abroad," a condition implied as the *raison d'être* for the Cuban revolution.[78] Without insurgency, according to this representation, Cuba cannot bring into existence other friendly revolutionary governments. Thus there was said to be no new supply of allies for Castro. He had no future. As a State Department report noted, Cuba's future is determined by the fact that "just a few short years ago, Cuba had 50,000 troops in Africa," and that now they have none, that "Cuban troops are out of Angola, and it is not controlled by a Marxist-Leninist state," that "Cuban troops have left Ethiopia and Somalia," that "Namibia is independent and democratic," that "there is peace in Central America," that "Castro lost the election [in Nicaragua] to Violetta Chamorro just as surely did Daniel Ortega," and that there is a "peace settlement in El Salvador, [which] was the death-knell for Cuban-style communism in Latin America."[79] According to this view, Cuba is completely isolated in the world, without friends, without influence, without a future. These are the signs of illegitimacy. In spite of the revolution's staying power, in spite of ties such as Cuba has with Hugo Chavez's Venezuela, which provides both significant financial and political support, and in spite of maintaining trade relations with many countries around the world, the US characterization remains the same. Cuba is isolated.

All US administrations over the last two decades have continually stressed that Castro and Cuba stand alone in the world after the Cold War. This is a consistent theme in the rhetoric. Sometimes it is stated directly that, "there is one outstanding example [in the Americas] where it is not totally free and where human rights are not respected, and that's Cuba." or that one should "[l]ook around the world. Fidel Castro is hopelessly isolated."[80] This theme is repeatedly developed during meetings of the Summit of the Americas. The first of these was held in 1994, and the most recent at this writing was in 2010. The US, which has blocked Cuba's participation in the Organization of American States (OAS), has repeatedly made it clear that 34 out of 35 nations in the Western Hemisphere have been represented at these meetings. The one country not invited to participate is Cuba, due to the fact that it is considered to be the only non-democratic country in the Americas and thus ineligible for participation with the other, legitimate governments in the OAS. At the 1994 meeting it was noted that "one nation in the Hemisphere continues to stand in unsplendid, and self-imposed, isolation from its sister nations of the region. That nation is Cuba. Cuba is the single glaring exception to the movement in Hemisphere toward greater political freedom, greater respect for human rights, and more open economics."[81] President George W. Bush has echoed this representation, saying in 2001 that he was "joined by leaders of 33 other democratic nations. Only one country in the Western Hemisphere is not represented, because that country, Cuba, is the only one that is not yet a democracy," and later, in announcing an "Initiative for a New Cuba" that "there is only one nation in our hemisphere that is not a democracy – only one. There is only one national leader whose position of power owes more to bullets than ballots."[82] Even Hugo Chavez of Venezuela, considered by the US to be a highly troublesome neighbor and the source of much US anxiety in the region, is not singled out in the way that Cuba is. After all, Chavez was elected to office and Venezuela maintains its membership in the OAS. The only retreat from the US position is that in 2009 the US removed its opposition to lifting Cuba's suspension in the Organization of American States. While the United States could not get the OAS to agree to explicitly state a set of specific conditions Cuba has to meet, it did get the agreement to call for "a process of dialogue" in line with OAS "practices, proposals and principles," a reference to human rights and democratization. In spite of the vote, Cuba stated that it has no interest in rejoining the group.

According to a representation of Cuba's troubles resulting from its isolation, blame is apportioned to Castro for bearing responsibility for failure. As President George H.W. Bush said, "let's make it clear: Cuba suffers because Castro refuses to change."[83] President Clinton has echoed the sentiment by attributing Cuba's problems to "the stubborn refusal of the Castro regime to have an open democracy and an open economy."[84] This stubborn refusal includes the fact that "the Government of Cuba has isolated itself," by "defying the trend toward democratic reform ... [by] refusing to permit its people to vote in free and fair elections, by refusing to permit freedom in the marketplace, by refusing to renounce support for violent revolutionary movements, by refusing to join the international community in curbing proliferation of nuclear weapons – in other words, by its own policy decisions, not as a result of US policy."[85] Consistently following this line of logic, President George W. Bush declared, "to improve relations, what needs to change is not the United States; what needs to change is Cuba. Cuba's Government must begin a process of peaceful democratic change.

They must release all political prisoners. They must have respect for human rights in word and deed and pave the way for free and fair elections."[86]

This understanding involves a representation in which the choice – to exclude Cuba from participation in the OAS, maintain an embargo, attempt to isolate Cuba – is posited as a truth. American leaders "have not been satisfied to call these outcomes choices that were contingent on preference, cultural biases or political fights. Instead they have sought to cloak them as the outcome of metaphysical categories." The implication is that any other possibilities or choices are viewed as "sinful, unnatural and unreasonable."[87] Therefore, Cuba can be considered as isolated and alone, trying to ignore the world around them. At the same time, Castro and his government can be viewed as trying to swim against the tide of history. It is not only implied in the presidential statements above that no government can do this and expect to survive, but also that to do so is a denial of what is the natural, or default position of nations. It is not the United States or any other country that has made a choice; their position is naturalized. Only Cuba, by this formulation, is making a choice, one that rejects what is normal. It follows from this that Cuba maintains an illegitimate pursuit, and this is why the revolution will inevitably fall.

A dichotomy been set up: one between legitimate, free and democratic states where human rights and civil liberties are respected, and dictatorships and totalitarian states where none of these qualities are present. In this global setting, the official rhetoric seeks to construct a Cuba that is precluded from having allies. In the 1990s the State Department pointed out that, "no government has stretched out a hand to stop the inevitable decay and disappearance of the Cuban dictator."[88] What is meant by this statement is that no single country had adopted a similar role to the Soviets. Yet these two things are by no means the same. To say that Cuba enjoyed no support because it did not reproduce this type of relationship with anyone else was an attempt to shift the object of focus from the presence of Cuba's global ties to the absence of Cuba's Soviet ties.

Of course, this characterization no longer holds true, as Cuba's relationship with Venezuela since the early 2000s has not only changed things considerably for Cuba, but also for the US representation of Cuba's isolation. The attempt to paint a picture of Cuba as a country that is isolated from all others is significantly weakened. As the State Department's *Background Notes* for Cuba in 2010 state, "Fifteen years after the demise of the Soviet Union the Cuban Government found in Hugo Chavez's Venezuela a new benefactor. The politically motivated preferential relationships with this country have replaced tourism as the main engine of growth for the Cuban economy since the second half of 2004."[89] One key element of this relationship has, in fact, reproduced one of the major elements of Soviet support for Cuba – the supply of oil at below market prices. Cuba, in exchange, provides medical and educational services, whereby Cuba sends doctors, nurses and teachers to Venezuela, with as many as 40,000 Cubans now working in Venezuela, a circumstance reminiscent of the time when Cuba enjoyed significant Soviet financial support. The relationship has moved beyond the initial oil-for-doctors swap, and in areas as diverse at food, education, medicine, oil, petrochemicals, agricultural goods, textiles, and other sectors, Cuba and Venezuela have vastly expanded their trade. This arrangement provides Cuba with hard currency (in part as a result of Cuba reselling Venezuelan oil on the world market, a similar arrangement made with the Soviet Union), and has made Venezuela one of Cuba's largest export markets, diminishing the incentive for Cuba to seek economic assistance and trade outlets with other countries.[90] Beyond this economic relationship, and indeed the basis for it, is the ideological solidarity of the two governments, which led to the development of the Bolivarian Alliance the Peoples of Our America, or ALBA. This organization, an association of eight socialist and social democratic governments (including Bolivia, Ecuador, and Nicaragua, as well as three Caribbean island nations), is seeking a level of regional economic integration and ideological solidarity that stands in direct opposition to US power and influence in the Western Hemisphere. Its operating principles are based on the ideas of social welfare, bartering and mutual economic aid, rather than trade liberalization, which is the model preferred by the US.[91] ALBA, and the support it has generated throughout the region, means that Cuba no longer stands quite so alone against the United States.

Beyond Venezuela and ALBA, Cuba maintains diplomatic relations with most countries in the world, more than 160 of them, and has strong economic ties with a number of countries, including much of Latin America and Western Europe, as well as China and Canada. Its nickel and sugar industries, along with pharmaceuticals, cigars, tourism and remittances from family members in the United States provide for a great deal of the Cuban economy. These circumstances of Cuba's economic relations mean that the US characterization of Cuba's isolation is at odds with its understanding of Cuba's economic prospects, and especially Venezuela's role in supporting the Cuban economy. If indeed Cuba maintains a lifeline via its relations with Venezuela, then it is not isolated and alone. Far from believing that there are no countries that support Cuba, US policy is based on the premise that there is too much support going to Cuba and that it must be stopped.

Moreover, the political support that Cuba maintains with respect to the US embargo further belies the assertion that Cuba is isolated. Rather, it is the United States that is isolated. For 19 years in a row, with the most recent vote at this writing in October of 2009, the UN General Assembly has passed a resolution condemning the US embargo on Cuba. The latest vote was 187 to 3 (each year the US receives a handful of votes supporting its position; in 2009 Israel and Palau joined the US in voting against the resolution). While the rhetoric from Washington repeatedly makes the claim that the US response to Cuba has been the correct one, both necessary and reasonable in a setting where Cuba has isolated itself, it can be more plausibly argued that the US is more isolated than Cuba. Only the United States maintains an embargo against Cuba. No other country in the world tries to isolate Cuba, and no other passes legislation aimed at the weakening of the Cuban economy and the removal of Fidel and Raúl Castro.

This problem of US isolation has been addressed in two ways. The first has been to accept the accusation and turn it into a virtue. By turning the tables and going on the offensive to claim the moral high ground, American officials have attempted to discredit those who engage the Cubans directly and rewrite its isolation as virtuous. By such a formulation, the embargo can be portrayed as a consistent or steadfast policy, which the United States pursues to reach a goal of returning freedom to Cuba. Former Congressman Robert Torricelli best summarized this view when he stated in 1996 that,

> There are those in the international community who believe that no matter how great the suffering, or how long the deprivation of freedom, that Cuba is an economic opportunity. The best course of action for their country is to take advantage of this moment, to realize profits, and to take advantage of the suffering of the Cuban people ... It is our own belief that it would be unconscionable to take advantage of the labor, the misery of the Cuban people for financial advantage ... I know that many are frustrated because the international community has not come to our side as we might have hoped and even expected. To me, that is a point of considerable pride ... In Europe, they [European powers] would insist upon the highest standard for human rights, basic freedoms, democratic governments, but in Latin America it is all right to have a dictatorship for 30 years, to imprison people, to deny basic freedom of speech or religion. For Latin America, there is a different standard, something that in Europe would never be tolerated. Our European friends should at least know that while they pursue their own policies, we understand them for what they are. We recognize the difference. And every person in Latin America should be appalled.[92]

Congressman Torricelli's statement tries to write any concern with success or failure of US policy out of existence. It also ignores entirely the argument that economic and political engagement may do more to liberalize Cuba than US hostility, all while depicting America's unilateral policy as virtuous. If, in this reading, the US is viewed as a solitary actor in the world, it is acting out of a commitment to a superior morality.

A second strategy the US government pursues to diminish the problem of its own isolation regarding Cuba is to shift the focus of the topic away from US policy and toward Cuba, in which emphasis is placed upon the common opposition to Cuba's lack of freedom, rather than the US embargo. American officials can point out how other countries agree with it in calling for democracy in Cuba. Many countries have done so, especially in Europe. The European Union, which adopted a Common Position regarding Cuba in 1996, states that the EU will "encourage the reform of internal legislation concerning political and civil rights ... the release of all political prisoners and the ending of the harassment and punishment of dissidents," and will "remind the Cuban authorities, both publicly and privately, of fundamental responsibilities regarding human rights, in particular freedom of speech and association."[93] The death in February 2010 of dissident Orlando Zapata Tamayo, who had been imprisoned in Cuba since 2003 for the crime of disrespecting authority, prompted several of condemnations of Cuba. The EU demanded that Cuba release all political prisoners, while the Deputy Prime Minister of Spain, Manuel Chaves, expressed Spain's view that "There is a deficit of human rights in that country [Cuba]."[94] The Polish parliament went so far as to pass a resolution condemning Cuba's actions, saying that "The Sejm of the Republic of Poland, representing the Polish tradition of fighting for freedom and recognizing the heritage of 'Solidarity,' condemns the actions of the Cuban authorities targeting the members of Cuban democratic opposition."[95] This move had been preceded in 2009 by 90 members of the Polish Parliament "adopting" 90 Cuban political prisoners, in which the Polish members of Parliament pledged to advocate for the release of the adopted prisoners, and be in contact with the families of the 90 political prisoners. As one member of Parliament, Adam Lipinski stated in supporting the action, "We are committed to the human rights of the Cuban people."[96]

In the years just following the end of the Cold War, the US repeatedly pointed out Cuba's global isolation. For example, in 1991, a State Department publication noted that "Germany and Czechoslovakia terminated trade ties with Cuba, citing its human rights practices" and that "Cuba isolated itself [by] voting against several crucial resolutions on Iraq." At an Ibero-American summit in Madrid in the following year, according to a State Department publication, other Latin American leaders "made it clear to Castro they wanted change in Cuba when they called for 'representative' democracy ... not Cuban-style democracy." Another highlighted instance involved the critical treatment of Cuba by the Russian government. President George H.W. Bush once pointed out that Russia not only cut off aid to Cuba and renegotiated all remaining commercial links, but that Russia's ambassador in Geneva met with human rights activists from Cuba and even voted in the UN to send a special human rights investigator to Cuba. "Imagine the change," said President Bush. "Russia condemning Fidel Castro."[97] This was cited as one of the most conclusive pieces of evidence of Cuban isolation, for there could be no clearer statement regarding the repressive and illegitimate nature of the Cuban regime than a rebuke from its former sponsor (Cuban-Russian relations have since warmed considerably, characterized by high level political contacts and commercial cooperation).

These examples of criticism of Cuba sought to pursue the strategy of trying to rhetorically co-opt other governments, asserting that there is a global community united against Castro's government. Since there are far more critics of US policy than defenders, those countries that criticize US policy cannot also serve as legitimizers of US policy without being appropriated. For example, American officials have admitted that many countries do not "totally support our policy toward Cuba. Many have called for the lifting of the US embargo." However, US officials have acknowledged this and enlisted it to serve American policy, characterizing it as merely a dispute over means to an already agreed-upon end. It is pointed out that "virtually all [the countries critical of the US embargo] agree that the solution to the Cubans' problems lies not in the fates or beyond Cuba's borders, but rather in themselves." Thus even critics of the US join it in calling for "a peaceful transition to a democratic pluralistic system which respects human rights and freedom of opinion."[98] The implication is that if those countries that object to US policy can agree on this judgment, then it must be true. In this type of argumentation, the US asserts its position as the natural one, and seeks to mute or tame the opposition of its critics by bringing them into agreement with the American position on the goal of Cuban democratization. The conclusion can then be reached that asserts that 1) the source of the problem in US-Cuban relations is Cuba, 2) the United States stands alongside other countries in making that assessment, and 3) Cuba is isolated in the world, not the United States.

The US response – Keep waiting

The years immediately following the collapse of the Soviet Union lent themselves well to US hopes, expectations and proclamations of imminent death of the Cuban revolution, and to representations of death, failure and isolation. The US government and much of the Cuban-American community in Florida seemed to share a sense of "next year in Havana." All one had to do to achieve a new Cuba was wait, just a little longer. The frustration of such unmet expectations, however, soon led to a situation where US policy revolved simply around waiting, but perhaps waiting for a long time – waiting for Fidel, and now Raúl, to step down, to die, to make room for a new, and of course, American-influenced government. This policy has been remarkably consistent over the 20-plus years since the fall of the Berlin Wall, reflecting both the hubris and hope that have informed US policy since 1959. Hubris in that US objectives and actions have been grounded in a belief that American success will result in benefitting, or uplifting, Cuba and its people, and that the US can and will do better for Cuba than Cubans have done for themselves. And hope in that by simply waiting for Fidel and Raúl to go, the US would eventually be able to welcome the emergence of a better, more tolerable, more acceptable government in Cuba, which seems as if it has been expected to arise almost naturally in the absence of the Castro brothers.

The official rhetoric that has accompanied this waiting game has been continually repeated, and remarkably consistent, over the past two decades. One would be hard pressed, absent some reference to a particular incident, to determine which president, member of Congress or other government official uttered which comment, or in which year. Presidential speeches or comments on Cuba are filled with the same phrases, promising that "the people of Cuba will be free. I will guarantee you that," or "a new day for Cuba will come," or "throughout the Americas, dictatorships have given way to democracy ... Cuba will follow this course of its neighbors," and "over time the overwhelming trend in the hemisphere will occur in Cuba as well."[99] These statements not only exhibit a degree of expectation, they also make a promise, a promise that demonstrates a sense of longing, expectation and entitlement. The sense of entitlement in US policy suggests that there is a "normal" condition that characterizes US-Cuban relations, but that it has been interrupted by Castro's revolution. The anticipated return to such a "normal" condition is what animates this promise. That promise extends to specific US actions as well, in which the US government explicitly pledges to work with Cubans and the international community to bring change to Cuba, either via the embargo, calling for change, refusing Cuban participation in the OAS, or planning for a transition in Cuba. The Commission for Assistance to a Free Cuba, which drafted a US plan to effect a democratic transition in Cuba, referenced the idea of the promise in its mission statement that "this plan is not an imposition but rather is a promise we will keep with the Cuban people."[100] This represents yet another example of what Lars Schoultz calls the "uplift mentality," the belief held in the US that Cuba "will welcome the opportunity to be guided toward a higher and better civilization by the United States of America."[101]

The continual repetition of the same language to describe US policy since the Cold War extends beyond the promise of a changing Cuba. The flip side of the promise is the demand, which has also been another common form of communication that US officials fall back upon – because it is familiar, it is so readily available, and in the absence of a change in policy, it represents one of the few options for US policymakers to employ in communicating about Cuba. As is the case with rhetoric promising a better future for Cuba, the language making demands of Cuba cannot be easily identified with a particular time or individual. They are relatively timeless. George W. Bush stated in 2008 that "If Cuba wants to join the community of civilized nations, then Cuba's rulers must begin a process of peaceful democratic change ... the first step must be to release all political prisoners. They must respect the human rights in word and in deed. And they must allow what the Cuban people have desired for generations: to pick their own leaders in free and fair elections. This is the policy of the United States, and it must not change until the people of Cuba are free."[102] His statement bears great resemblance to that of President Clinton, who proclaimed that "The Cuban people must receive the blessings of freedom they have been so long denied," or to Secretary of State Hillary Clinton's spokesperson, who stated in response to the death of Orlando Zapata Tamayo in a Cuban prison, that the incident "highlights the injustice of Cuba's holding more than 200 political prisoners who should now be released without delay."[103]

Even the very routine, mundane (and mandated) communications to Congress regarding Cuba follow the same pro forma structure. For example, every year since the passage of the Helms-Burton Act in 1996, the president (be it Clinton, Bush or Obama) issues similar notices to Congress as required by law stating "I hereby report that I have exercised my statutory authority to continue the national emergency declared in Proclamation 6867 of March 1, 1996, in response to the Cuban government's destruction of two unarmed U.S.-registered civilian aircraft in international airspace north of Cuba."[104] And every six months, the same law requires a note to Congress to suspend the lawsuits against the Cuban government that the law authorizes. Presidents Clinton, Bush and Obama have all used the same letter, word for word since the year 2000.

The repetition of US statements and actions brings to mind the plight of Estragon and Vladmir, in Samuel Beckett's play *Waiting for Godot*. These two characters simply wait and wait for the arrival of Godot, who, of course, never arrives. Yet they continue to hold out hope and wait, returning everyday to the same routine, the same conversation, the same unmet expectations. The play is riveting in spite of the fact that nothing happens, a similar circumstance to American policy. Little about it has substantially changed, yet it commands great attention both in the US and around the world, warranting the same question as Beckett's hopeless characters: How can one continue to do the same thing again and again despite any evidence that it will yield the desired results? Doing so only reveals the pointlessness and hopelessness of such efforts. "Waiting for Fidel" then, is the policy of letting time kill the Cuban revolution, which is personalized in terms of Fidel Castro, and now Raúl. President Clinton's lament that Castro "can't last forever. Nobody lives forever," or George W. Bush's that "one day the good Lord will take Fidel Castro away" reveal such hopelessness, the sheer ineffectiveness of a US policy that has tried to strangle Cuba economically but has not succeeded.[105]

Yet this hopelessness is recast by American policymakers. While Estragon and Vladmir wait, and stare their hopelessness in the face without acknowledging it, the American policy of waiting is represented in official discourse as successful, hopeful, steadfast and virtuous. The State Department claimed in 1992 that American policy toward Cuba was "a successful policy." It "succeeded in helping to significantly diminish Cuban support for insurgency abroad and terminate Cuba's special relationship with the Soviet Union." The result was that after the termination of the "six billion dollars in annual Soviet aid," the world was supposed to be witnessing "Cuba's economic collapse." Such success and hopefulness is attributed to the "long-standing American policy of economic and political isolation of Cuba," including embargo, suspension from the OAS, a US veto over international lending institutions which might provide loans to Cuba, and *The Cuban Democracy Act of 1992* and *Libertad Act of 1996*.[106] These measures, while failing in the ultimate goal of bringing about Castro's ouster, are written as a success. Moreover, the US approach is characterized as steadfast and virtuous. George W. Bush put it as plainly as anyone, stressing that "our Government has been very clear about our strategy, and that is, is that we will change the embargo strategy only when the Government of Cuba lets the people of Cuba express themselves freely. We will change our policy when the people running Cuba free people of conscience from the prisons. But until then we won't change."[107] Beckett's characters, exhibiting this sentiment, are rightly understood as stubborn, blind, and naïve, and inviting continual failure, while US policymakers have characterized a similar approach as hopeful, firm and successful.

American waiting is characterized as a virtue also because it is represented as being on the verge of success. The Cuban revolution was not expected to survive the US embargo, or the collapse of the Soviet Union, or the Special Period, or the stepping down of Fidel Castro. Even though it has survived each of these, there remains in the US a sense that "we're closer than ever" to a new Cuba. For example, when Fidel Castro stepped down in 2006, resigning his positions due to poor health (and then being officially succeeded by Raúl Castro in 2008), one possibility was that this would prompt a change in US policy. If anything could or would prompt such a change, it seemed that this could. The transition, however, was barely acknowledged in the White House. In a very brief press release, the president's statement simply said that he was monitoring the transfer of power and that the US stood prepared to offer humanitarian assistance if needed.[108] The succession in Cuba, however, offered opportunities for change. As a report from the Congressional Research Service noted in 2007, "In the context of Raúl Castro's succession, there are two broad policy approaches to contend with political change in Cuba: a stay the course or status-quo approach that would maintain the policy of isolating the Cuban government with comprehensive economic sanctions; and an approach aimed at influencing Cuban government and society through an easing of sanctions and increased contact and engagement."[109] The succession, however, did not elicit even a small change in US policy. Considering that the political succession in Cuba was quite stable, and that unrest has not resulted from the change, it becomes increasingly likely that the Cuban government can survive both Castros. Rather than being closer than ever to its stated goals, the United States may be in a position whereby "waiting for Fidel" and then "waiting for Raúl" may not be enough. The American hope and presupposition that Cuba will undergo a rapid democratic transition, and not a process of reform or economic change under a communist government, may leave the US unprepared to deal with the most likely scenarios of Cuba's political transition.

By the same token, when Soviet aid to Cuba came to an end with the collapse of the Soviet Union, the United States responded with the *Cuban Democracy Act*, to try and further pressure Cuba into reforms. The idea, as described by Congressman Robert Torricelli in 1992, was that the embargo was not something that has either "succeeded or failed, it has simply been frustrated, never allowed to work. No embargo against Cuba was ever going to succeed as long as the Soviet Union was willing to provide $4 or $5 billion worth of annual assistance."[110] It was only since the early 1990s, by such reasoning, that the embargo was given an opportunity to work. As Congressman Torricelli in 1995 claimed, "the embargo against Cuba is not 35 years old. It is now twenty-four months old."[111] By this reading, the American attempt at the isolation of Cuba was finally being given a chance to work the way it was intended to work, and would be expected to finally achieve the desired results in short order. This is effectively the same official rationale being made to the present day. When the Cuban Democracy Act and the Helms-Burton Act were originally adopted, casting the embargo in this light served to ennoble it with twin virtues. It was simultaneously represented in the discourse as both a new policy – untested, rather than failed – while at the same time it could be characterized as an old policy, unwavering and righteous. While any understanding of the embargo as "new" has clearly been put aside, a policy that can continue to be represented as one grounded in virtue remains strong, whether Fidel Castro sits atop the government or not. Such a characterization seeks to effect the production of an image of a policy that is based upon the strength of a principle – the opposition to totalitarianism – rather than a policy that has not achieved its stated aims.

The representations of American policy as successful – stemming from righteousness or imminent victory – as being responsible for the instigation of a coming change in Cuba, mask an inconsistency in US policy and expose the irony of its enduring pursuit. The inconsistency is that if American policymakers seek to take credit for the "collapse" of Cuba through vigilance in maintaining the embargo in spite of worldwide opposition, then it becomes more difficult to make the claim that the inherent problems of communism led to a breakdown of communist regimes around the world, with Cuba as the latest example of this "failed experiment." If the United States emerged victorious in the Cold War due the strength and quality of its foreign policy, then the US bears responsibility for the effects of that policy. In other words, according to the logic that proclaims American success, it is the United States, not the Cuban government, which currently impoverishes the Cuban people. This, of course, has been exactly the point of US policy, and as Louis Perez argues, it has indeed been successful.

> Sanctions were designed with malice of forethought, to make daily life in Cuba as difficult and desperate as possible, to inflict hardship and increase suffering, to deepen popular discontent with the goal of inciting a people to rebellion ... In varying degrees, the U.S. government did in fact achieve its purpose: Conditions in Cuba worsened. Scarcities increased. Hard times worsened. Cubans faced mounting shortages, increased rationing, and deteriorating services ... days were frequently filled with unrelieved hardship and adversity in the pursuit of even the most minimum needs of everyday life, day after day: hours on lines at

the local grocery store, hours waiting for public transportation, hours without electricity.[112]

US government officials since 1959 have repeatedly protested that the United States has no quarrel with the Cuban people, and have seemingly viewed their words and deeds to be grounded in such an understanding, but American actions have, to a great extent, focused US hostility to the revolution upon Cuba's people, and have caused them great harm. The notion of US success regarding Cuba exhibits a certain illogic in which a policy that is purportedly designed to help the Cuban people must first cause them hardship. It is reminiscent of the idea, expressed during the war in Vietnam, that it has become "necessary to destroy the village in order to save it." American words and deeds with respect to Cuba and the embargo are in fact remarkably inconsistent with one another.

Beyond inconsistency, American claims that "waiting for Fidel" is tantamount to victory in the struggle against the Cuban revolution exposes the tragic irony of such claims. First, there is the obvious fact that the failure of US policy is simply asserted to be victorious, and in spite of the fact that this assertion is convincing to no one but a handful of American politicians and Cuban exiles, it continues to be made. Second, and more importantly, is that US policy has not merely been ineffective, it has in fact aided and abetted the very outcome is sought to prevent: the survival of the revolution and the maintenance of support for it within Cuba. It is not simply the case, as noted earlier, that "a people utterly prostrate, preoccupied with matters of survival as the overriding reality of daily life, are not readily disposed to think about elections."[113] It is that the United States policy allowed for ordinary Cubans to understand their opposition to US policy a matter of national pride and national defense. As Louis Perez argues, "the United States challenged the Cubans on the grounds that the Cuban leadership was best prepared to defend: the ideal of patria, as a matter of national sovereignty and self-determination," such that "defending the nation became indistinguishable from defending the revolution and accelerated the centralization of power and facilitated the curtailment of civil liberties."[114] This effect of US policy, which has ingrained in Cuba the idea of resistance to the United States, has reinforced the simple fact that Cuba is far more likely to "outwait" the United States than the reverse.

The irony of the failure of US policy has generally been lost with respect to American policymakers, but in recent years a growing group of critics have begun to significantly change the debate. While the critics of US policy have been numerous outside of US government circles (both at home and abroad), they have begun to gain clout within government, reflecting the idea that US policy may be collapsing of its own irrelevance and ineffectiveness, and is more likely to do so than the Cuban revolution. In Congress every year, there are multiple bills introduced seeking to ease or eliminate travel restrictions to Cuba, and to end the embargo altogether (there has even been legislation introduced to allow Cuban baseball players to play professionally in the United States). The largest and most successful effort occurred in 2000, when Congress passed the *Trade Sanctions Reform and Export Enhancement Act*, with strong backing from agribusiness interests. This legislation allowed for US exports of food and medicine to go to any country embargoed by the US, although in the Cuban case, the law forbids any US public or private financing to facilitate any such sales.

In the absence of a strong lobby backing reform of US policy, efforts at further reform have failed in Congress, but the center of debate is shifting. In 2009, there were more than a dozen bills introduced in Congress to relax or end US restrictions regarding the embargo, and in years since restrictions were lifted for food and medicine, there have been well over one hundred such attempts in Congress. The proposed *Free Trade with Cuba Act* is emblematic of this effort. Introduced by Representative Charles Rangel in 2007 to lift the embargo and repeal both the Cuban Democracy Act and the Helms-Burton Act, the bill succinctly states the major problems that critics of US policy toward Cuba have identified over the years:

The Congress finds that –

(1) with the end of the Cold War and the collapse of the Soviet Union, Cuba is no longer a threat to the United States or the Western Hemisphere;
(2) the continuation of the embargo on trade between the United States and Cuba that was declared in February of 1962 is counterproductive, adding to the hardships of the Cuban people while making the United States the scapegoat for the failures of the communist system;
(3) in the countries of the former Soviet Union and the former Eastern bloc, China, and Vietnam, the United States is using economic, cultural, academic, and scientific engagement to support its policy of promoting democratic and human rights reforms; and
(4) the United States can best support democratic change in Cuba by promoting trade and commerce, travel, communications, and cultural, academic, and scientific exchanges.

An interesting feature of some of the legislation introduced has been an increasing effort to capture the terrain long claimed and held by advocates of the embargo, who have successfully associated their policies with the greatest virtues of American identity – freedom and democracy. In a nod to the long victorious hard-line policy advocates, Representative Charles Rangel called one of his bills to end all travel restrictions to Cuba the "Export Freedom to Cuba Act of 2009."[115] In another instance, on the House floor, Representative Jeff Flake stated that, "It is time for a get-tough policy with Cuba. It is time to allow Americans to travel there and spread freedom and influence. If we lift our travel ban, some say that Cuba will simply impose their own on us. But if somebody is going to limit my travel, it should be a communist, not my own government. We should let freedom ring here, and it will soon ring free in Cuba."[116] These efforts make an attempt to represent engagement as consistent with freedom and democracy, seeking to claim a rhetorical space that has been effectively exploited by advocates of the embargo. Whereas getting tough with Cuba has meant cutting off diplomatic relations and trade, in this context the argument is made that Cuban communism stands no chance in the face of American tourists and businesspeople being let loose upon the island, as that is where the real strength of the US lies. Moreover, the implication in Representative Flake's statement is that only totalitarian governments tell their citizens where they can and cannot travel. The US, by doing so, is not acting like a free country, but is instead acting like the adversaries it disdains, and thus it should change its policies.

While members of Congress have been willing to recognize US policy toward Cuba as a failure and try to reform or end it, this has not been the case in the executive branch, at least until President Obama and Secretary of State Hillary Clinton began to openly describe US policy toward Cuba as a failure in 2009.[117] Such explicit declarations, discussed in the next chapter, suggest that a change may be coming in US policy and actions, but it is unclear how easily a new approach can supplant the old one.

6 The presence of the past, or an Obama departure?

The past is never dead. It's not even past.

William Faulkner[1]

I do support the Cuban Democracy Act ... even though there's no longer any prospect of Russian missiles there, but that is our policy.

President Bill Clinton[2]

Historian Louis Perez, in an article entitled "The Circle of Connections," tells the story of Liborio, who in the days just after independence from Spain, was alone, cutting sugar cane in the field. He chopped through a row of cane to discover G-d, sitting in a little chair.

"Buenos dias, Liborio," said G-d. "I have come to see how my Cubans are doing."

Liborio stood with his clothes soaked with sweat, his hands cracked and bleeding, his feet bare and filthy, and thought for a long time about what he should say to G-d.

"First of all Señor," he said, "we are not longer subjects of the King of Spain. We are free men."

"I can see that," said G-d, looking at Liborio from head to foot. "The difference is astounding."

"But I wonder sometimes," Liborio continued, "why life is still so hard."

G-d smiled at him. "My son, nothing on this earth can be perfect, or nobody would want to go to heaven. Sugar is sweet, but man has to labor to take it from the ground. The ocean is wide and beautiful, but it has sudden storms and dangerous currents to pull you under and drown you. This Cuba is so beautiful, so I had to make the pests, all so that life here would be less than Paradise. Nothing can be perfect in this world."

Liborio pondered this, trying to fathom the wisdom of G-d's ways. "But nothing can mar the beauty of freedom," he said finally, "Surely freedom is perfect?"

G-d smiled again. "For that," he said, "I created the Americans."[3]

In telling this story, Perez sought to underscore, among other things, the persistent attention the US has devoted to Cuba throughout two centuries of shared history. In this time, he argues, through frequent contact and close encounters, both Cubans and North Americans have in part defined their worlds in relation to the other, and their connections have been intimate, bearing out the wisdom of John Quincy Adams.[4] For just as Adams predicted more than 175 years ago that Cuba could not divorce itself from American influence any more than the United States could ignore Cuba, his words continue to have relevance to this day.

If current US policies toward Cuba tend to be associated with a variety of newer representations – death, failure and isolation, arising out of a post-Cold War era in which communism is looked upon as an entity waiting to finally die – at a more fundamental level they are informed by long-standing historical interpretations and representations of the United States, Latin America, Cuba, Cubans and communism that continue to be reproduced today. There is a striking consistency in American behavior, embodying both of the themes outlined in this book: the presumption of regional superiority and the negation of communism in favor of liberal democracy. If, as it has been argued, the ascent of Castro prompted "the volatile combination of the Monroe Doctrine and the Cold War," it is the case that this volatile combination has yet to cease, long after the end of the Cold War, which should have seemingly removed the greatest impediment to a change in American behavior.

With respect to both of these themes, American policy reflects what Sheldon Wolin terms "the presence of the past," in which the past – practices, policies, statements, understandings – maintains a grasp on the present, influencing it greatly.[5] William Faulkner captured the idea more succinctly than anyone else, writing in *Requiem for a Nun* that, "The past is never dead. It's not even past." US policy toward Cuba is indeed a perfect example of this. Past policy, and the hold it exerts, maintains great significance in defining, ordering and understanding the present. American political leaders, businesspeople and members of the public who may oppose US policy toward Cuba have been unsuccessful in their efforts to change US policy precisely because of this circumstance. The past does not die easily. Those who have managed to keep US policy consistent for decades, who have sought to maintain the embargo and keep all possible economic and political pressure on Castro, their understanding is that the policy is not at all a relic of the past. It is very much relevant to, and a part of, the present. Consequently, US policy embraces a series of representations that serve to strengthen myths of American strength, superiority, justice and righteousness in action taken on behalf of the nation. As Wolin states, the main purpose of myth is "to fix certain meanings about matters that are alleged to be fundamental because they pertain to the identity and flourishing of the whole society. Societies try to express what they are about as political collectivities by appealing to or constructing their pasts and connecting that past with present arrangements of power." In other words, the language of identity and difference "is designed to privilege a certain past in order to legitimate a particular present."[6]

In the United States, the interpretation and construction of certain histories of American foreign policy have nourished a set of mythological understandings regarding America's proper role with respect to other countries. Continuous strands in official readings of these policies toward Cuba link a privileged past to present actions whose legitimacy rests upon that past. First of all, the presumption of American superiority and regional hegemony continues to be manifested in the discourse and the deeds of US foreign policy in the Western Hemisphere, reinforcing the hierarchy in which the United States maintains the "relative upper hand" over Latin America. As discussed in chapters two and three, this hierarchy is present in official American understandings regarding inter-American politics which continue to this day. The presumption of superiority and hegemony that the US maintains in the Western Hemisphere, or the idea that the United States bears a measure of responsibility for political affairs in the region, still remains as a part of US interaction with Latin American countries.

There continue to be occasional explicit references to the inferiority of Latin Americans, such as Jesse Helms' comment that "all Latins are volatile people," or the off-the-record comment told by a State Department official to Lars Schoultz that "what screws up in Latin America is the Latin American. And they'll *always* screw up, because *they're* screwed up."[7] These statements suggest that notions of Latin American inferiority based upon the language of race and/or underdevelopment have not entirely disappeared. More common, however, are representations informed by a "prejudice of equality," which involves the practice of rendering singularity or similarity out of difference, or in the words of Tzvetan Todorov, "identifying the other as purely and simply with one's own 'ego ideal.'"[8] Rooted in such imaginings of universal interests and ideals are the practices that effect "control-through-sameness."

The belief in US superiority is also reinforced by Washington's concerns with a post-Castro Cuba, in which the idea is readily accepted that political developments in Cuba, regardless of their character, are necessarily the concern of the United States. The first President Bush, describing the US response to such a circumstance, stated that "you'll see the United States do exactly what we should: Go down and lift those people up and say, 'We want to help you.'" His words are reminiscent of an earlier era, reflecting a consistency in the sentiment, if not the language, of American policymakers from the time of the Spanish-American War to the 1990s. Senator Albert Beveridge's exhortations to his contemporaries to serve "the betterment of man," and "the regeneration of the world," like Wilson's efforts to "make the world safe for democracy," reveal a similar attitude toward America's self-appointed role in the promotion of change for the better. President Obama, too, exhibits a consistency with the past, in saying about US policy toward Latin America that, "We will be partners in helping to alleviate poverty. But the American people have to get some positive reinforcement if they are to be engaged in the efforts to lift other countries out of the poverty that they're experiencing."[9] This desire to uplift others is something Lars Schoultz describes as a compulsion the US cannot seem to control. While decent in its intentions, it has created a resentment that stands in the way of mutual accommodation.[10]

With respect to Cuba, this attitude and understanding goes even further, fostering what Louis Perez calls a sense of entitlement that is still strongly exhibited in American actions. In only the past few years, Perez points out, there have been many US funded projects to plan for a post-Castro Cuba, including the development of a "Commission for Assistance to a Free Cuba," a "Cuba Transition Project," preparations for the reconstruction of the Cuban economy, and a program to study the restitution of nationalized property. "That the Americans in the twenty-first century could presume that planning the future of Cuba without the participation of any of the 11 million people who lived on the island was an attitude worthy of the arrogance of their predecessors in the nineteenth century."[11] Old habits are not easily modified.

In addition to the consistent reproduction of a presumption of US regional superiority, there continues to be, since the end of the Cold War, a reiteration and strengthening of a representation of Cuba that is characterized by difference, the denial of freedom, danger (to its own citizens) and illegitimacy, all a result of its communist system. Construed as the most telling features of the Cuban government, they continue to mark the country as an object of US disdain and hostility. President Obama's statements on Cuba, unsurprisingly, continue to reflect this outlook. In a statement in March 2010, responding to a Cuban crackdown on opposition to the government, Obama stated, "I remain committed to supporting the simple desire of the Cuban people to freely determine their future and to enjoy the rights and freedoms that define the Americas and that should be universal to all human beings." The fact that "Cuban authorities continue to respond to the aspirations of the Cuban people with a clenched fist," is characterized by the President as "deeply disturbing."[12] The president's comments, like others before his, are reflective of how American political leaders act as a self-appointed "community of judgment" regarding the legitimacy of the Cuban government.

Even though the Cold War is long since over, American policy and rhetoric is targeted at the same non-democratic challenge, with only the specifics of the current Cuban circumstance being altered in post-Cold War representations. It may be the case that there is no threat posed to the United States by Cuba's actions, but this is why "the very visibility of its mode of being as other" takes on added significance. That mode of being has always been considered illegitimate, but now it represents the sole provocation to Washington, and is thus the most salient feature of the revolution. The Cuban revolution's durability, its very survival, continues to represent a challenge to United States policy, which is increasingly implicated in the attempt to remove, first Fidel, and now Raúl Castro from power. At the same time, it challenges the dominant American understanding of the proper role each country should maintain in global and regional politics. In spite of the shift in the particulars of current representations, the discourse reproduces understandings of Cuba and Castro that dominated the Cold War. They are/ were both informed by the same sources: the absence of liberalism and the presence of communism in Cuba, leading to the same confrontation for the same reasons.

With respect to both US regional hegemony and US anti-communism, the representations, assumptions, judgments and understandings of these two domains have not altered substantially with respect to Cuba after the collapse of communism in Eastern Europe and the Soviet Union. American foreign policy reflects and supports these "surviving textual practices that give rise to systems of meaning and value" which are part of a relationship involving superiority/inferiority, strength/weakness, developed/ underdeveloped, democracy/communism, freedom/slavery, and legitimate/ illegitimate. Consequently, the political ramifications of these modes of representation, and the opposing understandings of the United States and Cuba they reinforce, also continue unabated. Even though the global context of the post-Cold War era is vastly different from that which preceded it, there is little that has changed with regard to the official American discourse concerning US and Cuban identities – what each state represents, practices and ultimately is.

As the representational practices that arose out of interaction in earlier eras survive, they perpetuate understandings that assert the truth and justice of American identity, and the illegitimacy of Cuban difference. The objectivity and justice of the American order is presupposed. Revolutionary Cuba, as a challenge to that order, is therefore considered to be the responsible agent for conflict, making the American response necessary, be it in the 1960s, 1980s, 1990s or today. Castro's actions, his experiment, have forced the US to adopt its policies. The perspective suggests that the United States does not take a proactive policy, but a reactive one, designed only to restore a non-communist order whose legitimacy is presumed. If Cuba is on the receiving end of a hostile US policy – embargo, isolation and denunciation – it has made such action necessary, reasonable and correct by virtue of both its actions and its presence. This lies at the center of President Clinton's claim, quoted at the beginning of the chapter, that even though there is no longer a physical threat from Cuba, US policy remains the same. By such a reading, the US government is not refusing to admit inconsistency, nor is it refusing to adapt to a changed world, for it is Cuba which refuses to change. There is nothing that the United States can alter. President George W. Bush argued this position forcefully, when he remarked in March of 2008 that, "reports of the supposed retirement of Cuba's dictator initially led many to believe that the time had finally come for the United States to change our policy on

Cuba and improve our relations with the regime. That sentiment is exactly backward. To improve relations, what needs to change is not the United States; what needs to change is Cuba."[13] Because US policies are postulated as serving goals of an open democracy and an open economy in Cuba, they require no modification. Were American policy not oriented toward effecting a restructuring of Cuban politics, it would symbolize assent for an illegitimate regime. Thus, the US response to Castro has been characterized as the correct one, both now and in the past.

As long as the discourse of US policy as it is constructed in Washington continues to support the same imaginings that have long been upheld – where the US is understood as democratic, free and legitimate, preserving human and civil rights, while Cuba is spoken of in terms of communism, non-democracy, the denial of freedom and illegitimacy, as a threat to its own citizens, international norms and peace, and as part of a place that is necessarily within the legitimate domain of American concerns – there is little reason to expect that the end of the Cold War should have automatically prompted a reappraisal or fundamental change in US policy toward Cuba. By virtue of Washington's current understandings of the conflict, there is little, if anything, to suggest a change. It appears to lie outside the realm of what is imagined as possible according to contemporary formulations of what the Cuban revolution does and is.

An Obama way for US-Cuban relations?

Does change appear to lie entirely outside the realm of US policy? The arrival of President Barack Obama in the White House has led to renewed discussion and speculation about whether the US will seek to improve and/or normalize relations with Cuba. During the election campaign, President Obama argued, to both great support and derision, that he would be willing to engage in talks with any of America's enemies, without preconditions. At one of the early Democratic party primary debates, Obama stated, in response to the question, "would you be willing to meet separately, without precondition, during the first year of your administration, in Washington or anywhere else, with the leaders of Iran, Syria, Venezuela, Cuba and North Korea?" that,

> I would. And the reason is this, that the notion that somehow not talking to countries is punishment to them – which has been the guiding diplomatic principle of this administration – is ridiculous. Now, Ronald Reagan and Democratic presidents like JFK constantly spoke to the Soviet Union at a time when Ronald Reagan called them an evil empire. And the reason is because they understood that we may not trust them and they may pose an extraordinary danger to this country, but we had the obligation to find areas where we can potentially move forward. And I think that it is a disgrace that we have not spoken to them.[14]

This approach to dealing with US adversaries represents a change with the recent past, in which engagement has been avoided with what the US has characterized as "rogue" or otherwise troublesome regimes, due to the perceived weakness of doing so. Fareed Zakaria has described Obama's approach, correctly, as a gamble, pointing out that, "Obama's outreach to the world is an experiment, and not just to see if the world will respond. He wants to demonstrate at home that engagement does not make America weak. For decades, it's been thought deadly for an American politician to be seen as seeking international cooperation. Denouncing, demeaning, and insulting other countries was a cheap and easy way to seem strong. In the battle of images, tough and stupid always seemed to win ... Obama is gambling that America is now mature enough to understand that machismo is not foreign policy"[15]

This outlook has appeared to inform President Obama's early approach to Cuba, resulting in a change to US policy only a few months after his inauguration. In April of 2009, the president announced that the US would eliminate the restrictions placed on travel and remittances. Cuban Americans became permitted to visit family members in Cuba without restrictions. Previously, there had been limitations placed on both the frequency and the duration of visits, even limitations on how heavy luggage could be that travelers carried. These were eliminated. In addition, Cuban Americans became able to send unlimited remittances to family members in Cuba. The limitations on the amount and frequency of remittances were removed, and US banks were granted permission to forward remittances to Cuba.[16]

These changes implemented by President Obama represented a significant reversal of the previous several years, during which travel and remittances for Cuban Americans had generally been subject to increasing restrictions. In fact, the administration went so far as to admit failure of previous US policy, and to point out that such failure was the catalyst for a change. The President wrote in an op-ed article that "we amended a Cuba policy that has failed for decades to advance liberty or opportunity for the Cuban people."[17] Secretary of State Hillary Clinton made the same point at the Summit of the Americas in 2009, "We are continuing to look for productive ways forward, because we view the present policy as having failed."[18] Even beyond the specifics of the provisions on travel and remittances, Obama's early move signaled a willingness to depart from the general thrust of US policy toward Cuba in the post-Cold War years. If the tenor since the early 1990s has been to tighten the embargo and further try to isolate Castro through efforts such as travel restrictions, the Cuban Democracy Act and the Helms-Burton legislation, Obama's policy change represented a move in the opposite direction. It did not lead to an immediate end to the embargo, or to normalization of relations, or even to the milder sanctions regime that existed under President Clinton, but it did represent a move in the opposite direction from the trend that had marked US policy for many years. To move beyond this initial move, President Obama has indicated that since the

United States made a significant first step, it is been incumbent upon Cuba to take the next step and reciprocate, as part of a gradual, mutual warming of relations. The type of reciprocity expected by the United States involves progress on human rights, elections, and the release of political prisoners, all longstanding demands of the United States.

While the progress in thawing US-Cuban relations has been limited since April 2009, the Obama Administration has continued to explore opportunities for engagement. In July of 2009, Obama began the resumption of immigration talks with Cuba. These talks, which began in 1994 in the wake of a wave of illegal Cuban immigration to the United States, were suspended by George W. Bush in 2003. In a similar vein, the two governments have held talks on the resumption of direct postal service between the two countries. In once such instance, in September of 2009, Cuban authorities invited a State Department official to turn her planned, brief visit to Cuba into a six-day stay that included meetings with not only government officials, but also opposition figures and people from Cuban civil organizations. Another change, albeit minor, involved turning off an electronic ticker sign that streamed anti-Castro messages from windows of the US interests section in Havana. The Cubans had installed large billboard with anti-US messages and black flags in front of the building to block the sign and keep the messages from being seen, but the Cubans removed the billboards once Obama came to office. These types of interactions have all given substance to the pronouncements that more than a cosmetic change to US policy is being contemplated and pursued. As Julia Sweig at the Council on Foreign Relations noted, "Look at the momentum; look at the pace of these steps. It's a departure from many, many years of practice."[19]

These shifts in US actions toward Cuba and the expanded dialogue between the two countries, all initiated in the first year of Obama's presidency, indicate an emerging break with the past. They reflect a change in US policy that President Obama says he seeks with Cuba, more than simply the tweaking of a few elements of US policy that the Administration wants to slightly modify. As the president said at the Summit of the America's meeting in 2009, "The United States seeks a new beginning with Cuba," and "I do believe that we can move U.S.-Cuban relations in a new direction."[20] His own view is that the change in travel and remittance restrictions was, "a good-faith effort, a show of good faith on the part of the United States that we want to recast our relationship."[21]

This shift, however, does not provide a full picture of current US policy. The presence of the past still looms large. In a speech to the Cuban American National Foundation in May of 2008, during his campaign for president, Obama stated that, "My policy toward Cuba will be guided by one word: Libertad. And the road to freedom for all Cubans must begin with justice for Cuba's political prisoners, the rights of free speech, a free press and freedom of assembly; and it must lead to elections that are free and fair." He also stated, in the same speech that, "Never, in my lifetime, have the people of

Cuba known freedom. Never, in the lives of two generations of Cubans, have the people of Cuba known democracy ... I won't stand for this injustice, you won't stand for this injustice, and together we will stand up for freedom in Cuba."[22] In other words, Obama is repeating the words of many of his predecessors, echoing US policy since 1959. This was not simply an empty campaign promise – to maintain continuity in America's pressure and opposition to Cuba – offered in the heat of a campaign to win votes. After all, President Obama has stuck to this formulation numerous times while in office. At the Summit of the Americas meeting in 2009, President Barack Obama declared: "The Cuban people are not free and that's our lodestone, our North Star, when it comes to our policy in Cuba."[23] And again, upon the death – from a hunger strike – of imprisoned Cuban dissident Orlando Zapata Tamayo, the President stated that, "I remain committed to supporting the simple desire of the Cuban people to freely determine their future and to enjoy the rights and freedoms that define the Americas and that should be universal to all human beings"[24] These statements, echoing words that go back decades, place the Cuban case in the in the larger context of US foreign policy and inter-American relations, in which "we all have a responsibility to see that the people of the Americas have the ability to pursue their own dreams in democratic societies."[25] There are many such examples of President Obama providing this characterization of US policies and goals, and they remain perfectly consistent with the remarks and policies of his predecessors.

These words suggest that the same objectives that have been sought for decades remain, and that they will continue to be openly declared. US goals are not being abandoned. In fact, their hold within the White House seems even to have been reasserted. As Abe Lowenthal observed, "After reversing some sanctions imposed by the Bush administration, the Obama government indicated that Cuba would have to make the next move before Washington considered any more steps toward rapprochement. Far from ushering in a new beginning, the Obama administration seemed to revert to the stance of several previous U.S. administrations: it would wait for Cuba to change."[26]

Still, there is a greater element of complexity, or tension, inherent in current US policy toward Cuba, far more so than during prior administrations, and this is evident in President Obama's approach to the country. This complexity and tension is manifested in two ways. The first of these is the suggestion that some element of engagement, rather than isolation, is a better strategy for achieving freedom and democracy in Cuba. Obama's May 2008 campaign speech to the Cuban American National Foundation spoke to the idea of engagement, demonstrating not only consistency with the past by holding out for Cuban freedom, but a departure as well by advocating a new strategy to achieve that goal. Obama stated, "Now I know what the easy thing is to do for American politicians. Every four years, they come down to Miami, they talk tough, they go back to Washington, and nothing changes in Cuba ... It's time for more than tough talk that never yields results. It's time for a new strategy ... It is time to pursue direct diplomacy, with friend and foe alike ... I would be willing to lead that diplomacy at a time and place of my choosing, but only when we have an opportunity to advance the interests of the United States, and to advance the cause of freedom for the Cuban people."[27] A further look at his statement made at the Summit of the Americas, about Cuban freedom being the lodestone of US policy, reveals a similar tilt. "What I think my entire administration has acknowledged is, is that the policy that we've had in place for 50 years hasn't worked the way we want it to. The Cuban people are not free."[28] In this understanding of the problem, the fundamental goals of US policy have not changed, only the means by which to achieve them. And Obama holds no great attachment to all the US policies toward Cuba he inherited. As he has stated, "we are not dug into policies that were formulated before I was born."[29]

This perspective understandably led to the presidential memorandum on travel and remittances, which stated, "Measures that decrease dependency of the Cuban people on the Castro regime and that promote contacts between Cuban-Americans and their relatives in Cuba are means to encourage positive change in Cuba. The United States can pursue these goals by facilitating greater contact between separated family members in the United States and Cuba and increasing the flow of remittances and information to the Cuban people."[30] Considering the failure of previous policies to achieve their state goals, the policy alteration represents a welcome departure to those who have been making this exact argument for years, only to have it ignored in Washington.

There is, however, an additional element of tension in US policy. It goes even further than the argument that the US is trying to achieve the same ends with different means. This tension appears more subtly in the President's language. This language offers a perspective that embodies the approach of political realism. Such an approach to US foreign policy is guided by aims that are more limited than current US policy toward Cuba. It argues that America "goes not abroad in search of monsters to destroy" (in the words of John Quincy Adams), and instead of pursuing goals such as democratization and regime change, places higher value on international order and stability, on appreciating the limits of US power and capabilities, as well as an understanding that the United States can engage in normal relations and conduct business with any country, even with governments it finds objectionable. It argues for an understanding that the United States does not have to try to undermine, overthrow or change a country's government simply because it does not like their foreign policy or their form of government. President Obama's foreign policy embodies a strong element of realist thinking as part of its larger strategic approach, far more so that was the case with George W. Bush. In a speech at West Point in 2009, laying out his case for how to conduct the war in Afghanistan, President Obama stated that, "As President, I refuse to set goals that go beyond our responsibility, our means, or our interests."[31] Fareed Zakaria points out how Obama has diverged from the trend among US presidents, who "cannot resist the temptation to become Winston Churchill. They gravitate to grand rhetoric about freedom and tyranny, and embrace the moral drama of their role as leaders of the free world." Instead, he argues persuasively that "Obama is a realist, by temperament, learning, and instinct. More than any president since Richard Nixon, he has focused on defining American interests carefully, providing the resources to achieve them, and keeping his eyes on the prize."[32]

The outlook is evident with respect to Cuba. The President's statements sometimes put aside the goal of democracy promotion, the end of the Castro brothers' rule, regime change, even the repeated calls for elections and a host of conditions required before the normalization of relations can occur. Instead the emphasis sometimes shifts in the Administration's statements, as well as the actual practice of US policy, toward a more limited set of goals – better country-to-country relations with Cuba, and finding avenues for cooperation in addressing a range of problems such as migration, broadcasting, postal service, telecommunications services, drug trafficking, the environment and economic development. These limited goals, in effect, recognize the fact of the Cuban revolution, and simply seek to make the best of the situation.

For example, Obama's campaign statement about meeting with leaders of hostile foreign nations without preconditions is grounded in the logic of realism. It argues that talks with adversaries are not concessions, that interests can be pursued and objectives reached in spite of mutual hostility, that the US cannot remake every government to its own liking, and that in the absence of remaking governments, it still makes sense to achieve some of what the US wants, even if it cannot have all that it wants. The policy changes involving travel and remittances also include elements of realism in them. The original logic of limiting such restrictions was to prevent the inflow of dollars to Cuba, based on an understanding that any financial transactions that brought money into Cuba would ultimately strengthen the regime and perhaps delay its collapse. The end of these restrictions implies that the United States government has less concern for the stated goal of such policies. It is possible to argue, as the President and Secretary of State have, that the policies have failed, that they forced Cuban Americans to pay too high a price for US foreign policy, that trying to encourage greater engagement is a better strategy to bring about democratic reform in Cuba. But in addition, the change in policy also carries with it an admission that the US now has a greater willingness, even if only a slightly greater willingness, to accommodate itself to Cuba and the fact of a revolutionary Cuban government, in order to accomplish some of its more limited objectives.

The understanding that the US government is willing to accept far less from its Cuba policy can be found in parts of Administration statements. "I'm prepared to have my administration engage with the Cuban Government on a wide range of issues, from drugs, migration, and economic issues, to human rights, free speech, and democratic reform."[33] In other words, the US has interests beyond democratization and human rights, and it is willing to talk and engage on these topics. Another example is that Obama has said, "My guidepost in U.S.-Cuba policy is going to be how can we encourage Cuba to be respectful of the rights of its people. And we do expect that Cuba will send signals that they're interested in liberalizing in such a way that not only do U.S.-Cuban relations improve, but so that the energy and creativity and initiative of the Cuban people can potentially be released."[34] Here again is an example of backing away for earlier, more maximal goals. This formulation says that the US can accommodate something less than the complete freedom of the Cuban people and democratic reform. It will instead settle simply for better treatment of citizens by the Cuban government. Such words say, in effect, that the US wants democracy in Cuba, but it will still seek better relations on a variety of other issues in the absence of this.

Just as policies and conditions in Cuba cannot be expected to change quickly, the same is true for US policy. A set of policies that have been in place for 50 years is not going to be dismantled quickly, especially without some reciprocity on the part of Cuba, which has been a key element in President Obama's statements. He has said, "if you take significant steps toward democracy, beginning with the freeing of all political prisoners, we will take steps to begin normalizing relations."[35] This is a departure from the recent past, in which US policy has reflected a tougher position, saying in effect that Cuba must democratize first and then the US would normalize relations. Current formulations take US policy closer back to the period just prior to the end of the Cold War, when freeing political prisoners was the last major precondition the US had attached to improved relations (all the others up to that point had involved Cuba's foreign policy: cutting ties to the Soviet Union, ending support for revolutionary movements, removing troops from Africa). After the Cold War is when the US began to demand a set of significant, additional internal changes to Cuba before normalization could occur. And to the extent that the US seeks a change in Cuba's internal arrangements, as opposed to its foreign policy, Cuba continues to exhibit little willingness to accommodate any such conditions as an avenue to better relations with the United States.

Perhaps President Obama's words and deeds that hint at a more realist approach to Cuba are emblematic of a slowly (very slowly) developing attitude of greater respect for Cuban sovereignty and independence. But for the most part, the same attitude that has reflected hierarchy in US-Cuban relations for years remains. As Lars Schoultz notes, this idea of respect is the key point for Cuba, without which much progress on country-to-country relations is likely. Washington, Schoultz points out, does not understand the idea of respect for Cuba. Pointing out how the United States has repeatedly demonstrated an arrogance toward Cuba – whether it has conducted spy plane overflights in Cuba, continually voiced the idea that the US merely seeks to help Cubans enjoy "the blessings of liberty," demanded democratization, or set up a commission to help transition Cuba to become a market democracy – Schoultz argues that they are policies that seek domination, even if it is supposedly benevolent domination. The government of Cuba, he points out, cannot countenance this circumstance. "The mere existence of a Commission for Assistance to a Free Cuba is proof that the United States still cannot concede to Cubans the right of self-determination, while Cubans apparently consider this concession the first step toward accommodation."[36]

Accommodation along the lines that the Cubans may expect will not come easy for the United States, if it comes at all. Though Obama promised to bring change to Washington, it is difficult to accomplish. The past has a hold on the present, and even if change is sought, the United States cannot and will not quickly divorce itself from its Cuba policy of the last 50 years. As this book has argued, American policy toward Cuba is bound up with American identity, and identity is not easily revised. While it should be pointed out that in considering policy toward Cuba, President Obama also has political considerations to take into account, and issues to address such as economic recovery, health care legislation, and financial services reform. But the political challenge involving Cuba is bigger than weighing priorities. Revising decades of words and deeds is not just a balancing act, it involves taking on the proponents of a settled policy that is grounded in a popular, well-supported sense of American identity.

Other worlds: Contingency and possible changes

In spite of the argument that the discourse of American foreign policy has served to render American behavior rational, reasonable, correct and necessary, the continuity in American representations and policy and the presupposed justice of them do not imply a deterministic interpretation of US policy. The thesis advanced here, that certain historical representations of Cuba, Latin America and communism have informed, led to and rendered comprehensible particular US policies, does not imply that any outcome or action by the US was predetermined. Nor is this discussion meant to suggest that US policy and the official discourse regarding Cuba must remain unchanged until Fidel and Raul Castro are among the departed. Rather, as representations are historical contingencies that reflect only one out of many possibilities, there is no reason why a shift in US policy is not possible. A rapprochement with Cuba, with Raul Castro still in power, is not out of the question. It would not represent a surprise to the argument advanced in this book, for identity and difference are not timeless constructs, but historical contingencies which can undergo varying degrees of modification.

What is crucial, however, to any such alteration is this: since identity is secured in relation to its opposites through discursive representational practices, a shift in US policy would require a concurrent shift in the discourse of Cuban-American relations and a focus upon newly-salient features of each country's identifying characteristics. Neither set of practices precludes or precedes the other; they are simultaneous happenings. One would not expect to see an end to the US embargo without an accompanying account of newly-emphasized identifying features of Cuba that would explain why it is not necessary to oust Raul Castro, or why engagement, as opposed to isolation, would better serve the achievement of democracy.

If President Obama or a subsequent administration were to break with current policy while Raul Castro remains in power (and even while Fidel Castro remains an important actor in Cuba), there are several scenarios that afford such a possibility, three of which are addressed here. The first, the opposite of the Vietnam-era strategy of declaring victory and getting out, would involve a US administration declaring victory over Castro and Cuban communism, rendering them inconsequential to the concerns of global politics and American foreign policy, then establishing normal diplomatic and commercial relations. In other words, declare victory and get in. Other examples of helping an enemy after its defeat, most notably Germany and Japan, provide for possible alternative understandings of an American relationship with Cuba. Once the threat from these countries was no longer judged to be significant, or represented as such, the US began a new relationship with each based upon close and cordial ties that has lasted for decades. The initial shift in US policy and was quite rapid, occurring over a period of only a few years. Additionally, in Japan the defeated wartime ruler, Emperor Hirohito, was allowed to maintain his position without threatening the official American acceptance of the new relationship.

By 1948 in Germany, the United States was engaged in a massive effort to save West Berlin from the Soviet blockade, expending its resources on a place that it had only recently sought to destroy. By 1950, US Secretary of State Dean Acheson declared that the US intended to defend Japan, stating that the country fell within the US "defensive perimeter." Far from sworn enemies of the United States, Germany and Japan became American allies and were incorporated into the economic and security regimes of the United States and Western Europe. What these cases suggest is that the possibility for a swift and thorough change in US policy is quite possible, and that such a change is accompanied by revised representations, emphasizing a set of non-threatening, perhaps even friendly characteristics previously ignored during times of conflict.

The weakness in this analogy is that is does not consider major differences in these two situations. The United States does not militarily occupy Cuba, dictating the terms of political and economic reorganization, nor is this a likely scenario. Moreover, Hirohito may have been permitted to remain emperor of Japan, but many other of that society's institutions were radically reformed or eliminated at the same time. Such discontinuity in Cuban society and politics would not be likely to accompany a shift in US policy toward Castro's Cuba.

A second possibility, the more plausible of the two, is one that has been cited more often than the one outlined earlier. It involves a replication of US policy toward China, in which the United States recognizes the country, conducts normal diplomatic relations with it, engages in trade, and does not try to overthrow it, even if a change in government might be ultimately desirable. The fundamental logic of this analogy is that if the United States can engage in such practices with China, which is also a communist country dominated by the party leadership, then so too can such a relationship be established with Cuba. In spite of the United States' differences with China in the 1950s and 1960s, Kissinger's secret visit and Nixon's surprise announcement brought a rapid change in US policy, and concurrently, representations of China. Instead of being regarded as an implacable enemy, China was regarded as a nation with whom the US could "live together on the same planet despite [our] differences," a country with which the US could "talk about these differences rather than fight about them."[37] From that point, the discourse of US relations with China changed dramatically, while at the same time, political relations were strengthened, business relations developed and student and cultural exchanges began.

The counterargument to this analogy includes the realist assessment that the stakes in America's relationship with China are much greater than they are with Cuba. The possibility of a refugee crisis in South Florida exists, but over the long term, China presents greater opportunities and dangers to the United States than does Cuba. Therefore, the current relationship with China, based on engagement, negotiation and continual dialogue is necessary, if not entirely palatable.

A response to these considerations might also make an appeal to the logic of realism, noting that the absence of a serious potential threat from Cuba might make it easier to reach an understanding with Castro, as the consequences for the US are minimal. Moreover, since the mid-1980s, almost every time the US and Cuba have undertaken negotiations to solve a particular problem, they have reached an agreement, be it in the area of migration, refugees, or even the removal of Cuban troops from Angola. Such has not been the case with China, which continues to confront the US over the export of advanced weapons technology, human rights, and the protection of intellectual property rights, in spite of many efforts to negotiate mutually acceptable solutions to these problems. In addition to these considerations, it is important to bear in mind Cuba's economic plight. Since Castro is in a weakened position domestically, and now might welcome an end to the US embargo, there may be greater possibilities for American political and economic gains.

The third option, which is what President Obama appears to be pursuing, is to argue that greater engagement advances the cause of Cuban freedom better than separation. The pursuit of this type of policy is reflected in the policy on travel and remittances and justified by arguing that United States can pursue it goals by "facilitating greater contact between separated family members in the United States and Cuba and increasing the flow of remittances and information to the Cuban people." This approach has already been discussed, so there is no need to revisit it. The point is simply that this option offers another possibility for a US rapprochement with Cuba. My own expectation is the president will at some point make a move to end the embargo and possibly normalize relations with Cuba, but he will argue that US goals have not changed. He will argue that the US seeks democratization, freedom, and market capitalism, but that the best way to achieve these objectives in Cuba is through active engagement with Cuba, via government contacts, commerce and tourism. Not only has the president acknowledged US policy toward Cuba to be a failure, but with each passing year, it becomes increasingly clear that the Cuban revolution will be able to outlast not only the rule of Fidel and Raul Castro, but also the fifty-plus years of American efforts to fatally undermine it.

Though reaching a *modus vivendi* with Castro would seemingly involve accepting the present Cuban government as it is, a condition repeatedly stated as unacceptable, this is not necessarily the case. As this book has argued, those elements which are seen as constituting Cuban identity are not inherent qualities, but historical and social constructions. If accepting the Cuban government as it is entails the perseverance of its present structures and personalities, it would not entail the perpetuation of how they are interpreted. After all, if the normalization of relations with Cuba were precluded primarily on the basis of principle – the presence of a communist dictatorship – then America's China policy would be rendered inconsistent or hypocritical. Yet it is the case that policies toward both Cuba and China are considered (officially) to be proper, each in its own right. The way in which they are represented makes each a distinct case, in which US actions are not uniformly guided by consistent notions of national interest or universal principle, but by understandings that are concerned with specific attributes of identity. The entity referred to as the Cuban Communist dictatorship is something that is also simultaneously Latin American, 'American,' and Cuban in ways that the Chinese government cannot be. In other words, the interpretation of it and its major characteristics are contingent upon a range of elements, none of which are themselves fixed.

What is central to either of these scenarios suggesting a possible change in US policy toward Cuba is that they could be rendered comprehensible, reasonable and correct in Washington's official language, as much as any current policy. An opening toward Cuba analogous to China would not have to be understood as the abandonment of US principles and interests. Rather it would be accompanied by a re-presentation of Cuban and American characteristics. Representations of Cuba might render it a defeated country, no longer a threat or danger to the US, but instead, in need of assistance in order to rebuild or prevent crisis or chaos. Raul Castro's role would likely be understood and written as diminished even if he remained in power, as his irrelevance and powerlessness would be evidenced in his acceptance by the same US government that vilified and distrusted Fidel and him for decades. The logic in such a project would be that if the United States government could accept him, then the challenge he represents to American interests, ideals or norms would have to be minimal or nonexistent.

US policymakers, by contrast, instead of stressing America's steadfast and principled opposition to a government that embodies reprehensible qualities, would be likely to begin using an adapted and modified language regarding the US relationship to such a reimagined Cuba. The US role would be spoken of as one of providing assistance, an outstretched hand or even guidance. Such a gesture would be characterized as magnanimous, rooted in strength and, like the first scenario, one which provides for an interpretation of American action as a sign of victory. Additionally, according to representations consistent with these actions, the presumption of American superiority would remain unchallenged.

Whether or not one or another of these different scenarios is likely, or will actually occur, involves a degree of speculation. But the possibilities for an alteration in policy and discursive constructions do exist. The central element in such possibilities is that any change must (and would) simultaneously reflect and encourage a shift in the respective representational practices and understandings of American and Cuban attributes that pertain to this longstanding conflict.

Cuba has never been a "normal" country to the United States. It was a territory that was coveted and sought throughout the nineteenth century, with Cuba's eventual union with the US seen as a natural inevitability. At the point when Spain was removed, the US advanced into what it saw as its proper role as a preeminent power on the island. However, since formal political control was untenable, the United States achieved what it could, establishing extensive influence and control in the country. When the Cubans finally rebelled against this state of affairs, and eliminated US influence from the island, the US then responded with a policy of punishment that remains in effect after more than 50 years. In other words, the past 200-plus years have involved a state of affairs in which US policy toward Cuba has been about the same thing: asserting and seeking a significant level of control in Cuba, enough to render the country almost as an extension of the US. It will be interesting to see how, under what circumstances, and when the United States can establish – not resume, but establish – a more normal relationship with Cuba, one that does not involve at its core such a strong desire to control, one that more closely resembles US policy toward other countries in Latin America and throughout the world.

Notes

1 Introduction

1 John Quincy Adams, in Walter LaFeber, ed., *John Quincy Adams and American Continental Empire: Letters, Speeches and Papers* (Chicago: Quadrangle Books, 1965) p. 130.
2 Wayne Smith, "Cuba's Long Reform," *Foreign Affairs*, March/April 1996, p. 110.
3 Hans Morgenthau, *Politics Among Nations: The Struggle for Power and Peace*, Sixth Edition, Revised by Kenneth Thompson (New York: Alfred A. Knopf, 1985); E.H. Carr, *The Twenty Years Crisis, 1919–1939* (London: Macmillan and Co. Ltd., 1962); Kenneth Waltz, *Theory of International Politics* (Reading MA, Addison-Wesley, 1979); and Robert Gilpin, *War and Change in World Politics* (Cambridge: Cambridge University Press, 1981).
4 G. John Ikenberry, "America's Liberal Grand Strategy: Democracy and National Security in the Post-War Era," *American Democracy Promotion: Impulses, Strategies and Impacts*, (New York: Oxford University Press, 2000); Thomas P.M. Barnett, *The Pentagon's New Map: War and Peace in the Twenty-First Century* (New York: Berkley Books, 2004); Fareed Zakaria, *The Future of Freedom: Illiberal Democracy at Home and Abroad*, (New York: W.W. Norton, 2003); and Michael Doyle, "Liberalism and World Politics," *The American Political Science Review*, December 1986, pp. 1151–69.
5 Robert Tucker, ed., *The Marx-Engels Reader*, 2nd Edition, (New York: W.W. Norton and Company, 1978); Lenin, *Imperialism, The Highest Stage of Capitalism* (New York: International Publishers, 1939); Fidel Castro, *Nothing Can Stop the Course of History*, an Interview by Jeffrey M. Elliot and Mervyn M. Dymally (New York: Pathfinder Press, 1986); Che Guevara, "Man and Socialism in Cuba," in *Che Guevara and the Cuban Revolution*, David Deutschmann, ed. (Sydney: Pathfinder/Pacific and Asia, 1987); In addition to the more orthodox Marxian view, I also include here the dependency theorists, Fernando Cardoso and Enzo Faletto, *Dependency and Development in Latin America* (Berkeley: The University of California Press, 1979); and World Systems Analysis, Immanuel Wallerstein, *The Modern World System* (New York: Academic Press, 1974).
6 William Connolly, *Identity/Difference: Democratic Negotiations of Political Paradox* (Ithaca: Cornell University Press, 1991); Michael Shapiro, *The Politics of Representation: Writing Practices in Biography, Photography, and Policy Analysis*, (Madison: The University of Wisconsin Press, 1988); Tzvetan Todorov, *The Conquest of America: The Question of the Other* (New York: Harper Perennial, 1992); Roland Barthes, *Mythologies*, translated by Annette Lavers (New York: Hill and Wang, 1972); David Campbell, *Writing Security: United*

States Foreign Policy and the Politics of Identity (Minneapolis: University of Minnesota Press, 1992); Cynthia Weber, *Simulating Sovereignty: Intervention, the State and Symbolic Exchange*, (Cambridge: Cambridge University Press, 1995); and Eldon Kenworthy, *America/Américas: Myth in the Making of US Policy Toward Latin America* (University Park: Pennsylvania State University Press, 1995).

7 Jutta Weldes, "Constructing National Interests: The Logic of US Security in the Postwar Era," Dissertation, University of Minnesota, 1993, p. 317–18.

2 Latin America – A different kind of place

1 General Shafter, a US army commander who fought in Cuba during the Spanish-American War, made this comment about the Cuban people while stationed there after the war, as part of the US occupying force. Louis Perez, *The U.S. and Cuba: Ties of Singular Intimacy* (Athens, GA: University of Georgia Press, 1990) p. 100.

2 Fredrick Pike, *The United States and Latin America: Myths and Stereotypes of Civilization and Nature* (Austin: University of Texas Press, 1992) p. 62.

3 Thomas Jefferson, Letter to James Monroe, October 24, 1823, in Thomas Karnes, ed., *Readings in the Latin American Policy of the United States* (Tucson: University of Arizona Press, 1972) p. 31.

4 John Quincy Adams, Letter to Hugh Nelson, April 28, 1823, in Walter LaFeber ed., *John Quincy Adams and American Continental Empire: Letters, Papers, Speeches*, (Chicago: Quadrangle Books, 1965) p. 129.

5 James Buchanan, Letter to Romulus M. Saunders, June 17, 1848, in William Manning, ed., *Diplomatic Correspondence of the United States: Inter-American Affairs, 1831–1860* (Washington DC: The Carnegie Endowment for International Peace, 1939) vol. 11, p. 57.

6 Shapiro, *The Politics of Representation*, p. 100.

7 Barthes, *Mythologies*, p. 110.

8 Eldon Kenworthy, *America/Américas*, p. 14.

9 Barthes, *Mythologies*, pp. 11, 102–19.

10 Said, *Orientalism*, (New York: Vintage Books, 1979), pp. 2–9. An example of this occurred in the US State Department until recently, where different regional bureaus are labeled in terms of the foreign territory, e.g. African Affairs, South Asian Affairs. Until 2000, there was only one bureau labeled in terms of the region's relationship to the US: Inter-American Affairs. It became the Western Hemisphere Bureau at that time.

11 *Congressional Record*, 58th Congress, Third Session, December 6, 1904, p. 19.

12 Connolly, *The Augustinian Imperative: A Reflection on the Politics of Morality*, (Newbury Park: Sage Publications, 1993) p. 76.

13 The term "community of judgment" comes from Weber, *Simulating Sovereignty*, p. 112.

14 Louis Perez, *Cuba in the American Imagination: Metaphor and the Imperial Ethos* (Chapel Hill: University of North Carolina Press, 2008), pp. 18–19.

15 "Enterprise for the Americas Initiative," Statement by President Bush, June 27, 1990, *Current Documents*, 1990, p. 816.

16 Louis Perez's, *Cuba in the American Imagination*, offers the most extensive collection and analysis of the images used to portray Cubans in the United States.

17 Arthur P. Whitaker, *The Western Hemisphere Idea: Its Rise and Decline*, (Ithaca: Cornell University Press, 1954).

18 Peter Bulkeley, *The Gospel Covenant* (1651), in Loren Baritz, *Sources of the American Mind*, v. 1 (New York: John Wiley and Sons Inc., 1966) p. 37; George

Bush, State of the Union Address, January 31, 1990, *Current Documents*, 1990, p. 2.

19 Alexis de Tocqueville, *Democracy in America*, vol. 2 (New York: Alfred A Knopf, 1966) pp. 36–37.

20 Andrei S. Markovits, "The Other 'American Exceptionalism' – Why Is There No Soccer in the United States?" *Praxis International*, July 1988, p. 125.

21 Lipset, S. M., *American Exceptionalism: A Double-Edged Sword* (New York: W.W. Norton and Company, 1996) p. 19.

22 Frederick Jackson Turner, "The Significance of the Frontier in American History," 1893, p. 5.

23 Daniel Bell, "The End of American Exceptionalism," Nathan Glazer and Irving Kristol, eds., *The American Commonwealth, 1976* (New York: Basic Books, 1976) p. 206.

24 Byron Shafer, *Is America Different?* (Oxford: Clarendon Press, 1991) p. 16.

25 Shapiro, *The Politics of Representation*, p. 100.

26 Reginald Horsman, *Race and Manifest Destiny: The Origins of American Racial Anglo-Saxonism* (Cambridge, MA: Harvard University Press, 1981) pp. 32–36.

27 Pott quoted in Horsman, *Race and Manifest Destiny*, p. 35.

28 Thomas Jefferson, Letter to William Ludlow, September 6, 1824, in Andrew Lipscomb and Albert Bergh, eds., *The Writings of Thomas Jefferson*, (Washington: The Thomas Jefferson Memorial Association, 1903, vol. 16, pp. 74–75.

29 Horsman, *Race and Manifest Destiny*, p. 90.

30 Bell, "The End of American Exceptionalism" p. 200.

31 Loren Baritz, *City on a Hill: A History of Ideas and Myths in America* (New York: John Wiley and Sons, Inc, 1964) pp. 3, 96.

32 Horsman, *Race and Manifest Destiny*, p. 86. Also, Lipset posits the idea that the US has its own "political religion," a phrase also used by Abraham Lincoln and Ralph Waldo Emerson, and argues that becoming American is a religious, that is, ideological act. Lipset, *American Exceptionalism*, 1996, p. 18.

33 *Congressional Record*, 56th Congress, 1st Session, January 9, 1900, p. 711. At the end of this very lengthy speech, applause broke out in the Senate galleries.

34 John O'Sullivan coined the term manifest destiny while arguing for the acquisition of Texas, stating that annexation was "the fulfillment of our manifest destiny to overspread the continent allotted by Providence for the free development of our yearly multiplying millions." John O'Sullivan, "Annexation," *The United States Magazine and Democratic Review*, July and August 1845, p. 5.

35 Henry R. Luce, "The American Century," *Life*, February 17, 1941, p. 65.

36 Message of the President to Congress, March, 12, 1947, and Statement by President June 27, 1950, Daniel Smith, ed., in *Major Problems in American Diplomatic History: Documents and Readings* (Boston: D.C. Heath and Co., 1965) vol. 2, pp. 612, 577.

37 President Kennedy's Inaugural Address, *Current Documents*, 1961, pp. 8–9.

38 Lyndon B. Johnson, State of the Union Address, *Current Documents*, 1966, p. 3.

39 Ronald Reagan, Address to the British Parliament, *Current Documents*, 1982, pp. 14–20.

40 Address by Ronald Reagan, November 22, 1982, *Current Documents*, 1982, p. 192.

41 *Public Papers of the Presidents of the United States, Ronald Reagan*, 1984, July 4, p. 1001.

42 Eldon Kenworthy, *America/Américas*, p. 7.

43 Jutta Weldes, "Constructing National Interests," pp. 144–52.

44 The words of Walter Lippmann, who was a frequent critic of the hypocrisy contained in this attitude, represents an excellent example of how ingrained was the idea of US superiority and disinterestedness. In spite of his disdain for the belief that American imperialism was at all different from anyone else's imperialism, his words nonetheless reveal the prejudices and myths of the day. He wrote that, "All the world thinks of the United States today as an empire, except the people of the United States ... We feel that there ought to be some other name for the civilizing work which we do so reluctantly in these backward countries." Walter Lippmann, "Empire: The Days of Our Nonage Are Over," Leiken and Rubin, eds., *The Central American Crisis Reader*, (New York: Summit Books, 1987) pp. 81–83.

45 NSC-68, in John Lewis Gaddis, ed., *Containment: Documents on American Policy and Strategy, 1945–1950* (New York: Columbia University Press, 1978) p. 390.

46 Weldes, "Constructing National Interests," pp. 516–17.

47 *Public Papers of the Presidents of the United States, Ronald Reagan, 1986*, p. 356.

48 *Congressional Record*, January 9, 1900, p. 711.

49 William J. Clinton, Remarks to the Cuban-American Community, June 27, 1995, John T. Woolley and Gerhard Peters, *The American Presidency Project* [online]. Santa Barbara, CA. http://www.presidency.ucsb.edu.

50 *The Cuban Liberty and Democratic Solidarity (Libertad) Act, Congressional Record*, 104th Congress, 1st Session, October 17, 1995, p. S15254.

51 The use of the terms black and Indian, as opposed to the more recent African-American and Native American, which are sometimes used here, is not an unselfconscious move. Such usage is intended not only to reflect the ongoing contemporary shift in terminology, but is also an attempt to engage an earlier era on some of its own terms, without relying solely on current formulations.

52 Barthes, *Mythologies*, p. 110; Campbell, *Writing Security*, p. 2.

53 Horsman, *Race and Manifest Destiny*; pp. 104–8.

54 Ronald Takaki, *Iron Cages: Race and Culture in 19th Century America* (Oxford: Oxford University Press, 1990) pp. 92–104.

55 Henry Knox, *American State Papers, Indian Affairs*, I (Washington: Gales and Seaton, 1832) p. 230.

56 William Henry Harrison, November 18, 1811, *American State Papers, Indian Affairs*, I, p. 776.

57 Charles Francis Adams, ed., *Memoirs of John Q. Adams*, vol. 7 (Philadelphia: J.B. Lippincott and Co., 1875) p. 90.

58 *Congressional Globe*, 27th Congress, 2nd Session, June 12, 1842, Appendix, p. 503; Horsman, *Race and Manifest Destiny*, p. 205.

59 Takaki, *Iron Cages*, pp. 176–78.

60 Takaki, *Iron Cages*, pp. 177–88.

61 Winthrop Jordan, *White Over Black: American Attitudes Toward the Negro, 1550–1812*, (Chapel Hill: University of North Carolina Press, 1968).

62 Horsman, *Race and Manifest Desitny*, p. 100.

63 Thomas Jefferson, *Notes on the State of Virginia* (Boston: Wells and Lilly, 1829) p. 150.

64 Benjamin Franklin, *Observations Concerning the Increase of Mankind*, 1751.

65 Stephen Jay Gould, *The Mismeasure of Man*, (New York: W.W. Norton and Co. 1981).

66 Craniometry is the measuring of skulls. It was believed that there was a correlation between superiority and brain size, with the top slot being occupied by white men, whose big brains provided them with greater intelligence and talent than blacks, women, Indians, etc. Polygeny is/was the theory that the different races

are actually members of different species, a view which caused great anguish in some religious circles. And recapitulation was the theory that individuals, in their own embryonic and juvenile growth, repeat the adult stages of their ancestors. Thus, white children actually pass through and then beyond the intellectual and developmental stages that characterize adults of "lower" races. Whites are, in this view, an "adult" race, blacks and others are "child" races – a scientific rationale for a paternalist and patronizing foreign policy.

67 Stephen Jay Gould, *Ever Since Darwin*, (New York: W.W. Norton and Co., 1977) pp. 217–18.
68 Gould, *The Mismeasure of Man*, pp. 35–50.
69 *Congressional Globe*, 30th Congress, 1st Session, January 4, 1848, p. 99.
70 Pike, *The United States and Latin America*, p. 49.
71 Pike, *The United States and Latin America*, p. 47.
72 Paul Horgan, *Great River: The Rio Grande in North American History*, v. 2, (New York: Rinehart and Co. Inc., 1954) p. 470.
73 John Douglas Pitts Fuller, *The Movement for the Acquisition of all Mexico 1846–1848*, (Baltimore: Johns Hopkins University Press, 1936) p. 41.
74 *Congressional Record*, 57th Congress, 1st Session, April 8, 1902, p. 3857. This statement is not a blatantly racist as it may seem. Tropical diseases such as malaria and yellow fever proved to be great obstacles to imperialist ventures by the US and European countries for many years. The attempt to construct the Panama Canal, for instance, was abandoned by the French before the Americans took it up due to the prevalence of disease among the people who had gone there to build it. While it represents a great arrogance to state that the climate is adapted to the white man, rather than the other way around, the concern with from disease was a serious one, albeit limited considering how close Cuba is to the United States.
75 LaFeber, *John Quincy Adams and American Continental Empire*, p. 130.
76 Perez, *Cuba in the American Imagination*, pp. 28–29.
77 Louis Perez, *Cuba Between Empires, 1878–1902* (Pittsburgh: University of Pittsburgh Press, 1983) p. 59.
78 Jules Benjamin, *The United States and the Origins of the Cuban Revolution*, (Princeton: Princeton University Press, 1990) pp. 8–9.
79 Perez, *Cuba Between Empires*, p. 62.
80 *Congressional Record*, 54th Congress, 1st Session, 1896, p. 2248.
81 James William Park, *Latin American Underdevelopment: A History of Perspectives in the United States, 1870–1965* (Baton Rouge: Louisiana State University Press, 1995) pp. 13–15.
82 Mark Peceny, "A Constructivist Interpretation of the Liberal Pacific Union: The Ambiguous Case of the Spanish-American War," Unpublished paper, 1996, p. 17.
83 Perez, *Cuba Between Empires*, pp. 198–222.
84 Perez, *Cuba Between Empires*, pp. 212–17.
85 What it meant for the Cubans to "govern themselves" could be many things, although perhaps one of the clearest and most amusing statements of what the US sought to achieve was summed up by General Leonard Wood, Governor-General of the island, who stated that "When people ask me what I mean by stable government, I tell them money at six percent." Walter LaFeber, *The American Age: United States Foreign Policy at Home and Abroad Since 1750* (New York: W.W Norton and Co. 1989) p. 198.
86 Rubin Francis Weston, *Racism in US Imperialism: The Influence of Racial Assumptions on American Foreign Policy, 1893–1946* (Columbia: University of South Carolina Press, 1973) p. 147.
87 Philip Jessup, *Elihu Root* (Dodd, Mead and Company, 1938) p. 288.

88 Louis Perez, *The U.S. and Cuba: Ties of Singular Intimacy* (Athens: University of Georgia Press, 1990) p. 100.
89 Perez, *Cuba Between Empires*, p. 272.
90 Perez, *Cuba Between Empires*, p. 273.
91 Weston, *Racism in US Imperialism*, p. 166.
92 Perez, *Cuba Between Empires*, pp. 272–73.
93 Jessup, *Elihu Root*, p. 288; and Perez, *Cuba Between Empires*, p. 273.
94 Perez, *Cuba Between Empires*, p. 272.
95 Perez, *Cuba in the American Imagination*, p. 107.
96 Gould, *The Mismeasure of Man*, pp. 116–17.
97 *Congressional Record*, 55th Congress, 2nd Session, April 16, 1898, pp. 3988–89.
98 *Congressional Record*, January 9, 1900, p. 711.
99 *Congressional Record*, 58th Congress, 2nd Session, pt. 1, December 12, 1903, pp. 167–68; Weston, *Racism in US Imperialism*, p. 170.
100 *Congressional Record*, 57th Congress, 1st Session, pt. 4, April 8, 1902, pp. 4123–25.
101 *Congressional Record*, 58th Congress, 2nd Session, pt. 1, December 12, 1903, pp. 167–68.
102 *Congressional Globe*, 28th Congress, 2nd Session, appendix, February 21–22, 1845, p. 397.
103 *Congressional Globe*, 29th Congress, 2nd Session, appendix, February 2, 1847, p. 281.
104 *Congressional Globe*, 32nd Congress, 3rd Session, appendix, March 15, 1853, p. 270.
105 Weston, *Racism in US Imperialism*, p. 159–60.
106 LaFeber, *The American Age: United States Foreign Policy at Home and Abroad Since 1750* (New York: W.W. Norton, 1989) p. 197.
107 The Platt Amendment can be found in Philip Brenner, *et al.*, *The Cuba Reader: The Making of a Revolutionary Society* (New York: Grove Press, 1988) pp. 30–31.
108 Perez, *Cuba Between Empires*, p. 279.
109 Weston, *Racism in US Imperialism*, p. 169.
110 Louis Perez, "The Circle of Connections," *Michigan Quarterly Review*, Summer 1994, p. 449.
111 John Rothchild, *Latin America Yesterday and Today* (New York: Praeger Publishers, 1974) pp. 440–47.
112 Karnes, *Readings in the Latin American Policy of the United States*, p. 242.
113 Walt Rostow, *The Stages of Economic Growth: A Non-Communist Manifesto* (Cambridge: Cambridge University Press, 1960); Gabriel Almond and Sidney Verba, *The Civic Culture* (Boston: Little, Brown, 1965); Samuel Huntington, *Political Order in Changing Societies* (New Haven: Yale University Press, 1968); Lucian Pye and Sidney Verba, *Political Culture and Political Development* (Princeton: Princeton University Press, 1965).
114 Cardoso and Faletto, *Dependency and Development in Latin America*, 1979Wallerstein, *The Modern World System*.
115 Park, *Latin American Underdevelopment*, pp. 159–62.
116 Perez, "The Circle of Connections," pp. 448–55.
117 Perez, *Ties of Singular Intimacy*, p. 227.
118 Deputy Undersecretary of State Murphy, May 19, 1958, *Current Documents*, 1958, p. 364; and Remarks by the President, May 14, 1958, *Current Documents*, 1958, p. 362.
119 Milton S. Eisenhower, Report to the President, December 27, 1958, *Current Documents*, 1958, p. 432.

120 Address by President Kennedy, March 13, 1961 (Alliance for Progress), *Current Documents*, 1961, p. 343.
121 Nelson A. Rockefeller, "The Rockefeller Report on the Americas," in Karnes, *Readings in the Latin American Policy of the United States*, p. 294.
122 Rockefeller, "The Rockefeller Report on the Americas," p. 296.
123 Statement by President Bush, July 2, 1990, *Current Documents*, 1990, p. 814.
124 Said, *Orientalism*, pp. 127–28.

3 Latin Americans as fellow travellers

1 John F. Kennedy, Remarks to the OAS Council, April 14, 1961, in *American Foreign Policy: Current Documents*, 1961, p. 263.
2 Richard Hofstadter, *The American Political Tradition* (New York: Alfred A. Knopf, 1985) p. 317.
3 Kenworthy, *America/Américas*, p. xiv.
4 William Connolly, "Identity and Difference in Global Politics," in Der Derian, James, and Shapiro, Michael, eds., *International/Intertextual Relations*, (Lexington, MA: Lexington Books, 1989). p. 327.
5 Kenworthy, *America/Américas*, p. xiv.
6 Whitaker, *The Western Hemisphere Idea*, p. 29.
7 Lipscomb and Bergh, *The Writings of Thomas Jefferson*, vol. 12, p. 356.
8 Thomas Jefferson, Letter to Governor Claiborne of Louisiana, October 29, 1808; Letter to Alexander von Humboldt, December 6, 1813; Letter to Clement Caine, September 16, 1811; in Lipscomb and Bergh, *The Writings of Thomas Jefferson*, vol. 12, p. 356, vol.14, p. 22, and vol. 13, p. 90.
9 The full text of Monroe's message to Congress (December 2, 1823) can be found in James D. Richardson, ed., *A Compilation of the Messages and Papers of the Presidents, 1787–1897*, 10 vols. (New York: Bureau of National Literature, Inc., 1897) vol. 2, pp. 776–89.
10 Kenworthy, *America/Américas*, p. 16.
11 Kenworthy, *America/Américas*, p. 16.
12 Harold Molineu, *US Policy toward Latin America* (Boulder: Westview Press, 1986) p. 19.
13 "Declaration of Solidarity for the Preservation of the Political Integrity of the American States Against the Intervention of International Communism" US Department of State, International Organization and Conference Series II, American Republics, no. 14, Publication 5692, (Washington DC: Government Printing Office, 1955) pp. 156–58.
14 Stephen Schlesinger and Stephen Kinzer, *Bitter Fruit: The Untold Story of the American Coup in Guatemala*, (Garden City New York: Doubledayand Co. 1982) pp. 142–43.
15 U.N. Ambassador Adlai Stevenson made these remarks in the U.N. protesting US innocence in the Bay of Pigs Invasion, which had begun that day. Statement to the U.N. General Assembly, April 17, 1961, *Current Documents*, 1961, p. 294.
16 Stevenson, Statements to the UN General Assembly, *Current Documents*, 1962, pp. 341, 343, 379; Dean Rusk, Address to the Nation, *Current Documents*, 1962, p. 336.
17 Kenworthy, *America/Américas*, p. 15.
18 Ronald Reagan, State of the Union Address, January 27, 1987, *Public Papers of the Presidents of the United States: Ronald Reagan, 1987*, vol. 1, p. 57.
19 Peter Kornbluh and Malcolm Byrne, *The Iran-Contra Scandal: The Declassified History* (New York: The New Press, 1993) p. 48.
20 One might also include another item which this analysis does not address: revolution. As the US is a nation born out of revolution, its leaders have often

expressed sympathy with fellow revolutionaries, but only of a particular sort. Those who would reproduce a limited, liberal, American-style revolution are, in theory, acceptable to the US. However, ever since the US achieved independence, its foreign policy has demonstrated more skepticism and wariness than it has support toward the revolutions of others.

21 Thomas Jefferson, Letter to James Madison, March 23, 1815, Lipscomb and Bergh, *The Writings of Thomas Jefferson*, vol. 14, p. 292.

22 Thomas Jefferson, Letter to James Monroe, October 24, 1823, Karnes, *Readings in The Latin American Policy of the United States*, pp. 30–31.

23 Henry Clay, Speech in the House of Representatives, March 24, 1818, in James B. Swain, ed., *The Life and Speeches of Henry Clay*, 2 vols. (New York: Greeley and McElrath, 1844) vol. 1, pp. 82,88.

24 Organization of American States, Eighth Meeting of Consultation of Ministers of Foreign Affairs of the American Republics, Punta del Este, January 1962, Final Act, p. 6.

25 "New Opportunities in Hemispheric Trade," US Department of State, *Dispatch*, August 26, 1991, p. 635.

26 Perez, *Cuba Between Empires*, p. 198.

27 Theodore Roosevelt, *The Works of Theodore Roosevelt, Vol. 17, State Papers as Governor and President*, (New York: Charles Scribner's Sons, 1925) pp. 456–57.

28 Adlai Stevenson, Statement to the U.N. General Assembly, April 17, 1961, *Current Documents*, 1961, p. 294.

29 John F. Kennedy, Address to the Nation, October 22, 1962, *Current Documents*, 1962, p. 403; George W. Bush, Remarks on the Situation in Cuba, May 21, 2008, *American Presidency Project*.

30 Rusk, Address to the Nation, *Current Documents*, 1962, p. 336.

31 Kenworthy, *America/Américas*, p. 22.

32 Connolly, *Identity/Difference*, p. 41.

33 Statement by President Bush, June 27, 1990, *Current Documents*, 1990, p. 809.

34 US Department of State, "President Bush's Address at the Signing of NAFTA," *Dispatch*, January 4, 1993, p. 1.

35 International American Conference, *Reports of Committees and Discussions Thereon*, v.4, *Historical Appendix, The Congress of 1826, at Panama, and Subsequent Movements Toward a Conference of American Nations* (Washington: Government Printing Office, 1890) p. 304.

36 Connolly, *Identity/Difference*, p. 93.

37 John F. Kennedy, Remarks before the Council of the OAS, April 14, 1961, *Current Documents*, 1961, p. 263.

38 *Bush on Cuba: Selected Statements by the President* (Miami: Cuban American National Foundation, 1991) p. 67.

39 *Public Papers of the Presidents of the United States Dwight D. Eisenhower, 1960–1961*, (July 11), p. 571.

40 James Monroe, Message to Congress, in Richardson, *A Compilation of the Messages and Papers of the Presidents, 1787–1897*, vol. 2, pp. 776.

41 Kennedy, May 24, 1961, *Current Documents*, 1961, p. 310.

42 "Update of US Policy toward Cuba," *Dispatch*, November 7, 1994, p. 751.

43 The theme of fathers and children has not figured prominently in official rhetoric. There was a State Department official in the 1920s, commenting on the exercise of American power in Latin America, who stated that, "as these young nations grow and develop a greater capacity for self-government, and finally take their places upon an equal footing with the mature, older nations of the world, ... they will come to see the United States with different eyes, and to have for her something of the respect and affection with which a man regards the instructor

of his youth and a child looks upon the parent who has molded his character." Such overt references like this one, however, have been rare. (See Walter LaFeber, *Inevitable Revolutions*, 1st Edition [New York: W.W. Norton, 1983] p. 301).

44 Michael Hunt, *Ideology and US Foreign Policy*, (New Haven: Yale University Press, 1987) p. 61.

45 Hunt, *Ideology and US Foreign Policy*, pp. 59–60.

46 Benjamin, *The United States and the Origins of the Cuban Revolution*, pp. 55–57; Kenworthy, *America/Américas*, p. 33; Hunt, *Ideology and US Foreign Policy*, pp. 63–68; Perez, *Cuba in the American Imagination*.

47 This mythology was actually reproduced in real life. The year before war with Spain broke out, a young Cuban woman named Evangelina Cisneros was arrested and imprisoned. She was guilty, according to the Hearst press which made a sensation of the story, of nothing more than trying to protect her virtue from an unscrupulous Spanish officer. Hearst not only ran the most yellow of stories in his paper about the affair, he also launched a campaign to "Enlist the Women of America!" in behalf of Evangelina. Appeals were sent to the Pope and the Queen of Spain, and petitions were signed by thousands. Not stopping at that, Hearst also sent one of his reporters, Karl Decker, to Cuba with orders to rescue the girl "at any hazard." Under a banner headline reading "An American Newspaper Accomplishes at a Single Stroke What the Best Efforts of Diplomacy Failed Utterly to Bring About in Many Months," Decker's story recounted how he climbed up to the roof of a house in order to break in to the prison, then broke the bars across a window, lifted Evangelina out, hid her for days in Havana, then smuggled her out to safety. The fanfare surrounding the escape was significant, and the two were greeted with a procession on Broadway and a reception at Madison Square Garden. The whole incident prompted Governor Stephens of Missouri to suggest that Hearst send 500 reporters down to Cuba to free the entire island. (Thomas Paterson, ed., *American Imperialism and Anti-Imperialism*, [New York: Thomas Y. Crowell Company, Inc., 1973] pp. 23–24.)

48 Perez, *Cuba in the American Imagination*, p. 87.

49 Weldes, "Constructing National Interests," pp. 471–72.

50 *The Public Papers and Addresses of Franklin D. Roosevelt*, vol. 2 (New York: Random House, 1938) pp. 11–16.

51 James Blaine, Letter to President Arthur, February 3, 1882, William Appleman Williams, ed., *The Shaping of American Diplomacy: Readings and Documents in American Foreign Policy*, (Chicago: Rand McNally and Company, 1965) pp. 380–81.

52 "NAFTA: A Bridge to a Better Future for the United States and the Hemisphere, *Dispatch*, September 13, 1993, p. 626.

53 Barack Obama, Proclamation 8495 – Pan American Day and Pan American Week 2010, April 9, 2010, American Presidency Project.

54 McKinley's War Message to Congress, Julius Muller, ed., *Presidential Messages and State Papers*, Vol. 8 (New York: The Review of Reviews Company, 1917) pp. 2957–63.

55 Weldes, "Constructing National Interests," p. 472.

56 *Public Papers of the Presidents of the United States Ronald Reagan, 1986*, (March 16) vol. 1, p. 352.

57 Kenworthy, *America/Américas*, p. 31.

58 George W. Bush, Remarks on the Colombia Free Trade Agreement, April 7, 2008, American Presidency Project.

59 Todorov, *The Conquest of America*, pp. 127–32.

60 George Bush, Address Before the Council of the Americas, May 22, 1990, *Current Documents*, 1990, p. 809.

61 "US-Mexican Relations and NAFTA," *Dispatch*, June 28, 93, p. 458.

4 Cuba, the Cold War foe

1 Jeanne Kirkpatrick, *Cuba and the Cubans* (Miami: Cuban-American National Foundation, 1983) p. 7.
2 US Department of State, "Tasks for US Policy in the Hemisphere," Current Policy No. 282, June 3, 1981, p. 2. Enders was referring to the upheaval in Central America, and the belief in the Reagan administration that its "source" was Cuba.
3 US Department of State, "Human Rights in Castro's Cuba," Special Report No. 153, December 1986.
4 Connolly, *Identity/Difference*, p. 64.
5 Barthes, *Mythologies*, p. 110.
6 Connolly, *Identity/Difference*, p. 64.
7 Committee of Santa Fe, Lewis Tambs, ed., "A New Inter-American Policy for the Eighties" (Washington DC: Council for Inter-American Security, 1980), p. 2.
8 Committee on the Present Danger, *Alerting America: The Papers of the Committee on the Present Danger* (Washington: Pergamon Brasseys, 1984), pp. 3, 177.
9 Committee of Santa Fe, "A New Inter-American Policy ...," p. 15.
10 Jeanne Kirkpatrick, "Dictatorships and Double Standards," *Commentary*, November 1979, pp. 34–45; Paul Nitze, "Strategy for the 1980," *Foreign Affairs*, Winter 1980, pp.82–101; Norman Podhoretz, *The Present Danger: "Do We Have the Will to Reverse the Decline of American Power?"* (New York: Simon and Schuster, 1980); Richard Pipes, *US-Soviet Relations in the Era of Detente* (Boulder: Westview Press, 1981); Eugene Rostow, "The Case Against SALT II," *Commentary*, 1979, pp. 23–32; Colin Gray, "SALT II: The Real Debate," *Policy Review*, 1979, 10, pp. 7–22.
11 Committee of Santa Fe, "A New Inter-American Policy ...," pp. v, 1.
12 Caspar Weinberger, "Rearming America," pp. 29, 35.
13 Alexander Haig, *Caveat: Realism, Reagan, and Foreign Policy* (New York: Macmillan, 1984) pp. 25–27.
14 Ronald Reagan, *An American Life* (New York: Simon and Schuster, 1990) pp. 219, 266.
15 Jorge Dominguez points out that every president from Eisenhower to Reagan engaged in, or considered, military confrontation with or over Cuba. Eisenhower authorized the first efforts to overthrow Castro at the Bay of Pigs. Kennedy carried out the plan and prepared to go to war with the Soviets during the missile crisis. Johnson invaded the Dominican Republic to prevent another Cuba. Nixon confronted the Soviets and Cubans over the Soviet use of Cienfuegos harbor for strategic submarines. Ford faced Cuban intervention in Angola, and only Congress stopped him from responding. Carter faced intervention in Ethiopia as well as the discovery of a larger, more complex Soviet military presence in Cuba. He also authorized the rebuilding of US forces in southern Florida. And Reagan threatened an invasion of Cuba and staged a massive display of military force in the Caribbean and Central America, invading Grenada where US troops fought against Cuban troops. See Jorge Dominguez, "US-Cuba Relations in the mid-1980's: Issues and Policies," *Journal of Interamerican Studies and World Affairs*, February 1985, vol. 27, no. 1, pp. 17–18.
16 Committee of Santa Fe, "A New Inter-American Policy ...," pp. ii, 1, 3–10, 17, 45.
17 Haig, *Caveat*, pp. 26–27, 122.
18 Jeanne Kirkpatrick, *The Reagan Phenomenon* (Washington DC: American Enterprise Institute, 1983) pp. 31–32, 195.
19 Caspar Weinberger, "US Defense Policy Requirements," Address to American Newspaper Publishers Association, *Current Documents*, 1981, p. 39; and

Weinberger, "We Must Make America Strong Again," Remarks before the Council on Foreign Relations, in *Current Documents*, 1981, p. 45.

20 Reagan, *An American Life*, pp. 238–39.

21 Committee on the Present Danger, *Alerting America*, p. 3.

22 Committee of Santa Fe, "A New Inter-American Policy ...," pp. 8–9.

23 Committee of Santa Fe, "A New Inter-American Policy ...," p. 46.

24 Shapiro, *The Politics of Representation*, p. 89.

25 Shapiro, *The Politics of Representation*, p. 93.

26 Shapiro, *The Politics of Representation*, p. 101.

27 Reagan, *An American Life*, p. 267.

28 Reagan, *An American Life*, pp. 237–38.

29 Haig, *Caveat*, p. 29.

30 Haig, *Caveat*, p. 29.

31 Reagan, *An American Life*, p. 555.

32 Reagan, *An American Life*, pp. 238, 267.

33 Kirkpatirck, *The Reagan Phenomenon*, p. 31.

34 US Department of State, "Cuba's Renewed Support for Violence in Latin America," Special Report No. 90, December 14, 1981, p. 2.

35 Ronald Reagan, "Strategic Importance of El Salvador and Central America," March 10, 1983, US Department of State Current Policy No. 464, p. 1.

36 Reagan, "Strategic Importance of El Salvador and Central America," p. 1.

37 US Department of State, "El Salvador: The Search for Peace," July 16, 1981, Current Policy 296, p. 1.

38 *Public Papers of the Presidents of the United States, Ronald Reagan*, 1983 (April 27) p. 606.

39 At one point, the president made an appearance in Congress in April of 1983 to address a joint session on Central America. In another instance in March of 1986, he made a televised address to the nation to warn of the danger posed by communism in Nicaragua. *Public Papers of the Presidents*, 1983 (April 27) pp. 601–7; and 1986 (March 16) pp. 352–57.

40 Kirkpatrick, *The Reagan Phenomenon*, p. 46.

41 Caspar Weinberger, *Fighting for Peace* (New York: Warner Books, 1990) pp. 30–32; and Robert McFarlane, *Special Trust* (New York: Cadell and Davies, 1994) pp. 176–81.

42 Martha Cottam, *Images and Intervention: U.S. Policies in Latin America* (Pittsburgh: University of Pittsburgh Press, 1994) p. 10.

43 Cottam, *Images and Intervention*, p. 10.

44 Cottam, *Images and Intervention*, p. 11.

45 Cottam, *Images and Intervention*, p. 21.

46 US Departments of State and Defense, *The Challenge to Democracy in Central America*, 1986, pp. 8, 13.

47 US Department of State, "The Role of Cuba in International Terrorism and Subversion," Congressional Testimony by Undersecretary of Defense for Policy, March, 11, 1982, *Current Documents*, 1982, p. 1408.

48 US Department of State, "US Security Interests in Latin America," February 22, 1983, *Current Documents*, 1983, p. 1241.

49 "The Cuban Challenge to the Hemisphere," *Current Documents*, 1983, p. 1376.

50 William LeoGrande, *Cuba's Policy in Africa, 1959–1980* (Berkeley: Institute of International Studies, 1980); Jorge Dominguez, *To Make A World Safe for Revolution* (Cambridge: Harvard University Press, 1989); Wayne Smith, *Castro's Cuba: Soviet Partner or Non-Aligned?* (Washington DC: The Woodrow Wilson International Center for Scholars, 1984).

51 US Departments of State and Defense, "The Challenge to Democracy in Central America," June 1986, p. 8.

52 "US Security Interests in Latin America," *Current Documents,* 1983, p. 1239.
53 "Cuba's Renewed Support ...," pp. 6–7.
54 "El Salvador: The Search for Peace," p. 1.
55 US Department of State, "Dealing with the Reality of Cuba," Current Policy No. 443, December 14 1982, p. 1.
56 "Cuba's Renewed Support ...," pp. 3–4.
57 US Department of State, "Communist Interference in El Salvador," Special Report No. 80, February 23, 1981, *Current Documents,* 1981, p. 1236. (Hereafter referred to as "White Paper.")
58 "White Paper," pp. 1231–36.
59 "White Paper," pp. 1231.
60 James Petras, "Blots on the White Paper: The Reinvention of the 'Red Menace,'" in Gettleman *et al., El Salvador: Central America in the New Cold War,* 1981, p. 243.
61 Campbell, *Writing Security,* p. 2.
62 George H.W. Bush, "US Policy in the Hemisphere," Address before the Council of the Americas, June 3, 1981, *Current Documents,* 1981, p. 1196.
63 "Tasks for US Policy in the Hemisphere," p. 2.
64 Ronald Reagan, "Viva Cuba Libre: Cuba Si, Castro, No," Address before Cuban Independence Day Parade, *Current Documents,* 1983, p. 1326.
65 "Tasks for US Policy in the Hemisphere," p. 2; and "Cuba's Renewed Support..," p. 6.
66 Reagan, "Strategic Importance of El Salvador and Central America," 1983, pp. 1–2.
67 Dean Rusk, "Communist Threat to US Through the Caribbean," Address at the Eighth Meeting of Consultation of Ministers of Foreign Affairs of the American States, Punta del Este, Uruguay, January 25, 1962, p. 894.
68 Richard Drinnon, *Facing West: The Metaphysics of Indian Hating and Empire Building* (Minneapolis: University of Minnesota Press, 1980) p. 262.
69 Cottam, *Images and Intervention,* p. 33.
70 *Public Papers of the Presidents of the United States, Dwight D. Eisenhower,* January 3, 1961, p. 891.
71 Rusk, "Communist Threat to US Through the Caribbean," January 25, 1962, p. 892.
72 Reagan, "Viva Cuba Libre," p. 1326.
73 "Dealing With the Reality of Cuba," p. 2.
74 Reagan, "Viva Cuba Libre," p. 1326.
75 Reagan, "Viva Cuba Libre," p. 1326.
76 "Cuba's Renewed Support ..." pp. 2–4.
77 An example, perhaps one of the best, of this fear/attitude is the movie, *The Manchurian Candidate,* in which soldiers who had been taken prisoner during the Korean War were unknowingly brainwashed while held captive by quite villainous yet sophisticated Chinese Communists. They are given a mission, set to begin when the trigger, planted in the soldier's brains, is set off by a particular image. Their assignment is to carry out a plot to ensure that the US presidency is assumed by a secret communist agent. The enemy in the movie is at once evil enough to hatch the plan, genius enough to brainwash captives who have no recollection of it, and patient enough to wait years for the right time to act.
78 Reagan, "Strategic Importance of El Salvador ...," p. 2.
79 Drinnon, *Facing West,* pp. 368–69.
80 "Cuba's Renewed Support ...," p. 3; Reagan, "Viva Cuba Libre," p. 1327; and Fred Ikle, "Defending our Fourth Border," April 12, 1983, *Current Documents,* 1983, p. 1308.

81 The Munich analogy involves the interpretation of a given event in terms of drawing an historical parallel to the meeting of the great powers in Munich in 1938. In this meeting, Hitler's ambitions to incorporate part of Czechoslovakia into Germany was agreed to by France and Great Britain, provided Hitler demanded no more territory be added to Germany. Since this agreement did not stop Hitler's demands, the subsequent meaning of Munich came to be that one should not accommodate or appease an aggressor, as this will only fuel his ambitions and provide the example that aggression will be rewarded.
82 Schlesinger and Kinzer, *Bitter Fruit*, p. 11.
83 Kennedy, Inaugural Address, *Current Documents*, 1961, p. 15.
84 *Public Papers of the Presidents of the United States, Ronald Reagan*, 1986 (March 16) p. 353.

5 Waiting for Fidel ... and now Raúl

1 *Public Papers of the Presidents of the United States, George Bush*, 1992, (May 20), p. 805.
2 William J. Clinton, Interview with José Diaz-Balart of Telemundo, November 4, 2000, John T. Woolley and Gerhard Peters, *The American Presidency Project* [online], Santa Barbara, CA, http://www.presidency.ucsb.edu/index.php. (accessed June 3, 2010).
3 US House of Representatives, *The Cuban Liberty and Democratic Solidarity (Libertad) Act* Hearings, p. 21.
4 *Public Papers of the Presidents of the United States, George Bush*, 1992, (October 23) p. 1939.
5 After the collapse of communism in Eastern Europe and Russia, there were a host of articles and books written suggesting/hoping that the beginning of the end was at hand for Castro. These included titles such as Sarah Kaufmann Purcell, "Collapsing Cuba," *Foreign Affairs*, Spring 1992, pp. 130–45; Howard Wiarda, "Is Cuba Next? Crises of the Castro Regime," *Problems of Communism*, Jan/Apr 1991, pp. 84–93; Andres Oppenheimer, *Castro's Final Hour: The Secret Story Behind the Coming Downfall of Communist Cuba* (New York: Simon and Schuster, 1992); and Carmelo Mesa-Lago and Horst Fabian, "Analogies Between East European Socialist Regimes and Cuba: Scenarios for the Future," in Mesa-Lago ed., *Cuba After the Cold War* (Pittsburgh: University of Pittsburgh Press, 1993) pp. 353–79; as well as many others. Castro's continued hold on power then prompted a series of articles looking to explain why and how he managed to persevere. Jorge Dominguez, "The Secrets of Castro's Staying Power," *Foreign Affairs*, Spring 1993, pp. 97–107; Donald Schulz, "Can Castro Survive?" *Journal of Interamerican Studies and World Affairs*, Spring 1993, pp. 89–117; Enrique Baloyra, "Socialist Transitions and Change in Cuba," in *Conflict and Change in Cuba*, pp. 38–63; and Isabella Thomas, "Cuba: Change and the Perception of Change," *The World Today*, May 1995, pp. 99–101.
6 *Newsweek*, December 26, 1994/January 2, 1995, p. 68.
7 Rubén Berríos, "Why America Should Lift Its Cuban Embargo," *Contemporary Review*, Oct 1994, p. 183.
8 Walter Russell Mead, "Rum and Coca-Cola: The United States and the New Cuba," *World Policy Journal*, Fall 1995, pp. 32, 48–49.
9 Louis Perez, "Thinking Back on Cuba's Future: The Logic of *Patria*," *NACLA Report on the Americas*, March/April 2009, pp. 14–15.
10 George W. Bush, Fact Sheet: Encouraging Freedom, Justice, and Prosperity in Cuba, October 24, 2007, *American Presidency Project*, http://www.presidency. ucsb.edu. (accessed June 3, 2010).

11 Congressman Tiahrt's resolution, House Concurrent Resolution 132 (H. Con.Res.132, May 20, 2009), which specified 50 different objectionable actions taken by the Cuban government, stated that "With respect to the totalitarian government of Cuba, the United States should pursue a policy that insists upon freedom, democracy, and human rights, including the release of all political prisoners, the legalization of political parties, free speech and a free press, and supervised elections, before increasing United States trade and tourism to Cuba." Senator Ensign's legislation, the Cuba Transition Act of 2006 (S.3769, August 1, 2006), authorized the president to provide financial assistance for democracy building in Cuba, with aid targeted toward political prisoners and their families, and "independent" journalists, worker activists, youth groups, charities, etc.

12 Richard Kerry, *The Star-Spangled Mirror: America's Image of Itself* (Savage, MD: Rowman and Littlefield Publishers, Inc., 1990) pp. 1, 7.

13 Shapiro, *The Politics of Representation*, p. 90.

14 Campbell, *Writing Security*, p. 195.

15 Campbell, *Writing Security*, p. 196.

16 "Cuba: Current Assessment and US Policy," *Dispatch*, August 16, 1993, p. 577.

17 Barack Obama, "Remarks to the Summit of the Americas in Port of Spain, Trinidad and Tobago," April 17, 2009; "Choosing a Better Future in the Americas," April 16, 2009; Bush, Remarks on the Situation in Cuba," March 7, 2008; and Remarks on the Situation in Cuba," May 21, 2008; all from the *American Presidency Project*.

18 William Connolly, "The Dilemma of Legitimacy," in *Legitimacy and the State*, p. 227.

19 Address by President Bush Before the Council of the Americas, May 22, 1990, *Current Documents*, 1990, p. 810.

20 Sheldon Wolin, *The Presence of the Past: Essays on the State and the Constitution* (Baltimore: Johns Hopkins University Press, 1989) p. 192.

21 The comment about electing good men comes from Woodrow Wilson, who said that "I am going to teach the South American republics to elect good men." Paul Drake, "From Good Men to Good Neighbors: 1912–32," Abraham Lowenthal, ed., *Exporting Democracy: The United States and Latin America* (Baltimore: The Johns Hopkins University Press, 1991), p. 13.

22 Connolly, *Identity/Difference*, p. 66.

23 US Department of State, "Cuba," *Background Notes*, November 1994, p. 4.

24 *Background Notes*, 1994, pp. 3, 7.

25 Wayne Smith, "A Pragmatic Cuba Policy," *Foreign Service Journal*, April 1991, p. 23.

26 Michael Shapiro, "Textualizing Global Politics," Der Derian and Shapiro, eds., *International/Intertextual Relations*, p. 13.

27 *Background Notes*, 1994, p. 4; US Department of State, "US Policy Toward Cuba," *Dispatch*, August 5, 1991, p. 583.

28 US Department of State, "Cuba," *Background Notes*, 2010.

29 *Background Notes*, 1994.

30 George H.W. Bush, *Bush on Cuba: Selected Statements by the President* (Miami: Cuban American National Foundation, 1991) p. 65.

31 *Public Papers of the Presidents of the United States, George Bush*, 1992, (October 23) pp. 1939–40; and William J. Clinton, 1994, (August 19), p. 1684; George W. Bush, "Remarks on the Situation in Cuba," March 7, 2008, *American Presidency Project*.

32 "Cuba: Current Assessment and US Policy," p. 578.

33 George W. Bush, "Remarks on the 100th Anniversary of Cuba Independence," May 20, 2002, *American Presidency Project*.

34 US House of Representatives, *The Cuban Liberty and Democratic Solidarity (Libertad) Act*, Hearings, p. 7; US *Congressional Record*, November 1, 2007 (Senate), p. S13655.

35 *Congressional Record, The Cuban Liberty and Democratic Solidarity (Libertad) Act*, 104th Congress, October 17, 1995, p. S15254.

36 Shapiro, *The Politics of Representation*, p. 102.

37 US Department of State, "Cuba," *2009 Country Reports on Human Rights Practices*.

38 Campbell, *Writing Security*, p. 9.

39 Campbell, *Writing Security*, p. 195.

40 *Public Papers of the Presidents of the United States, William J. Clinton*, 1994, (May 3) p. 975.

41 Examples include Cabrera Infante, *Mea Cuba* (London: Faber and Faber, 1994); Rufo Lopez-Fresquet, *My Fourteen Months with Castro* (Cleveland: World Publishing Company, 1966); Armando Valladares, *Against All Hope: The Prison Memoirs of Armando Valladares* (New York: Alfred A. Knopf, 1986); and the movie *Impoper Conduct* (New York: Cinevista Video, 1984).

42 *Congressional Record*, 110th Congress, May 21, 2008, p. S4706.

43 *Congressional Record*, 104th Congress, 1st Session, p. S14995; US House of Representatives, *Libertad Act* Hearings, pp. 36–37; US House of Representatives, *The Cuban Democracy Act of 1992*, Hearings, pp. 44–47.

44 Shapiro, *The Politics of Representation*, p. 93.

45 Dean Rusk, January 25, 1962, *Current Documents*, p. 892.

46 Weber, *Simulating Sovereignty*, pp. 14–15.

47 Weber, *Simulating Sovereignty*, p. 81.

48 George H.W. Bush, Statement on the 90th Anniversary of Cuban Independence, May 20, 1992, American Presidency Project.

49 US Department of State, Ambassador Rice's Remarks on U.N. Resolution on Cuba, October 29, 2009.

50 Weber, *Simulating Sovereignty*, p. 92, 115.

51 US House of Representatives, *The Cuban Democracy Act of 1992*, Hearings, p. 25.

52 Campbell, *Writing Security*, p. 12.

53 Perez, *Cuba in the American Imagination*, pp. 13–14.

54 Jutta Weldes and Diana Saco, "From Soviet Puppet to Decaying Cadaver: The U.S. Construction of the Cuban Security Problematic" Unpublished Paper, 1993.

55 *Public Papers of the Presidents of the United States, George Bush*, 1992, (May 20) p. 805; 1991, (December 19) p. 1647; 1992, (October 23) p. 1941; 1991, (December 26) p. 1658.

56 William J. Clinton, Remarks to the Cuban-American Community, June 27, 1995, American Presidency Project; US Department of State, "The Cuban Democracy Act: One Year Later," Statement by Alexander Watson, Assistant Secretary of State for Inter-American Affairs before the House Foreign Affairs Committee, November 18, 1993, *Dispatch*, December 6, 1993, p. 853.

57 *Background Notes*, 2010.

58 US House of Representatives, *Libertad Act* Hearings, p. 3.

59 *Public Papers of the Presidents of the United States, George Bush*, 1992, pp. 2190–91.

60 Edward Gonzalez and David Ronfeldt, *Storm Warnings for Cuba* (Santa Monica, CA: RAND, 1994).

61 Gonzalez and Ronfeldt, *Storm Warnings for Cuba*, p. xiv.

62 Commission for Assistance to a Free Cuba, Report to the President, July 2006, pp. 91–93.

63 Of course, this same assumption could serve to justify a conciliatory gesture on the part of the US toward Cuba, but this is impacted by other circumstances, which are discussed in the following chapter.

64 "US Policy Toward Cuba," p. 580.

65 James A. Baker III, *The Politics of Diplomacy*, 1995, p. 586.

66 *Public Papers of the Presidents of the United States, George Bush*, 1992, (May 20) p. 805.

67 William J. Clinton, Interview With Dan Rather of CBS News, December 18, 2000, *American Presidency Project*.

68 George W. Bush, Remarks Announcing the Initiative for a New Cuba, May 20, 2002; and Remarks at the Department of State, October 24, 2007, *American Presidency Project*. Interestingly, President Obama has departed from this characterization of Cuba. In fact, he has gone so far as to declare US policy a failure, for failing to achieve the desired objectives of freedom and democracy in Cuba. (See his Remarks to the Summit of the Americas, April 17, 2009, *American Presidency Project*.)

69 "The Cuban Democracy Act: One Year Later," p. 853.

70 US Senate, Committee on Foreign Relations, *The Cuban Democracy Act of 1992*, Hearings, August 5, 1992, p. 3.

71 Such success, in fact, was the often the focus of books and articles regarding Cuba. See William Leogrande, "The Limits of Success," in Dominguez, ed., *Cuba: Internal and International Affairs* (Beverly Hills: Sage Publications, 1982) pp. 167–92; Jorge Dominguez, *To Make A World Safe for Revolution*; Raymond Duncan, *The Soviet Union and Cuba*, 1985; and the collection by George Fauriol and Eva Loser eds., *Cuba: The International Dimension*, 1990.

72 The premier example of this is, of course, Francis Fukuyama, *The End of History and the Last Man* (New York: Free Press, 1992).

73 Critiques of Fukuyama can be found in Samuel Huntington, "No Exit: The Errors of Endism," *The National Interest*, Fall 1989, no. 17, pp. 3–10; Leon Wieseltier, "Spoilers at the Party," *The National Interest*, Fall 1989, no. 17, pp. 12–16; and Timothy Burns, ed., *After History? Francis Fukuyama and His Critics* (Lanham, MD: Rowman and Littlefield, 1994).

74 William J. Clinton, Remarks to the Community in Detroit, October 22, 1996, *American Presidency Project*; *Public Papers of the Presidents of the United States, George Bush*, 1992, (December 15) p. 2189.

75 *Bush on Cuba*, pp. 60, 64.

76 William J. Clinton, Remarks to the Community in Detroit, October 22, 1996, *American Presidency Project*.

77 These states are often included together as rogue or outlaw states. See, for example, Samuel Huntington, "The Clash of Civilizations" *Foreign Affairs*, Summer 1993, vol. 72, no. 3, pp. 22–49.

78 US Department of State, "The Cuban Democracy Act and US Policy Toward Cuba," Statement by Robert Gelbard, Principal Deputy Assistant Secretary for Inter-American Affairs before the Subcommittee, August 10, 1992, *Dispatch*, August 17, 1992, p. 658.

79 "The Cuban Democracy Act and US Policy Toward Cuba," p. 658.

80 *Bush on Cuba*, p. 67; and *Public Papers of the Presidents of the United States, George Bush*, 1992, (March 4) p. 377.

81 "Update on US Policy Toward Cuba," Address by Alexander Watson, Assistant Secretary for Inter-American Affairs, *Dispatch*, November 7, 1994, p. 751.

82 George W. Bush, The President's Radio Address, April 21, 2001; and Remarks Announcing the Initiative for a New Cuba, May 20, 2002, *American Presidency Project*. The Initiative for a New Cuba was only a modest revision to the policy President Bush inherited. It sought to facilitate humanitarian assistance by

religious groups operating in Cuba, resume direct mail service between the US and Cuba, and provide some scholarship opportunities, but it made no major substantive changes to the embargo.

83 *Public Papers of the Presidents of the United States, George Bush*, 1992, (October 23) pp. 1939–40.
84 William J. Clinton, The President's News Conference, August 19, 1994, *American Presidency Project*.
85 "US Policy Toward Cuba," p. 580.
86 George W. Bush, Remarks on the Situation in Cuba, March 7, 2008, *American Presidency Project*.
87 John Vasquez, "The Post-Positivist Debate: Reconstructing Scientific Enquiry and International Relations Theory after Enlightenments's Fall," in *International Relations Theory Today*, pp. 220–21.
88 "The Cuban Democracy Act and US Policy Toward Cuba," p. 657.
89 US State Department, *Background Notes*, 2010.
90 Hernan Yanes, "The Cuba-Venezuela Alliance: 'Emancipatory Neo-Bolivarismo' or Totalitarian Expansion?" Institute for Cuban & Cuban-American Studies, University of Miami, Occasional Paper Series, December 2005, pp. 1, 15; US State Department, *Background Notes*, 2010.
91 The election of leftist leaders throughout Latin America and the development of ALBA have generated frustration and disbelief in Washington that a variation of the socialist left has been revived in the region.
92 US House of Representatives, *Libertad Act* Hearings, p. 2.
93 Common Position of 2 December 1996 defined by the Council on the basis of Article J.2 of the Treaty on European Union, on Cuba (96/697/CFSP), http://eur-lex.europa.eu/LexUriServ/LexUriServ.do?uri = CELEX:31996E0697:EN:NOT (accessed May 25, 2010).
94 "Dissident's Death Raises Cries for Cuba to Open Up," *USA Today*, February 25, 2010, p. 8A.
95 Capitol Hill Cubans, Resolution of the Polish Sejm on the Internal Situation of the Republic of Cuba, March 19, 2010, http://www.capitolhillcubans.com/2010/03/resolution-of-polish-sejm.html, (accessed May 25, 2010).
96 Cuban Democratic Directorate, "90 Members of Polish Parliament Adopt 90 Cuban Political Prisoners," December 17, 2009, http://www.directorio.org/pressreleases/note.php?note_id = 2623, (accessed May 25, 2010).
97 "US Policy Toward Cuba," p. 580; "The Cuban Democracy Act and US Policy Toward Cuba," p. 657; *Public Papers of the Presidents of the United States, George Bush*, 1992, (March 4) p. 377.
98 "Update on US Policy Toward Cuba," p. 751.
99 George H.W. Bush, Remarks at a Republican Party Fundraising Dinner in Orlando, Florida, April 20, 1990; George W. Bush, Remarks on the Situation in Cuba, March 7, 2008; William J. Clinton, Remarks to the Cuban-American Community, June 27, 1995; Barack Obama, The President's News Conference in Port of Spain, Trinidad and Tobago, April 19, 2009, *American Presidency Project*.
100 Commission for Assistance to a Free Cuba, Mission Statement, http://2005-9.cafc.gov/mission/index.htm, (accessed May 18, 2010).
101 Lars Schoultz, *That Infernal Little Cuban Republic: The United States and the Cuban Revolution* (Chapel Hill: University of North Carolina Press, 2009) p. 557.
102 George W. Bush, Remarks to the Council of the Americas May 7, 2008, *American Presidency Project*.
103 Remarks on Signing the Cuban Liberty and Democratic Solidarity (LIBERTAD) Act of 1996, March 12, 1996, *American Presidency Project*; US Department of

State, Death of Cuban Dissident Orlando Zapata Tamayo, Office of Public Diplomacy and Public Affairs, February 24, 2010.

104 George W. Bush, Message to the Congress on Continuation and Expansion of the National Emergency With Respect to Cuba, February 26, 2004, *American Presidency Project*.

105 William J. Clinton, Interview With Jose' Diaz-Balart of Telemundo, November 4, 2000; George W. Bush, Remarks at the Naval War College Newport, Rhode Island, June 28, 2007, *American Presidency Project*.

106 "The Cuban Democracy Act and US Policy Toward Cuba," p. 657; "The Cuban Democracy Act: One Year Later," *Dispatch*, December 6, 1993, p. 853; "Update on US Policy Toward Cuba, p. 752; "The Cuban Democracy Act and US Policy Toward Cuba," p. 658.

107 George W. Bush, Remarks Following a Meeting With Cuban American Community Leaders in Coral Gables, Florida October 10, 2008, *American Presidency Project*.

108 George W. Bush, Statement on Cuba, August 3, 2006, *American Presidency Project*.

109 Mark P. Sullivan, "Cuba's Political Succession: From Fidel to Raul Castro," CRS Report to Congress, October 23, 2007, p. 6.

110 US Senate, *The Cuban Democracy Act of 1992*, Hearings, p. 13.

111 US House of Representatives, *Libertad Act* Hearings, p. 17.

112 Perez, "Thinking Back on Cuba's Future," p. 14.

113 Perez, "Thinking Back on Cuba's Future," pp. 14–15.

114 Perez, "Thinking Back on Cuba's Future," p. 15.

115 H.R. 1528, Export Freedom to Cuba Act of 2009, Sponsored by Representative Charles Rangel of New York, Introduced 3/16/2009.

116 *Congressional Record*, 110th Congress, 1st Session, December 18, 2007, p. H16649.

117 Barack Obama: "Choosing a Better Future in the Americas," April 16, 2009, American Presidency Project; "Clinton Impresses Audiences by Saying US Policies Have Failed," *New York Times*, April 18, 2009.

6 The presence of the past, or an Obama departure?

1   William Faulkner, *Requiem for a Nun* (New York: Random House, 1951).

2   *Public Papers of the Presidents of the United States, William J. Clinton, 1994*, (May 20), p. 1140.

3   Louis Perez, "The Circle of Connections," pp. 437–438.

4   Perez, "The Circle of Connections," pp. 438, 455. Adams is quoted at the beginning of Chapter 1. He said that "Cuba can gravitate only toward the North American Union, which cannot cast her off from its bosom."

5   Wolin, *The Presence of the Past: Essays on the State and the Constitution*, (Johns Hopkins University Press, 1989).

6   Wolin, *The Presence of the Past*, pp. 2–3.

7   Kenworthy, *America/Américas*, p. 29 (italics in original).

8   Todorov, *The Conquest of America*, p. 165.

9   Barack Obama, Remarks to the Summit of the Americas in Port of Spain, Trinidad and Tobago, April 17, 2009, *American Presidency Project*.

10 Lars Schoultz, *That Infernal Little Cuban Republic*, p. 567.

11 Perez, *Cuba in the American Imagination*, p. 274.

12 Barack Obama, Statement on the Situation in Cuba, March 24, 2010, *American Presidency Project*.

13 George W. Bush, Remarks on the Situation in Cuba, March 7, 2008, *American Presidency Project*.

14 "Transcript of Fourth Democratic Debate," *New York Times*, July 24, 2007 [online].

15 Fareed Zakaria, "Obama's Big Gamble," *Newsweek*, September 26, 2009.

16 Barack Obama, Memorandum on Promoting Democracy and Human Rights in Cuba, April 13, 2009, *American Presidency Project*.

17 Barack Obama, "Choosing a Better Future in the Americas," April 16, 2009, *American Presidency Project*.

18 "Clinton Impresses Audiences by Saying US Policies Have Failed," *New York Times*, April 18, 2009.

19 "In Further Sign of Thaw, U.S. Official Meets Cuban Authorities," New York Times, September 30, 2009.

20 Barack Obama, Remarks to the Summit of the Americas, *American Presidency Project*.

21 Barack Obama, The President's News Conference with President Felipe de Jesus Calderon Hinojosa of Mexico in Mexico City, Mexico, April 16, 2009, *American Presidency Project*.

22 Barack Obama, Remarks to the Cuban American National Foundation in Miami, Florida, May 23, 2008, *American Presidency Project*.

23 Barack Obama, Remarks to the Summit of the Americas, *American Presidency Project*.

24 Barack Obama, Statement on the Situation in Cuba, *American Presidency Project*.

25 Barack Obama, Remarks to the Summit of the Americas, *American Presidency Project*.

26 Abraham F. Lowenthal, "Obama and the Americas: Promise, Disappointment, Opportunity," *Foreign Affairs*, July/August 2010, p. 116.

27 Barack Obama, Remarks to the Cuban American National Foundation, *American Presidency Project*.

28 Barack Obama, Remarks to the Summit of the Americas, *American Presidency Project*.

29 Barack Obama, The President's News Conference with President Calderon of Mexico, *American Presidency Project*.

30 Barack Obama, Memorandum on Promoting Democracy and Human Rights in Cuba, *American Presidency Project*.

31 Barack Obama, "The Way Forward in Afghanistan and Pakistan," Address at the United States Military Academy at West Point, December 1, 2009.

32 Fareed Zakaria, "The Post-Imperial Presidency," *Newsweek*, December 14, 2009, p. 37.

33 Barack Obama, Remarks to the Summit of the Americas, *American Presidency Project*.

34 Barack Obama, The President's News Conference with President Calderon of Mexico, *American Presidency Project*.

35 Barack Obama, Remarks to the Cuban American National Foundation, *American Presidency Project*.

36 Schoultz, *That Infernal Little Cuban Republic*, p. 567.

37 *Public Papers of the Presidents of the United States, Richard M. Nixon*, January 20, 1972.

Bibliography

Adams, Charles Francis, ed., *Memoirs of John Q. Adams*, vol. 7, (Philadelphia: J.B. Lippincott and Co., 1875).

Aguilar, Luis, "Castro's Last Stand: Can Cuba Be Freed Without a Bloodbath?" *Policy Review*, Summer 1990, no. 53, pp. 74–77.

Almond, Gabriel, and Sidney Verba, *The Civic Culture* (Boston: Little, Brown, 1965).

American State Papers, Indian Affairs, I (Washington: Gales and Seaton, 1832).

Amnesty International, *Report, 1994* (London: Amnesty International, 1994).

Anderson, Benedict, *Imagined Communities: Reflections on the Origin and Spread of Nationalism*, Revised edition (London: Verso, 1991).

Baker III, James A., *The Politics of Diplomacy: Revolution, War and Peace, 1989–1992*, (New York: G.P. Putnam's Sons, 1995).

Baloyra, Enrique, and Morris, James, eds., "Socialist Transitions and Change in Cuba", *Conflict and Change in Cuba*, (Albuquerque: University of New Mexico Press, 1993).

Baritz, Loren, *City on a Hill: A History of Ideas and Myths in America* (New York: John Wiley and Sons, Inc., 1964).

Baritz, Loren, *Sources of the American Mind*, vol. 1 (New York: John Wiley and Sons Inc., 1966).

Barnett, Thomas P. M., *The Pentagon's New Map: War and Peace in the Twenty-First Century* (New York: Berkley Books, 2004).

Barthes, Roland, *Mythologies*, Translated by Annette Lavers (New York: Hill and Wang, 1972).

Batista, Fulgencio, *The Growth and Decline of the Cuban Republic* (New York: The Devin-Adair Company, 1964).

Bell, Daniel, "The End of American Exceptionalism," in Nathan Glazer and Irving Kristol, eds., *The American Commonwealth, 1976* (New York: Basic Books, 1976) pp. 193–224.

Benjamin, Jules, "Interpreting the U.S. Reaction to the Cuban Revolution, 1959–60," *Cuban Studies*, 1989, vol. 19, pp. 145–65.

Benjamin, Jules, *The United States and the Origins of the Cuban Revolution* (Princeton: Princeton University Press, 1990).

Bernell, David, "The Curious Case of Cuba in American Foreign Policy," *Journal of Interamerican Studies and World Affairs*, Summer 1994, vol. 36, no. 2, pp. 65–103.

Berríos, Rubén, "Why America Should Lift Its Cuban Embargo," *Contemporary Review*, October 1994, vol. 265, no. 1545, pp. 182–85.

Berrios, Reuben, and Lillian Thomas, "Taking Orders from Little Havana," *Bulletin of the Atomic Scientists*, September/October 1994, vol. 50, no. 5, pp. 20–21.

Black, George, *The Good Neighbor: How the United States Wrote the History of Central America and the Caribbean* (New York: Pantheon Books, 1988).

Blasier, Cole, *The Hovering Giant* (Pittsburgh: University of Pittsburgh Press, 1985).

Blasier, Cole, and Mesa-Lago, Carmelo, eds., *Cuba in the World* (Pittsburgh: The University of Pittsburgh Press, 1979).

Booth, Ken, and Steve Smith, *International Relations Theory Today* (Cambridge: Polity Press, 1995).

Brenner, Phillip, LeoGrande, Rich, and Seigel eds., *The Cuba Reader: The Making of a Revolutionary Society* (New York: Grove Press, 1988).

Brenner, Philip, and Peter Kornbluh, "Clinton's Cuba Calculus," *NACLA Report on the Americas*, Sept/Oct 1995, vol. 29, no. 2, pp. 33–40.

Bulkeley, Peter, *The Gospel Covenant* (1651), Loren Baritz, ed., *Sources of the American Mind*, vol. 1 (New York: John Wiley and Sons Inc., 1966).

Burns, Timothy, ed., *After History? Francis Fukuyama and His Critics* (Lanham, MD: Rowman and Littlefield, 1994).

Bush on Cuba: Selected Statements by the President (Cuban American National Foundation, 1991).

Bush, George W., Remarks on the Situation in Cuba, May 21, 2008, *American Presidency Project*.

Campbell, David, *Writing Security: United States Foreign Policy and the Politics of Identity* (Minneapolis: The University of Minnesota Press, 1992).

Capitol Hill Cubans, Resolution of the Polish Sejm on the Internal Situation of the Republic of Cuba, March 19, 2010, http://www.capitolhillcubans.com/2010/03/resolution-of-polish-sejm.html, (accessed May 25, 2010).

Cardoso, Fernando, and Faletto, Enzo, *Dependency and Development in Latin America* (Berkeley: The University of California Press, 1979).

Carr, E. H., *The Twenty Years Crisis, 1919–1939* (London: Macmillan and Co. Ltd., 1962).

Castro, Fidel, "History Will Absolve Me," in Rolando Bonachea and Nelson Valdes eds., *Revolutionary Struggle 1947–1958: Volume I of the Selected Works of Fidel Castro* (Cambridge: The MIT Press, 1972) pp. 164–221.

—— *Nothing Can Stop the Course of History*, an Interview by Jeffrey M. Elliot and Mervyn M. Dymally (New York: Pathfinder Press, 1986).

Castro, Fidel, and Che Guevara, *To Speak the Truth*, Mary-Alice Waters, ed. (New York: Pathfinder Press, 1992).

Centro de Estudios Sobre America, ed., *The Cuban Revolution into the 1990's: Cuban Perspectives*, Latin American Perspectives Series, No. 10 (Boulder: Westview Press, 1992).

"Clinton Impresses Audiences by Saying US Policies Have Failed," *New York Times*, April 18, 2009.

Clinton, William J., Remarks to the Cuban-American Community, June 27, 1995, John T. Woolley and Gerhard Peters, *The American Presidency Project* [online]. Santa Barbara, CA. http://www.presidency.ucsb.edu.(accessed June 3, 2010).

Commission for Assistance to a Free Cuba, Mission Statement, http://2005–9.cafc.gov/mission/index.htm, (accessed May 18, 2010).

Commission for Assistance to a Free Cuba, Report to the President, July 2006.

Committee of Santa Fe, "A New Inter-American Policy for the Eighties," Lewis Tambs, ed. (Washington D.C.: Council for Inter-American Security, 1980).

Committee on the Present Danger, *Alerting America: The Papers of the Committee on the Present Danger* (Washington: Pergamon Brasseys, 1984).

Congressional Globe, 27th Congress, 2nd Session, appendix, June 12, 1842, p. 503.

——, 28th Congress, 2nd Session, appendix, February 21–22, 1845, p. 397.

——, 29th Congress, 2nd Session, appendix, February 2, 1847, p. 281.

——, 30th Congress, 1st Session, January 4, 1848, p. 99.

——, 32nd Congress, 3rd Session, appendix, March 15, 1853, p. 270.

Congressional Record, 54th Congress, 1st Session, 1896, p. 2248.

——, 55th Congress, 2nd Session, April 16, 1898, pp. 3988–89.

——, 56th Congress, 1st Session, January 9, 1900, p. 711.

——, 57th Congress, 1st Session, April 8, 1902, p. 3857.

——, 57th Congress, 1st Session, April 8, 1902, pp. 4123–25.

——, 58th Congress, 2nd Session, pt. 1, December 12, 1903, pp. 167–68.

——, 58th Congress, 3rd Session, December 6, 1904, p. 19.

——, 104th Congress, 1st Session, p. S14995

——, 104th Congress, 1st session, October 11–18, 1995, p. S21554.

——, 110th Congress, 1st Session, December 18, 2007, p. H16649.

——, 110th Congress, 2nd Session, May 21, 2008, p. S4706.

Connolly, William, *The Augustinian Imperative: A Reflection on the Politics of Morality*, (Newbury Park: Sage Publications, 1993).

——, *Identity/Difference: Democratic Negotiations of Political Paradox* (Ithaca: Cornell University Press, 1991).

——, "Identity and Difference in Global Politics," in Der Derian, James, and Shapiro, Michael, eds., *International/Intertextual Relations* (Lexington, MA: Lexington Books, 1989).

——, ed., *Legitimacy and the State* (New York: New York University Press, 1984).

Cottam, Martha, *Images and Intervention: U.S. Policies in Latin America* (Pittsburgh: University of Pittsburgh Press, 1994).

Crozier, Michel, Samuel Huntington, and Joji Watanuki, *The Crisis of Democracy: Report of the Governability of Democracies to the Trilateral Commission* (New York: New York University Press, 1975).

Cuban Democratic Directorate, "90 Members of Polish Parliament Adopt 90 Cuban Political Prisoners," December 17, 2009, http://www.directorio.org/pressreleases/note.php?note_id = 2623, (accessed May 25, 2010).

Debray, Regis, *Revolution in the Revolution?* (New York: Grove Press, 1967).

del Aguila, Juan M., *Cuba: Dilemmas of a Revolution*, (Boulder: Westview Press, 1988).

Der Derian, James, and Shapiro, Michael, eds., *International/Intertextual Relations* (Lexington, MA: Lexington Books, 1989).

"Dissident's Death Raises Cries for Cuba to Open Up," *USA Today*, February 25, 2010, p. 8A.

Dominguez, Jorge, ed., *Cuba: Internal and International Affairs* (Beverly Hills: Sage Publications, 1982).

——, "It Won't Go Away: Cuba on the U.S. Foreign Policy Agenda," *International Security*, Summer 1983, vol. 8, no. 1, pp. 113–28.

——, "US-Cuba Relations in the mid-1980's: Issues and Policies," *The Journal of Interamerican Studies and World Affairs*, February 1985, vol. 27, no. 1, pp. 17–34.

——, "Cuba in the 1980's," *Foreign Affairs*, Fall 1986, vol. 65, no. 1, pp. 118–35.

——, *To Make A World Safe for Revolution* (Cambridge: Harvard University Press, 1989).

——, "The Secrets of Castro's Staying Power," *Foreign Affairs*, Spring 1993, vol. 72, no. 2, pp. 97–107.

Dominguez, Jorge, and Hernandez, Rafael, eds., *U.S.-Cuban Relations in the 1990's*, (Boulder: Westview Press, 1989).

Doyle, Michael, "Liberalism and World Politics," *The American Political Science Review*, December 1986, vol. 80, no. 4, pp. 1151–69.

Draper, Theodore, *Castro's Revolution* (New York: Praeger, 1962).

Drinnon, Richard, *Facing West: The Metaphysics of Indian Hating and Empire Building* (Minneapolis: University of Minnesota Press, 1980).

Duncan, Raymond, *The Soviet Union and Cuba: Interests and Influence* (New York: Praeger Publishers, 1985).

——, "Castro and Gorbachev: Politics of Accommodation," *Problems of Communism*, March/April 1986, vol. 35, no. 2, pp. 45–57.

Erisman, Michael, *Cuba's International Relations* (Boulder: Westview Press, 1985).

Fagen, Richard, "Cuba and the Soviet Union," *The Wilson Quarterly*, Winter 1978, vol. 2, no. 1, pp. 69–78.

Falcoff, Mark, and Robert Royal, eds., *Crisis and Opportunity* (Washington D.C.: The Ethics and Public Policy Center, 1984).

Falk, Pamela, *Cuban Foreign Policy* (D.C. Heath Company, 1987).

Faulkner, William, *Requiem for a Nun* (New York: Random House, 1951).

Fauriol, Georges, and Loser, Eva, *Cuba: The International Dimension*, New Brunswick: Transaction Publishers, 1990).

Feinsilver, Julie, "Cuba as World Medical Power," *Latin American Research Review*, vol. 24, no. 2, 1989, pp. 1–34.

Foucault, Michel, *Discipline and Punish* (New York: Random House, 1977).

——, *Power/Knowledge: Selected Interviews and Other Writings, 1972–1977*, Colin Gordon, ed., (New York: Pantheon Books, 1980).

Franklin, Benjamin, *Observations Concerning the Increase of Mankind*, 1751.

Fukuyama, Francis, *The End of History and the Last Man* (New York: Free Press, 1992).

Fuller, John Douglas Pitts, *The Movement for the Acquisition of all Mexico 1846–1848*, (Baltimore: Johns Hopkins University Press, 1936).

Gaddis, John, Lewis, ed., *Containment: Documents on American Policy and Strategy, 1945–1950* (New York: Columbia University Press, 1978).

Gettleman, Marvin, ed., *El Salvador: Central America in the New Cold War* (New York: Grove Press, 1981).

Gilpin, Robert, *The Political Economy of International Relations* (Princeton: Princeton University Press, 1987).

Gilpin, Robert, *War and Change in World Politics* (Cambridge: Cambridge University Press, 1981).

Gonzales, Edward, and David Ronfeldt, *Storm Warnings for Cuba* (Santa Monica, CA: RAND, 1994).

Gould, Stephen Jay, *Ever Since Darwin*, (New York: W.W. Norton and Co., 1977)

——, *The Mismeasure of Man* (New York: W.W. Norton and Co., 1981).

Gray, Colin, "SALT II: The Real Debate," *Policy Review*, 1979, no. 10, pp. 7–22.

Guevara, Ernesto Che, "Man and Socialism in Cuba," *Che Guevara and the Cuban Revolution: Writings and Speeches of Ernesto Che Guevara*, David Deutschmann, ed. (Sydney: Pathfinder/Pacific and Asia, 1987).

Gunn, Gillian, "Will Castro Fall?" *Foreign Policy*, Summer 1990, no. 79. pp. 132–50.

——, "Cuba in Crisis," *Current History*, February 1991, vol. 90, no. 553, pp. 101–4, 133–35.

Haig, Alexander, *Caveat: Realism, Reagan, and Foreign Policy* (New York: Macmillan, 1984).

Halebsky, Sandor, and John Kirk, *Cuba: Twenty-Five Years of Revolution* (New York: Praeger Publishers, 1985).

——, eds., *Cuba in Transition: Crisis and Transformation*, Latin American Perspectives Series, No. 9 (Boulder: Westview Press, 1992).

Halliday, Fred, *The Making of the Second Cold War* (London: Verso Press, 1983).

Harries, Owen, "An Offer Castro Couldn't Refuse-or Survive," *The National Interest*, Summer 1996, pp. 126–28.

Hofstadter, Richard, *The American Political Tradition* (New York: Alfred A. Knopf, 1985).

Horgan, Paul, *Great River: The Rio Grande in North American History*, v. 2, (New York: Rinehart and Co. Inc., 1954).

Horowitz, Irving Louis, *Cuban Communism*, 8th ed. (New Brunswick: Transaction Publishers, 1995).

Horsman, Reginald, *Race and Manifest Destiny: The Origins of American Racial Anglo-Saxonism* (Cambridge, MA: Harvard University Press, 1981).

Hunt, Michael, *Ideology and US Foreign Policy* (New Haven: Yale University Press, 1987).

Huntington, Samuel, *Political Order in Changing Societies* (New Haven: Yale University Press, 1968).

——, "No Exit: The Errors of Endism," *The National Interest*, Fall 1989, no. 17, pp. 3–10.

——, "The Clash of Civilizations" *Foreign Affairs*, Summer 1993, vol. 72, no. 3, pp. 22–49.

Ikenberry, G. John, "America's Liberal Grand Strategy: Democracy and National Security in the Post-War Era," *American Democracy Promotion: Impulses, Strategies and Impacts*, (New York: Oxford University Press, 2000).

Immerman, Richard, *The CIA in Guatemala: The Foreign Policy of Intervention* (Austin: The University of Texas Press, 1982).

Improper Conduct (New York: Cinevista Video, 1984).

"In Further Sign of Thaw, U.S. Official Meets Cuban Authorities," *New York Times*, September 30, 2009.

Infante, Cabrere, *Mea Cuba* (London: Faber and Faber, 1994).

Inter-American Commission on Human Rights, OAS, *The Situation of Human Rights in Cuba* (Washington, D.C.: Organization of American States, 1983).

International American Conference, *Reports of Committees and Discussions Thereon, vol. 4, Historical Appendix, The Congress of 1826, at Panama, and Subsequent Movements Toward a Conference of American Nations* (Washington: Government Printing Office, 1890).

Jefferson, Thomas, *Notes on the State of Virginia* (Boston: Wells and Lilly, 1829).

Jessup, Philip, *Elihu Root* (Dodd, Mead and Company, 1938).

Jordan, Winthrop, *White Over Black: American Attitudes Toward the Negro, 1550–1812* (Chapel Hill: University of North Carolina Press, 1968).

Kaplowitz, Donna Rich, ed., *Cuba's Ties to a Changing World* (Boulder: Lynne Rienner Publishers, 1993).

Karnes, Thomas, ed., *Readings in the Latin American Policy of the United States* (Tucson: University of Arizona Press, 1972).

Karol, K.S., *Guerrillas in Power: The Course of the Cuban Revolution* (New York: Hill and Wang, 1970).

Kennan, George (X), "The Sources of Soviet Conduct," *Foreign Affairs*, July 1947, vol. 25, no. 4, pp. 566–82.

Kenworthy, Eldon, *America/Americas: Myth in the Making of US Policy Toward Latin America*, (University Park: Pennsylvania State University Press, 1995).

Keohane, Robert, *After Hegemony: Cooperation and Discord in the World Political System* (Princeton: Princeton University Press, 1984).

——, ed., *Neorealism and Its Critics*, (New York: Columbia University Press, 1986).

Kerry, Richard, *The Star-Spangled Mirror: America's Image of Itself and the World* (Savage, MD: Rowman and Littlefield Publishers, Inc., 1990).

Kirkpatrick, Jeanne, "Dictatorships and Double Standards," *Commentary*, November 1979, vol. 68, no. 5, pp. 34–45.

——, *Cuba and the Cubans* (Miami: Cuban-American National Foundation, 1983).

——, *The Reagan Phenomenon* (Washington: American Enterprise Institute, 1983a).

Kline, Michael, "Castro and 'New Thinking' in Latin America," *Journal of Interamerican Studies and World Affairs*, 1990, vol. 32, no. 1, pp. 83–118.

Kornbluh, Peter, and Malcolm Byrne, *The Iran-Contra Scandal: The Declassified History* (New York: The New Press, 1993).

Krauthammer, Charles, "The Unipolar Moment," *Foreign Affairs*, Winter 1991, vol. 70, no. 1, pp. 23–33.

LeFeber, Walter, ed., *John Quincy Adams and American Continental Empire: Letters, Papers, Speeches*, (Chicago: Quandrangle Books, 1965).

——, *Inevitable Revolutions: The United States in Central America*, 1st Edition (New York: W.W. Norton, 1983).

——, *The American Age: United States Foreign Policy at Home and Abroad Since 1750* (New York: W.W. Norton, 1989).

——, *Inevitable Revolutions: The United States in Central America*, 2nd Edition (New York: W.W. Norton, 1993).

Landau, Saul, "Notes on the Cuban Revolution," *The Socialist Register*, 1989, pp. 278–306.

Leiken, Robert, and Barry Rubin eds., *The Central American Crisis Reader* (New York: Summit Books, 1987).

Lenin, V.I., *Imperialism, The Highest Stage of Capitalism* (New York: International Publishers, 1939).

LeoGrande, William, *Cuba's Policy in Africa, 1959–1980* (Berkeley: Institute of International Studies, 1980).

——, "Evolution of the Nonaligned Movement," *Problems of Communism*, January/February 1980, vol. 29, no. 1, pp. 35–52.

——, "Cuban-Soviet Relations and Cuban Policy in Africa," in Carmelo Mesa-Lago and June Belkin, eds., *Cuba in Africa* (Pittsburgh: University of Pittsburgh Press, 1982), pp. 13–50.

——, "Cuba Policy Recycled," *Foreign Policy*, Spring 1982, no. 46, pp. 105–19.

——, "Cuba and Nicaragua: From the Somozas to the Sandinistas," in Barry B. Levine, ed., *The New Cuban Presence in the Caribbean* (Boulder: Westview, 1983), pp. 43–58.

The Life and Speeches of Henry Clay, 2v, (New York: Greeley and MacElrath, Tribune Buildings, 1844).

Lippmann, Walter, "Empire: The Days of Our Nonage Are Over," in Leiken and Rubin eds, *The Central American Crisis Reader* (New York: Summit Books, 1987) pp. 81–83.

Lipscomb, Andrew, and Albert Bergh, eds., *The Writings of Thomas Jefferson*, Vols. 12–16. (Washington: The Thomas Jefferson Memorial Association, 1903).

Lipset, S.M., *American Exceptionalism: A Double-Edged Sword* (New York: W.W. Norton and Company, 1996).

——, "American Exceptionalism Reaffirmed," in Byron Shafer ed., *Is America Different?* (Oxford: Clarendon Press, 1991) pp. 1–45.

Lopez-Fresquet, Rufo, *My Fourteen Months with Castro* (Cleveland: World Publishing Company, 1966).

Lowenthal, Abraham, ed., *Exporting Democracy: The United States and Latin America* (Baltimore: The Johns Hopkins University Press, 1991).

——, "Obama and the Americas: Promise, Disappointment, Opportunity," *Foreign Affairs*, July/August 2010.

Luce, Henry R., "The American Century," *Life*, February 17, 1941, vol. 10, no. 7, pp. 61–65.

Luxenberg, Alan, "Did Eisenhower Push Castro into the Arms of the Soviets?" *Journal of Interamerican Studies and World Affairs*, Spring 1988, vol. 30, no. 1, pp. 37–71.

Manning, William, ed., *Diplomatic Correspondence of the United States: Inter-American Affairs, 1831–1860*, Vol. 11 (Washington D.C.: Carnegie Endowment for International Peace, 1939).

Markovits, Andrei S., "The Other 'American Exceptionalism' – Why Is There No Soccer in the United States?" *Praxis International*, July 1988, vol. 8, no. 2, pp. 125–50.

McFarlane, Robert, *Special Trust* (New York: Cadell and Davies, 1994).

Mead, Walter Russell, "Rum and Coca-Cola: The United States and the New Cuba," *World Policy Journal*, Fall 1995, vol. 12, no. 3, pp. 29–53.

Mesa-Lago, Carmelo, ed., *Revolutionary Change in Cuba* (Pittsburgh: University of Pittsburgh Press, 1971).

——, ed., *Cuba After the Cold War* (Pittsburgh: University of Pittsburgh Press, 1993).

Meyer, Karl, and Sculz, Tad, *The Cuban Invasion* (New York: Frederick A. Praeger, 1962).

Mills, C. Wright, *Listen Yankee* (New York: McGraw Hill Book Company Inc., 1960).

Molineu, Harold, *US Policy toward Latin America* (Boulder: Westview Press, 1986).

Morgenthau, Hans, *Politics Among Nations: The Struggle for Power and Peace*, Sixth Edition, Revised by Kenneth Thompson (New York: Alfred A. Knopf, 1985).

Morley, Morris, *Imperial State and Revolution* (Cambridge: Cambridge University Press, 1987).

Morris, Charles, *Our Island Empire: A Hand-Book of Cuba, Porto Rico, Hawaii, and the Philippine Islands* (Philadelphia: J.B. Lippincott Company, 1899).

Muller, Julius, ed., *Presidential Messages and State Papers,* 10v, (New York: The Review of Reviews Company, 1917).

Murray, Mary, *Cuba and the United States,* An Interview with Cuban Foreign Minister Ricardo Alarcon, (Melbourne: Ocean Press, 1992).

Nearing, Scott, and Joseph Freeman, *Dollar Diplomacy: A Study in American Imperialism* (New York: B.W. Huebsch Inc., 1925).

Newfarmer, Richard, ed., *From Gunboats to Diplomacy: New US Policies for Latin America* (Baltimore: The Johns Hopkins University Press, 1984).

The New York Times, "Obama Declares U.S. Will Pursue Thaw with Cuba," April 18, 2009, p. A1.

Newsweek, December 26, 1994/January 2, 1995, vol. 125, no. 1.

Nitze, Paul, "Strategy for the 1980," Foreign Affairs, Winter 1980, vol. 59, no. 1, pp. 82–101.

Obama, Barack, "The Way Forward in Afghanistan and Pakistan," Address at the United States Military Academy at West Point, December 1, 2009.

Oppenheimer, Andres, *Castro's Final Hour: The Secret Story Behind the Coming Downfall of Communist Cuba* (New York: Simon and Schuster, 1992).

Organization of American States, Eighth Meeting of Consultation of Ministers of Foreign Affairs of the American Republics, Punta del Este, January 1962, Final Act, p. 6.

O'Sullivan, John, "Annexation," *The United States Magazine and Democratic Review,* July and August 1845, vol. 17, no. 85, pp. 5–10.

Park, James William, *Latin American Underdevelopment: A History of Perspectives in the United States, 1870–1965* (Baton Rouge: Louisiana State University Press, 1995).

Pastor, Manual, Jr. and Zimbalist, Andrew, "Cuba's Economic Conundrum," *NACLA Report on the Americas,* Sept/Oct 1995, vol. 29, no. 2, pp. 7–12.

Pastor, Robert A., *Whirlpool: U.S. Foreign Policy toward Latin America and the Caribbean* (Princeton: Princeton University Press, 1992).

Paterson, Thomas G., ed., *American Imperialism and Anti-Imperialism* (New York: Thomas Y. Crowell Company, Inc., 1973).

Payne, Douglas, Mark Falcoff, and Sarah Kaufmann Purcell, eds., *Latin America: US Policy After the Cold War* (New York: Americas Society, 1991).

Peceny, Mark, "A Constructivist Interpretation of the Liberal Pacific Union: The Ambiguous Case of the Spanish-American War," Unpublished paper, 1996.

Perez, Louis, *Cuba Between Empires, 1878–1902* (Pittsburgh: University of Pittsburgh Press, 1983).

——, *The U.S. and Cuba: Ties of Singular Intimacy* (Athens: University of Georgia Press, 1990).

——, "History, Historiography, and Cuban Studies: Thirty Years Later," in Damien J. Fernandez, ed., *Cuban Studies Since the Revolution* (Gainesville: University of Florida Press, 1992), pp. 53–78.

——, "The Circle of Connections: One Hundred Years of Cuba-US Relations, *Michigan Quarterly Review,* Summer 1994, vol. 33, no. 3, pp. 437–55.

——, *Cuba in the American Imagination: Metaphor and the Imperial Ethos* (Chapel Hill: University of North Carolina Press, 2008).

——, "Thinking Back on Cuba's Future: The Logic of *Patria,*" *NACLA Report on the Americas,* March/April 2009.

Petras, James, "Blots on the White Paper: The Reinvention of the 'Red Menace,'" in Gettleman ed., *El Salvador: Central America in the New Cold War* (New York: Grove Press, 1981).

Pike, Fredrick, *The United States and Latin America: Myths and Stereotypes of Civilization and Nature* (Austin: University of Texas Press, 1992).

Pilzer, Paul Zane, *Unlimited Wealth: The Theory and Practice of Economic Alchemy* (New York: Crown Publishers, 1990).

Pipes, Richard, *US-Soviet Relations in the Era of Detente* (Boulder: Westview Press, 1981).

Podhoretz, Norman, *The Present Danger: "Do We Have the Will to Reverse the Decline of American Power?"* (New York: Simon and Schuster, 1980).

The Public Papers and Addresses of Franklin D. Roosevelt, vol. 2 (New York: Random House, 1938).

Public Papers of the Presidents of the United States, Dwight D. Eisenhower, 1960–61, (Washington D.C.: Government Printing Office).

Public Papers of the Presidents of the United States, George Bush, 1991, 1992, (Washington D.C.: Government Printing Office).

Public Papers of the Presidents of the United States, Richard Nixon, 1972, (Washington D.C.: Government Printing Office).

Public Papers of the Presidents of the United States, Ronald Reagan, 1983, 1984, 1986, 1987 (Washington D.C.: Government Printing Office).

Public Papers of the Presidents of the United States, William J. Clinton, 1993, 1994, (Washington D.C.: Government Printing Office).

Purcell, Susan Kaufmann, "Is Cuba Changing?" *The National Interest*, Winter 1988–89, no. 14, pp. 43–53.

——, "Cuba's Cloudy Future, *Foreign Affairs*, Summer 1990, vol. 68, no. 3, pp. 114–30.

——, "Collapsing Cuba," *Foreign Affairs*, Winter 1992, vol. 71, no. 1, pp. 130–45.

Pye, Lucian, and Sidney Verba, *Political Culture and Political Development* (Princeton: Princeton University Press, 1965).

Rabkin, Rhoda, *Cuban Politics: The Revolutionary Experiment* (New York: Praeger Publishers, 1991).

Reagan, Ronald, "Strategic Importance of El Salvador and Central America," March 10, 1983, US Department of State Current Policy No. 464.

——, *An American Life* (New York: Simon and Schuster, 1990).

Richardson, James D., ed., *A Compilation of the Messages and Papers of the Presidents, 1787–1897*, 10 vols. (New York: Bureau of National Literature, Inc., 1897).

Rieff, David, "Cuba Refrozen" *Foreign Affairs*, July/August 1996, vol. 75, no. 4, pp. 62–76.

Robbins, Carla Anne, *The Cuban Threat* (New York: McGraw Hill Book Co., 1983).

——, "Dateline Washington: Cuban-American Clout," *Foreign Policy*, Fall 1992, no. 88, pp. 162–82.

Rogin, Michael, *Fathers and Children: Andrew Jackson and the Subjugation of the American Indian* (New York: Vintage Books, 1975).

Roosevelt, Theodore, *The Works of Theodore Roosevelt, Vol. 17, State Papers as Governor and President*, (New York: Charles Scribner's Sons, 1925).

Rostow, Eugene, "The Case Against SALT II," *Commentary*, 1979, vol. 67, no. 2, pp. 23–32.

Rostow, W.W., *The Stages of Economic Growth: A Non-Communist Manifesto* (Cambridge: Cambridge University Press, 1960).

Rothchild, John, *Latin America Yesterday and Today* (New York: Praeger Publishers, 1974).

Rusk, Dean, Address at the Eighth Meeting of Consultation of Ministers of Foreign Affairs of the American States, Punta del Este, Uruguay, January 25, 1962, reprinted as Appendix I, US Senate, "Communist Threat to US Through the Caribbean," Hearings before the Judiciary Committee, March 29, April 26, June 1, and July 27, 1961, Part 13 (Washington DC: Government Printing Office, 1962) pp. 889–95.

Said, Edward, *Orientalism* (New York: Vintage Books, 1979).

Schlesinger, Stephen, and Kinzer, Stephen, *Bitter Fruit: The Untold Story of the American Coup in Guatemala*, (Garden City, New York: Doubleday and Co., 1982).

Schoultz, Lars, *National Security and United States Policy in Latin America* (Princeton: Princeton University Press, 1987).

——, *That Infernal Little Cuban Republic: The United States and the Cuban Revolution* (Chapel Hill: University of North Carolina Press, 2009).

Schulz, Donald, "Can Castro Survive?" *Journal of Interamerican Studies and World Affairs*, Spring 1993, vol. 35, no. 1, pp. 89–117.

——, ed., *Cuba and the Future* (Westport: Greenwood Press, 1994).

Shafer, Byron, ed., *Is America Different?* (Oxford: Clarendon Press, 1991).

Shapiro, Michael, *Language and Political Understanding: The Politics of Discursive Practices* (New Haven: Yale University Press, 1981).

——, ed., *Language and Politics* (New York: NYU Press, 1984).

——, *The Politics of Representation: Writing Practices in Biography, Photography, and Policy Analysis*, (Madison: University of Wisconsin Press, 1988).

Shearman, Peter, *The Soviet Union and Cuba*, Chatham House Papers, no. 38 (London: Royal Institute of International Affairs, 1987).

Smith, Daniel, ed., *Major Problems in American Diplomatic History: Documents and Readings*, 2v, (Boston: D.C. Heath and Company, 1965).

Smith, Gaddis, *The Last Years of the Monroe Doctrine, 1945–1993* (New York: Hill and Wang, 1994).

Smith, Wayne, *Castro's Cuba: Soviet Partner or Non-Aligned?* (Washington DC: The Woodrow Wilson International Center for Scholars, 1984).

——, *The Closest of Enemies* (New York: Norton Co., 1987).

——, "A Pragmatic Cuba Policy," *Foreign Service Journal*, April 1991, vol. 68, no. 2, pp. 22–25.

——, "Castro: To Fall or Not to Fall?" *SAIS Review*, Summer-Fall 1992, vol. 12, no. 2, pp. 97–110.

——, "Cuba's Long Reform," *Foreign Affairs*, March/April 1996, vol. 75, no. 2, pp. 99–112.

Suchlicki, Jaime, "Soviet Policy in Latin America: Implications for the United States," *Journal of Interamerican Studies and World Affairs*, Spring 1987, vol. 29, no. 1, pp. 25–46.

——, "Myths and Realities in US-Cuban Relations," *Journal of Interamerican Studies and World Affairs*, Summer 1994, vol. 36, no. 1, pp. 103–13.

Sullivan, Mark P., "Cuba's Political Succession: From Fidel to Raul Castro," CRS Report to Congress, October 23, 2007.

Swain, James B., ed., *The Life and Speeches of Henry Clay*, 2 vols. (New York: Greeley and McElrath, 1844).

Szulc, Tad, *Fidel: A Critical Portrait* (New York: William Morrow and Co. Inc., 1986).

Takaki, Ronald, *Iron Cages: Race and Culture in 19th Century America* (Oxford: Oxford University Press, 1990).

Thomas, Isabella, "Cuba: Change and the Perception of Change," *The World Today*, May 1995, vol. 51, no. 5, pp. 99–101.

Tocqueville, Alexis de, *Democracy in America*, vol. 2 (New York: Alfred A Knopf, 1966).

Todorov, Tzvetan, *The Conquest of America: The Question of the Other* (New York: Harper Perennial, 1992).

"Transcript of Fourth Democratic Debate," *New York Times*, July 24, 2007 [online] http://www.nytimes.com/2007/07/24/us/politics/24transcript.html, (accessed April 16, 2010).

Tucker, Robert, ed., *The Marx-Engels Reader*, Second Edition, (New York: W.W. Norton and Company, 1978).

Tulchin, Joseph, and Hernandez, Raphael, eds., *Cuba and The United States: Will the Cold War in the Caribbean End?* (Boulder: Lynne Rienner Publishers, 1991).

Turner, Frederick Jackson "The Significance of the Frontier in American History," 1893.

"UN Urges US to End Ban on Cuba," *New York Times*, November 3, 1995, Section A, page 8.

US Department of State, International Organization and Conference Series II, American Republics, no. 14, Publication 5692, (Washington DC: Government Printing Office, 1955) pp. 156–58.

——, *American Foreign Policy: Current Documents*, (Washington DC: Government Printing Office, 1957–91).

——, "Communist Interference in El Salvador," Special Report No. 80, February 23, 1981.

——, "Tasks for US Policy in the Hemisphere," Current Policy No. 282, June 3, 1981.

——, "El Salvador: The Search for Peace," Current Policy No. 296, July 16, 1981.

——, "Cuba's Renewed Support for Violence in Latin America," Special Report No. 90, December 14, 1981.

——, "Dealing with the Reality of Cuba," Current Policy No. 443, December 14 1982.

——, "Strategic Importance of El Salvador and Central America," March 10, 1983, Current Policy No. 464.

——, "The United States and Cuba" Current Policy no. 646, December 17, 1984.

——, "Human Rights in Castro's Cuba," Special Report No. 153, December 1986.

——, "Cuba: 'Our Last Adversary," Current Policy no. 1085, May 13, 1988.

——, "US Policy Toward Cuba," Statement by Bernard W. Aronson, Assistant Secretary for Inter-American Affairs, before the Subcommittee on Western Hemisphere Affairs, House Foreign Affairs Committee, July 11, 1991, in *Dispatch*, August 5, 1991.

——, "New Opportunities in Hemispheric Trade," *Dispatch*, August 26, 1991, p. 635.

——, "The Cuban Democracy Act and US Policy Toward Cuba," Statement by Robert Gelbard, Principal Deputy Assistant Secretary for Inter-American Affairs before the Subcommittee, August 10, 1992, in *Dispatch*, August 17, 1992.

——, "President Bush's Address at the Signing of NAFTA," *Dispatch*, January 4, 1993.

——, "US-Mexican Relations and NAFTA," *Dispatch*, June 28, 1993.

——, "Cuba: Current Assessment And US Policy," Robert S. Gelbard, Deputy Assistant Secretary for Inter-American Affairs, Statement before the Senate Select Committee on Intelligence, July 29, 1993, in *Dispatch*, August 16, 1993, Vol 4., No. 33.

——, "NAFTA: A Bridge to a Better Future for the United States and the Hemisphere, *Dispatch*, September 13, 1993.

——, "The Cuban Democracy Act: One Year Later," Statement by Alexander Watson, Assistant Secretary of State for Inter-American Affairs before the House Foreign Affairs Committee, November 18, 1993, in *Dispatch*, December 6, 1993.

——, "Update on US Policy Toward Cuba," Address by Alexander Watson, Assistant Secretary for Inter-American Affairs, October 28, 1994, in *Dispatch*, November 7, 1994.

——, "Cuba," *Background Notes*, November 1994, Vol. 5, No, 14.

——, *Country Reports on Human Rights Practices for 1994*, (Washington DC: Government Printing Office, 1995).

——, "Cuba," *2009 Country Reports on Human Rights Practices* [online] http://www.state.gov/g/drl/rls/hrrpt/2009/wha/136108.htm, (accessed May 15, 2010).

——, Ambassador Rice's Remarks on U.N. Resolution on Cuba, October 29, 2009.

——, Death of Cuban Dissident Orlando Zapata Tamayo, Office of Public Diplomacy and Public Affairs, February 24, 2010.

——, "Cuba," *Background Notes*, 2010 [online] http://www.state.gov/r/pa/ei/bgn/2886.htm, (accessed May 15, 2010).

US Departments of State and Defense, "The Challenge to Democracy in Central America," June 1986.

US House of Representatives, Committee on Foreign Affairs, *The Cuban Democracy Act of 1992*, Hearings, March 18, 25, April 2, 8, May 21, June 4, 5, 1992 (Washington DC: Government Printing Office, 1993).

US House of Representatives, Committee on International Affairs, *The Cuban Liberty and Democratic Solidarity (Libertad) Act of 1995*, Hearings, March 16, 1995 (Washington DC: Government Printing Office, 1995).

US Senate, Committee on Foreign Relations, *The Cuban Democracy Act,* Hearings, August 5, 1992, (Washington DC: Government Printing Office, 1992).

Valladares, Armando, *Against All Hope: The Prison Memoirs of Armando Valladares* (New York: Alfred A. Knopf, 1986).

Vasquez, John, "The Post-Positivist Debate: Reconstructing Scientific Enquiry and International Relations Theory after Enlightenment's Fall," Booth and Smith, eds., *International Relations Theory Today* (Cambridge: Polity Press, 1995).

Wallerstein, Immanuel, *The Modern World System* (New York: Academic Press, 1974).

——, "The World-System After the Cold War," *Journal of Peace Research*, February 1993, vol. 30, no. 1, pp. 1–6.

Walt, Stephen, *The Origins of Alliances*, (Ithaca: Cornell University Press, 1987).

Waltz, Kenneth, *Theory of International Politics* (Reading MA, Addison-Wesley, 1979).

The Washington Post, "U.S., Cuba Held Extended Talks; State Department Official Discloses 6 Days of Meetings on Island," September 30, 2009, p. A4.

Weber, Cynthia, "Writing Sovereign Identities: Wilson Administration Intervention in the Mexican Revolution," *Alternatives*, vol. 17, no. 1992, pp. 313–37.

——, *Simulating Sovereignty: Intervention, the State and Symbolic Exchange*, (Cambridge: Cambridge University Press, 1995).

Weinberg, Albert, *Manifest Destiny: A Study of Nationalist Expansionism in American History* (Baltimore: The Johns Hopkins University Press, 1935).

Weinberger, Caspar, "Rearming America," US Department of Defense, 1981.

——, *Fighting for Peace* (New York: Warner Books, 1990).

Weldes, Jutta, "Constructing National Interests: The Logic of US National Security in the Post War Era," Dissertation, University of Minnesota, 1993.

Weldes, Jutta, and Diana Saco, "From Soviet Puppet to Decaying Cadaver: The U.S. Construction of the Cuban Security Problematic" (Paper delivered at the annual meeting of the International Studies Association, Acapulco, Mexico, March, 1993).

Wendt, Alexander, "Anarchy is What States Make of It: The Social Construction of Power Politics," *International Organization*, Spring 1992, vol. 46, no. 2, pp. 391–425.

Weston, Rubin Francis, *Racism in US Imperialism: The Influence of Racial Assumptions on American Foreign Policy, 1893–1946* (Columbia: University of South Carolina Press, 1973).

Whitaker, Arthur P., *The Western Hemisphere Idea: Its Rise and Decline* (Ithaca: Cornell University Press, 1954).

Wiarda, Howard, "Is Cuba Next? Crises of the Castro Regime," *Problems of Communism*, Jan/Apr 1991, pp. 84–93.

Wieseltier, Leon, "Spoilers at the Party," *The National Interest*, Fall 1989, no. 17, pp. 12–16.

Williams, William Appleman, ed., *The Shaping of American Diplomacy: Readings and Documents in American Foreign Relations*, 2v, Second Edition (Chicago: Rand McNally and Co., 1965).

Wolin, Sheldon, *The Presence of the Past: Essays on the State and the Constitution* (Baltimore: Johns Hopkins University Press, 1989).

Woolley, John T., and Gerhard Peters, *The American Presidency Project* [online]. Santa Barbara, CA. http://www.presidency.ucsb.edu, (accessed June 3, 2010).

Yanes, Hernan, "The Cuba-Venezuela Alliance: 'Emancipatory Neo-Bolivarismo' or Totalitarian Expansion?" Institute for Cuban & Cuban-American Studies, University of Miami, Occasional Paper Series, December 2005.

Zakaria, Fareed, *The Future of Freedom: Illiberal Democracy at Home and Abroad*, (New York: W.W. Norton, 2003).

——, "Obama's Big Gamble," *Newsweek*, September 26, 2009.

——, "The Post-Imperial Presidency," *Newsweek*, December 14, 2009.

Index

For Product Safety Concerns and Information please contact our EU
representative GPSR@taylorandfrancis.com
Taylor & Francis Verlag GmbH, Kaufingerstraße 24, 80331 München, Germany